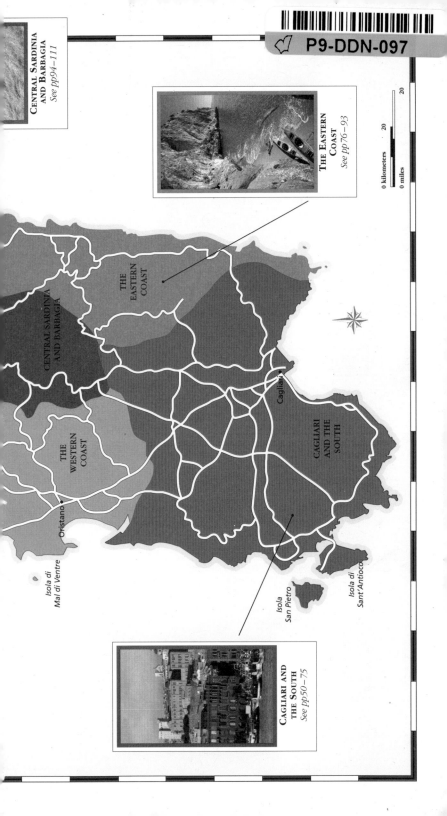

CENTRAL SARDINIA
AND BARBAGIA
See pp94–111

P9-DDN-097

THE EASTERN
COAST
See pp76–93

0 kilometers   20

0 miles   20

CENTRAL SARDINIA
AND BARBAGIA

THE
EASTERN
COAST

Cagliari

THE
WESTERN
COAST

CAGLIARI
AND THE
SOUTH

Oristano

Isola di
Mal di Ventre

Isola
San Pietro

Isola di
Sant'Antioco

CAGLIARI AND
THE SOUTH
See pp50–75

EYEWITNESS *TRAVEL GUIDES*

SARDINIA

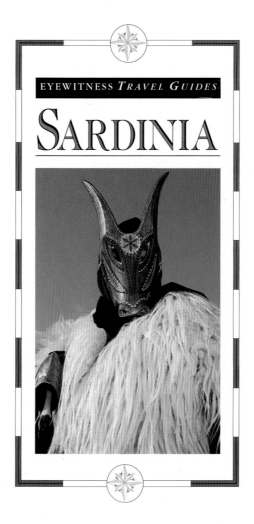

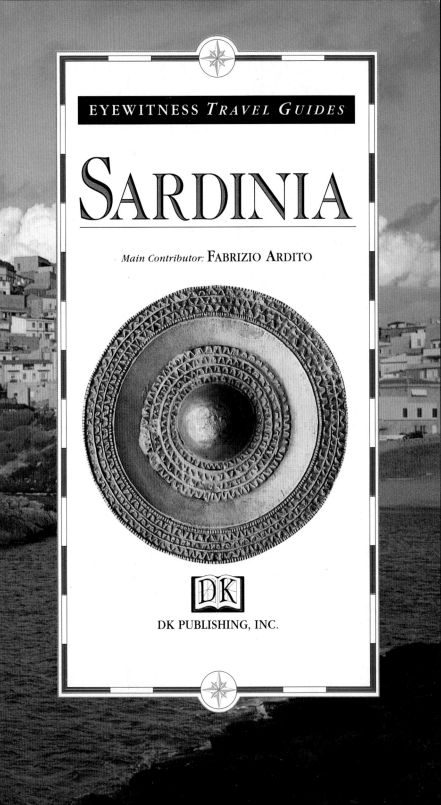

EYEWITNESS *TRAVEL GUIDES*

SARDINIA

Main Contributor: FABRIZIO ARDITO

DK

DK PUBLISHING, INC.

A DK PUBLISHING BOOK

Produced by Fabio Ratti
Editoria Libraria e Multimediale
Milano, Italy

PROJECT EDITOR Diana Georgiacodis
EDITORS Anna Lia Deffenu, Giovanni Francesio,
Renata Perego, Laura Recordati
DESIGNERS Paolo Gonzato, Stefania Testa,
Studio Matra
MAPS Paul Stafford
PICTURE RESEARCH Fabio De Angelis, Riccardo Villarosa

Dorling Kindersley Ltd
PROJECT EDITOR Fiona Wild
EDITOR Francesca Machiavelli
US EDITOR Mary Sutherland
DTP Cooling Brown
DTP DESIGNER Ingrid Vienings
PRODUCTION David Proffit
MANAGING EDITORS Fay Franklin, Georgina Matthews
MANAGING ART EDITOR Annette Jacobs
SENIOR MANAGING EDITOR Vivien Crump
DEPUTY ART-DIRECTOR Gillian Allan

MAIN CONTRIBUTOR Fabrizio Ardito
ADDITIONAL CONTRIBUTORS Patrizia Giovannetti, Raffaella Rizzo

ILLUSTRATORS Giorgia Boli, Alberto Ipsilanti,
Daniela Veluti, Nadia Viganò
•
ENGLISH TRANSLATION Richard Pierce
•
Film outputting bureau Press Data (London)
Reproduced by FGV (Milano), Lineatre Service (Milano)
Printed and bound by Mondadori (Italy)

First American Edition, 1998
2 4 6 8 10 9 7 5 3 1

Published in the United States by
DK Publishing, Inc.,
95 Madison Avenue, New York, New York 10016

Copyright © 1998 Dorling Kindersley Limited, London
Visit us on the World Wide Web at htttp://www.dk.com

Library of Congress Cataloging-in-Publication Data
Sardinia. –– 1st American ed.
    p.   cm. –– (Eyewitness travel guides)
Includes index.
ISBN 0-7894-2868-7
1. Sardinia (Italy) –– Guidebooks. I. Series.
DG975.S3S358 1998   97-32280
914.5'904929 –– dc21   CIP
•

Every effort has been made to ensure that the information in this
book is as up-to-date as possible at the time of going to press.
However, details such as telephone numbers, opening hours, prices,
gallery hanging arrangements, and travel information are liable to
change. The publishers cannot accept responsibility
for any consequences arising from the use of this book.

We would be delighted to receive any corrections and
suggestions for incorporation in the next edition. Please write to:
Senior Editor, Eyewitness Travel Guides,
DK Publishing, Inc., 95 Madison Avenue, New York, New York 10016.

◁ **The promontory of Castelsardo on the northern coast**

CONTENTS

HOW TO USE
THIS GUIDE *6*

**Sheep grazing in pastures filled
with spring flowers**

INTRODUCING
SARDINIA

**A prehistoric tower of the Santu
Antine nuraghe at Torralba**

The beach at Stintino on the tip of the western coast

Flamingos wintering in the ponds and marshes of Sardinia

Knight on horseback during the Sa Sartiglia festival at Oristano

A bird's-eye view of the city of Alghero

HOW TO USE THIS GUIDE

THIS GUIDE HELPS you get the most from your visit to Sardinia, providing expert recommendations as well as detailed practical information. *Introducing Sardinia* sets the island in its geographical, historical, and cultural context. The five area chapters in *Sardinia Area by Area* describe the main sights and monuments in detail, with maps, pictures, and illustrations. *Travelers' Needs* offers recommendations on hotels, restaurants, and bars as well as features on what to eat, drink and where to shop. The *Survival Guide* contains practical information on everything from transportation to safety.

SARDINIA AREA BY AREA

Sardinia has been divided into five main sightseeing areas, each coded with a colored thumb tab for quick reference. A map illustrating how the island has been divided can be found on the inside front cover of this guide. The sights covered within the individual areas have been plotted and numbered on a *Pictorial Map*.

Each area can be identified quickly by its color coding.

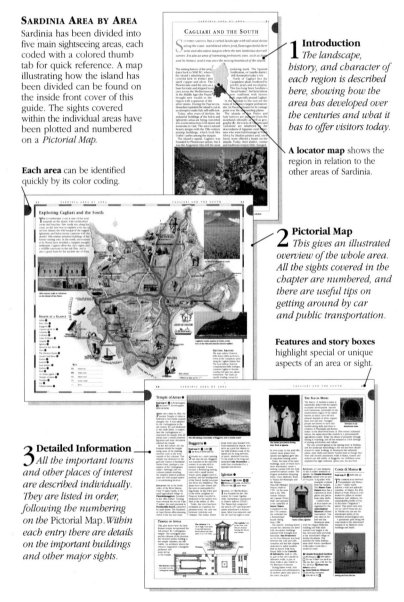

1 Introduction
The landscape, history, and character of each region is described here, showing how the area has developed over the centuries and what it has to offer visitors today.

A locator map shows the region in relation to the other areas of Sardinia.

2 Pictorial Map
This gives an illustrated overview of the whole area. All the sights covered in the chapter are numbered, and there are useful tips on getting around by car and public transportation.

Features and story boxes highlight special or unique aspects of an area or sight.

3 Detailed Information
All the important towns and other places of interest are described individually. They are listed in order, following the numbering on the Pictorial Map. *Within each entry there are details on the important buildings and other major sights.*

4 Major Towns
All the important towns are described individually. Within each entry there is further detailed information on important buildings and other sites. The Town Map *shows the location of the main sights.*

A Visitors' Checklist gives you the practical details to plan your visit, including travel information, the address of the tourist office, market days, and festivals.

The Town Map shows all major and minor roads. The key sights are plotted, along with train and bus stations, parking areas, churches, and tourist information offices.

5 Street-by-Street Map
Towns or districts of special interest to the visitor are given a bird's-eye view in detailed 3D with photographs and descriptions of the most important sights.

A suggested route for a walk covers the most interesting streets in the area.

Opening hours, telephone number and transit details for the sight are given in the Visitors' Checklist.

6 The Top Sights
These are given two or more pages. Historic buildings are dissected to reveal their interiors, while the photographs highlight the most interesting features.

Stars indicate sights that visitors should not miss.

INTRODUCING
SARDINIA

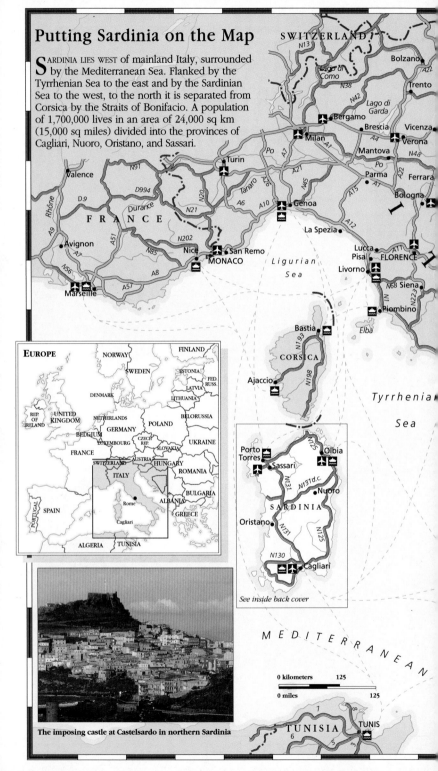

Putting Sardinia on the Map

Sardinia lies west of mainland Italy, surrounded by the Mediterranean Sea. Flanked by the Tyrrhenian Sea to the east and by the Sardinian Sea to the west, to the north it is separated from Corsica by the Straits of Bonifacio. A population of 1,700,000 lives in an area of 24,000 sq km (15,000 sq miles) divided into the provinces of Cagliari, Nuoro, Oristano, and Sassari.

SWITZERLAND
N13
Lago di Como
Bolzano
A22
Trento
N42
N38
Lago di Garda
N48
Bergamo
Brescia
Vicenza
Verona
Milan
Mantova
Turin
Po
A7
A1
A21
A22
Parma
Ferrara
Valence
N91
Tanaro
A26
A45
A1
Po
A15
Bologna
Rhône
D9
D994
N20
A6
A10
Genoa
A13
A14
La Spezia
A12
FRANCE
Durance
N21
Lucca
A11
FLORENCE
Avignon
A51
N202
Nice
Pisa
A9
A7
N85
San Remo
Livorno
N68
Siena
MONACO
Ligurian
Sea
N223
A57
A8
Piombino
N1
Marseille
Elba

EUROPE

NORWAY
FINLAND
SWEDEN
ESTONIA
FED. RUSS.
DENMARK
LATVIA
LITHUANIA
REP. OF IRELAND
UNITED KINGDOM
NETHERLANDS
BELORUSSIA
POLAND
BELGIUM
GERMANY
LUXEMBOURG
CZECH REP
SLOVAKIA
UKRAINE
FRANCE
SWITZERLAND
AUSTRIA
HUNGARY
ROMANIA
ITALY
SPAIN
Rome
ALBANIA
BULGARIA
GREECE
PORTUGAL
Cagliari
ALGERIA
TUNISIA

Bastia
N193
CORSICA
N198
Ajaccio

Tyrrhenian
Sea

Porto Torres
N125
Olbia
Sassari
N131 d.c.
Nuoro
N131
Oristano
SARDINIA
N125
N31
N130
Cagliari

See inside back cover

MEDITERRANEAN

0 kilometers   125

0 miles   125

The imposing castle at Castelsardo in northern Sardinia

TUNISIA
TUNIS

Satellite view of Northern Italy and Sardinia

KEY

☐	Area covered by this guide
⚓	Ferry port
✈	Airport
▬	Highway
▬	Major road
- -	Ferry routes
·–·–	International borders

A PORTRAIT OF SARDINIA

T HE VERY ISOLATION OF THIS LARGE ISLAND *set in the middle of the Mediterranean has shaped its unique character. For thousands of years Sardinia has stood on the sidelines of mainstream Mediterranean historical events, remaining a singular world to itself. Even the Romans found it a difficult place to subdue.*

The experience of invasion from across the water over the centuries has left a legacy that is still evident today. The roads tend to follow valleys inland rather than tracing a scenic path along the beautiful coastline. There are yachting marinas and harbors, but fishing is not a mainstay of the economy and, even in peacetime, Sardinia has never really become a seafaring nation. Over the years Sardinia's shores have seen the arrival of Phoenicians, Romans, Genoans battling for supremacy with Pisans and Arabs, the Spanish, and finally the House of Savoy. The different cultures have contributed to the art, architecture, and cultural life of Sardinia, and evidence is scattered throughout the island: prehistoric dwellings and

Detail of a mural at Orgosolo

fortresses from the earliest known inhabitants, ancient rock-cut tombs, and Romanesque churches which resemble those of Pisa or Lucca. Introduced artistic styles were often taken up and developed with distinctive Sardinian character – the altar paintings in the Spanish *retablo* tradition, for instance. In 1848 this untamed island became part of the newly created nation of Italy.

The 20th century brought with it dreams of industrialization and new-found prosperity, as well as the beginnings of a tourist industry.

However, the Sardinia that brings the visitors is a land of white beaches and deep blue sea, which does not really represent the essence of the place. The coastline is certainly beautiful, apart from some stretches

The stately procession of Sant'Efisio passing through Pula

◁ **The rugged cliffs of Punta Cristallo**

where random building spoiled the views. But the interior is stunningly beautiful too, and deserves further exploration. The natural scenery is extremely varied, providing totally different environments and habitats for plants, animals, and birds. In some areas there are fertile alluvial plains, in others steep mountains of granite and limestone where panoramas change from horizontal to vertical in the space of a few miles.

PEOPLE, LANGUAGE, AND MUSIC

Human settlements have existed in the interior for thousands of years, and Sardinia is studded with the traces of ancient pastoral civilizations, further proof that the people have always tended to prefer to live in the comparative safety of the mountainous interior rather than along the coasts. The passing of the seasons is still marked by the stages in the agricultural year, and by celebrations of successful harvests. Ancient traditions – now deeply rooted in Catholicism

Hand loom at the Museo Etnografico in Nuoro

but showing traces of far older religions – are manifested in numerous festivals, which are often based on the very close relationship between the people of the island and their natural environment.

A number of very different dialects can be heard in the interior of the island, and the Sardinian language still has a clear Latin base – the word *domus* is used to mean a house, for instance, instead of the Italian *casa*. Years of Spanish rule mean that in some towns on the west coast you can still hear Catalan spoken on the streets, and, on the island of Sant'Antioco in the southwest, the traditions and the cooking reflect a Ligurian heritage.

Music features strongly in Sardinian life, and feast days, weddings, and ordinary everyday events, especially in the interior, are always celebrated with music. Musicologists and musicians – such as Peter Gabriel, who recorded the music of the Tenores de Bitti group in his world music series – have described traditional Sardinian music as unique in Europe. Today it is undergoing something of a revival. There is a great deal of vocal and instrumental variety; based on the sound of the *launeddas*, a cane wind instrument, and polyphonic music for

Fishermen at work on Isola Rossa

Decanting ewes' milk after the morning milking

four voices. The most well-known exponents of the art are the Canto a Tenores, who perform regularly to growing numbers.

ECONOMIC DEVELOPMENT

In an uneasy position between the past and the future, the economy of Sardinia is complex. Agriculture and shepherding used to be the key factors in the economy, and there was also a mining boom in certain areas after unification, particularly around Sulcis, an abundant source of both coal and metals. But the Sardinian mining industry declined, especially after World War II and is unlikely to recover. Other plans for promoting industry have badly affected the environment and have been abandoned. However, attempts in the 1950s to eradicate malaria, by treating marshy areas with pesticides, produced impressive results: in a short space of time the coast became habitable.

TOURISM IN SARDINIA TODAY

Interest in creating the facilities needed for tourism in Sardinia was initially subdued, and services were slow to take off. The gradual development of

Traditional bread from the Sulcis region

tourism has, however, made the island famous, opening up Sardinia to the outside world, as well as increasing awareness of its history, local culture, arts, and handicrafts.

The island's varied wildlife was perhaps bound to be affected by increasing numbers of visitors, and wildlife and marine parks have now been established to protect unique habitats and their flora and fauna. The vast, wild Gennargentu range is also now a protected National Park. In recent years, the rare monk seàl, thought to be extinct, has been sighted once again off the western coast, an indication that it is possible for tourism and ecology to co-exist in comfort. Sardinia possesses some of the most pristine scenery in Europe that, like its other special qualities, can only be fully appreciated by visiting the island.

The stacks on the Masua and Nebida coastlines

Marine Life of Sardinia

Prawn

THE WATERS around Sardinia are considered to be the cleanest in Italy and are rich in flora and fauna. The generally healthy sea-beds are havens for both scuba divers and naturalists. The sheer cliffs along the coast are home to dozens of species of nesting birds and birds of prey. Years of marine research in the Golfo di Orosei, on the eastern coast, have finally confirmed the return of the fabled monk seal, once so widespread in the area that caves and inlets were named after it. Dolphins and other large sea mammals, such as small whales, can occasionally be seen in the northwestern waters and the Straits of Bonifacio. In recent years the area has been declared an international marine preserve.

Neptune grass (Posidonia oceanica) *is a sea plant with shaggy leaves that grows down to a depth of 30–35 m (100–115 ft). Sea grass, as it is also known, has flowers, which is unusual for a marine plant.*

Rocks of volcanic origin

The striped *sarago*, a common fish in the Mediter-ranean, combs the seabed in search of prey.

Rocks are covered with seaweed such as *Cystoseira.*

Sardinian coral *can be various shades of red or white and lives on the rocky seabed, between 15– 100 m (50–140 ft) below sea level.*

The lobster *is a crustacean that lives mostly along the rocky shores but can also be found at depths of up to 100 m (328 ft). The meat is a local delicacy.*

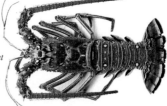

The sea anemone *attaches itself to rocks in shallow water. Its decep-tively delicate tentacles contain stinging cells, enabling it to capture small fish and crustaceans.*

Gorgonian coral *survives because the water is so clean. The flexible branches may be white, yellow, or red, and can grow to be 1m (3 ft) tall.*

BIRDS OF THE COASTLINE

The cliffs along the Sardinian coastline provide an ideal habitat for birds. Wild pigeons build safe nests here and raise their young without being disturbed. Herring gulls, Audouin's gulls, and cormorants perch on the rocks between bouts of fishing. Farther up the cliff edge, birds of prey such as the peregrine falcon, the red kite, and the rare griffon vulture, build their nests.

Cormorants on the cliff ledges

Audouin's gull

Herring gull

Peregrine falcon

Red kite

UNDERWATER MEDITERRANEAN

The Mediterranean Sea has a rich and varied ecosystem, sustained by warm currents and clean waters. There is coral and myriad species of seaweed, a wide variety of fish, crustaceans, and mollusks, and marvelous rock formations for snorkelers and scuba divers to enjoy.

Cracks and crevices in the rocks make an ideal habitat for the moray eel.

Fronds

Brown meagres move in schools to defend themselves from predators by day. At night they hunt mollusks, small fish, and prawns.

Dolphins *are frequently seen riding the waves at the bow of a boat in the warm waters around Sardinia, particularly in the clear sea of the Maddalena along the northern shore.*

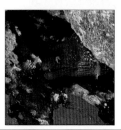

The moray eel *has powerful teeth and poisonous mucus. It also has an excellent ability to camouflage itself, making it one of the most dangerous creatures in the Mediterranean Sea.*

Monk seals, *once thought to be extinct, have returned to the Golfo di Orosei where they live in grottoes and solitary caves.*

The Sardinian Coastline

Grains of quartz on Is Arutas

WASHED BY THE CLEAR blue waters of the Mediterranean, Sardinia offers a varied coastline of sculpted cliffs and coves. Secluded inlets alternate with golden sand dunes, where wild lilies and cistus bloom, or rugged cliffs that plummet into the sea. The best-known resort is the world-famous Costa Smeralda where visitors come to enjoy luxury villas and lovely, sandy beaches. Other popular areas are the coast south of Olbia, including the sheltered Cala Gonone and the southeastern tip of the island, near Villasimius (easily accessible from Cagliari). Several stretches of coastline have remained untouched, such as the isolated coves between Orosei and Arbatax, and the southwestern area between Baia Chia and Oristano.

At Capo Caccia, *sheer limestone cliffs, 168 m (551 ft) high, jut out from the sea.*

Between Bosa and Alghero *the spectacular coastline is punctuated by cliffs of volcanic origin, covered with mastic trees.*

Around Piscinas *the coast is known for its impressive wind-carved sand dunes. The sand is an ideal habitat for juniper and tamarisk.*

The cliffs on the island of San Pietro*, eroded by sea and wind, are of pink and gray trachyte. Crevices and ledges offer useful shelter to rare birds like Eleonora's falcon.*

Isola dell'Asinara

GOLFO DELL'ASINARA

Porto Torres

THE NORTH AN
THE COSTA
SMERALDA

Alghero

MAR DI
SARDEGNA

THE
WESTERN
COAST

⑤ Bosa Marina

④ Is Arutas

Oristano

③ Piscinas Dunes

② Cala Domestica

Isola di
San Pietro

CAGLIARI
AND
THE SOUTH

① Cagliari

Isola di
Sant'Antioco

GOL
CAG

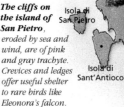

The Costa Smeralda *is characterized by granite cliffs shaped by wind and water erosion, and by inlets with clear water – paradise for scuba divers, snorkelers, and surfers.*

In the Golfo di Orosei *the limestone cliffs plunge into the sea. Isolated coves can be reached only by boat or a long hike on foot through the maquis.*

0 kilometers   40

0 miles   40

The Arbatax coast *is famous for the reddish color of the porphyry rock and the steely gray color of the older granite, jutting out in pinnacles from the sea.*

SARDINIA'S TEN BEST BEACHES

Most lively ①
Il Poetto, just outside Cagliari, is the largest and liveliest beach on the island. Locals throng here on weekends and throughout the summer.

Most hidden beach ②
Cala Domestica, protected by a Saracen tower, is invisible from the sea. In World War II it was used as a German military base.

Best dunes ③
At Piscinas there are 9 km (5 miles) of sand dunes covered with maquis vegetation. Some are as tall as 50 m (164 ft), the highest in Europe.

Most tropical ④
The beach at Is Arutas is made of tiny grains of quartz. A forest of pine trees forms a green backdrop to the sand.

Cleanest sea ⑤
Bosa Marina, unchanged since the 1950s, has won medals for being the cleanest beach in Italy.

Best windsurfing ⑥
A strong and constant breeze from the mouth of the Liscia river makes Porto Pollo (*Porto Puddu* in Sardinian dialect) perfect for windsurfing.

Best coral beach ⑦
The beach on the island of Budelli consists of pieces of shells, coral, and marine microorganisms. Note, however, that these must not be taken as souvenirs.

Best beach for young people ⑧
La Cinta, 1 km (half a mile) long, is a favorite with the trendy younger set. It is ideal for soaking up the sun and for windsurfing.

Most remote beach ⑨
Berchida, with its white beach and red rocks, can be reached only via a long sandy track through the shrubby maquis.

Most inaccessible beach ⑩
The secluded Cala Luna, with its white sand, pink oleanders, and green mastic trees, is accessible only by boat or on foot.

The Flora and Fauna of Sardinia

FROM THE RUGGED GENNARGENTU massif to the Campidano plains, from the Nurra hills to the wind-eroded rocks of the Gallura area, Sardinia offers a great variety of natural habitats for wildlife. The forests, especially in the north, are dominated by cork oaks, for centuries a useful source of raw material. The Mediterranean maquis is permeated with the scents of mastic trees, cistus, myrtle, and strawberry trees. Despite decades of farming, the fauna is still varied and interesting. Deer and wild boar abound in the scrub and forests and the rocks are home to the moufflon. The small Monte Arcosu preserve retains a tiny population of rare Sardinian deer, and the island of Asinara is the home of wild donkeys. In the spectacular Giara di Gesturi plateau, wild horses graze freely. Assorted reptiles can also be found but no vipers.

Donkey at Gesturi

The moufflon is an ancient inhabitant of the island. It has a thick coat and impressive curving horns.

Sardinian deer are stocky, with smaller horns than their mainland counterparts.

Foxes can still be seen on Monte Limbara and Gennargentu.

Mountain

Woods

Marshl

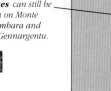

The Sardinian horse is a compact animal native to the island. The horses roam on the Giara di Gesturi plateau and on the Capo Caccia headland.

The Kermes oak (Quercus coccifera) thrives mostly on the southern coastline.

The cork oak (Quercus suber), important to the economy, dominates the forest of Gallura (see p151).

Sardinian boar live in various parts of the island. They are smaller and stouter than species on mainland Italy.

The holm oak (Quercus ilex) *predominates in almost all medium-altitude woods.*

THE MEDITERRANEAN MAQUIS

This thick, often impenetrable, shrubby vegetation (*macchia* in Italian) thrives in the coastal and mountainous regions of Sardinia. The shrubs – including myrtle, arbutus (strawberry tree), and blackthorn – flower in spring, rest in summer, and revive again in autumn. Even in winter the island looks green, with splashes of color from berries. In recent years the area of maquis has increased, as a result of forest fires that encourage plenty of new growth.

Myrtle in flower

Strawberry tree

White cistus flowers

The kite's habitat is the wooded upland valleys.

THE SARDINIAN TERRAIN

The southwestern corner of Sardinia began to emerge from the sea over 500 million years ago.

Turtles, which may grow up to as much as 1 m (3 ft) in length, are dying out because their eggs are highly prized.

Plain

Mastic trees (Pistacia lentiscus) *grow on the coast, on Monte Limbara, and the Gennargentu.*

The flamingo *winters in the coastal marshes and lagoons, and now nests on Sardinia.*

The white-headed duck, *which nests among reeds, is a rare sight on the Sardinian marshland.*

Prickly pears (Opuntia) *are a characteristic feature everywhere along the coastline.*

The Nuraghi

THERE ARE OVER 7,000 NURAGHI in Sardinia, their distinctive truncated cones a familiar part of the landscape. Little is known about their builders, a civilization that flourished on the island from 1800 to 500 BC (in some areas the nuraghic peoples resisted the Romans long after this date). Initially a nuraghe consisted of a single tower made of huge blocks of stone laid without mortar. Later, more towers were added, with connecting ramparts, resulting in more complex structures such as the Losa nuraghe at Abbasanta, the Santu Antine at Torralba, and the Su Nuraxi at Barùmini. Nuraghi served as both dwelling and fortress, and the towers were often surrounded by a village and wall. There is no trace of any written language, but over 1,500 bronze figures have been found in tombs and near holy wells. The figures, and other finds, are now on display in Sardinia's archaeological museums.

Bronze quiver

Tribal chief
This bronze figure comes from the nuraghic village of Santa Vittoria, at Serri, one of the largest in Sardinia. It is a portrait of a prince at prayer.

Simple nuraghe
This is the most commonly seen and simplest form of nuraghe, consisting of a single tower with a chamber made of inwardly stepped circular tiers of stones. At times these nuraghi had more than one level.

The central tower is in the shape of a truncated cone.

The rampart incorporates three defense towers.

Outer defense wall

Sassari

Nuoro

Oristano

Cagliari

● Principal Nuraghic Sites

The Losa Nuraghe at Abbasanta
This nuraghe is in three parts and is surrounded by a rampart with small towers. The oldest tower dates from before 1500 BC. There is a fine panoramic view of the Gennargentu mountains from the terrace.

Maiori Nuraghe at Tempio Pausania
*This ground-floor room of the Maiori nuraghe
in northern Sardinia could be illuminated only
by light filtering in from the outside.*

NURAGHIC BURIALS

The nuraghic peoples built monumental
tombs known as Tombe dei Giganti
(Tombs of Giants) to bury their dead.
Each tomb consisted of a long covered
corridor constructed with huge slabs of
stone. The shape represented the horn
of the Bull God. A monolithic oval stele,
with an opening at the base, formed the
front face. Two rows of stones on either
side, forming an arch, completed the
burial chamber. The central, arched
stele could sometimes be as high as
3 m (10 ft). The area around a typical
Tomba dei Giganti was often surrounded by long rows of menhirs.

**The Tomb of Giants at Li Lolghi is one of the
most famous prehistoric sites in Sardinia**

The central tower
had three super-
imposed chambers.

The side towers
were built at a
later stage, in the
early Iron Age.

The rampart
created a solid
defense system.

SANTU ANTINE NURAGHE
The central tower of this roughly
triangular nuraghe is surrounded
by a three-sided rampart with three
towers. It was built in different stages
in the 9th–8th centuries BC. The huge
complex was later dedicated to the
Roman emperor Constantine.

*This
reconstruction
shows the original layout of Santu
Antine. The central tower was the
main fortress and dwelling,
protected by the external towers.*

Arrubiu Nuraghe
*This consists of a massive fortress built in red
stone covering an area of about 7 acres at
the edge of a plateau dominating the
Flumendosa valley. Imposing external
ramparts with five towers protected the
inner courtyard and the central nuraghic
construction, which was 16 m (52 ft) high.*

Music and Dance in Sardinia

THE MUSIC of Sardinia ranks among the oldest in the Mediterranean. This is demonstrated by the nuraghic bronze figure (8th–7th centuries BC) from Ittiri, now in the Museo Archeologico in Cagliari *(see p58)*. The bronze represents a musician playing the *launeddas*, a three-piped Sardinian wind instrument still used in processions and dances. It is a difficult instrument to play and requires a special breathing technique. It consists of three flutes of varying length: *su tumbu* (the longest), *sa mancosa,* and *sa mancosedda*. The *Canto a Tenores* is unaccompanied four-part polyphonic music for male voices: *sa boghe* (the soloist, who also directs the group); *sa contra* and *su basso* (accompanying voices with guttural sounds); and *sa mesa boghe* (a soft, low voice that serves to blend the different sounds). Dance has always been a fundamental part of religious feasts and festivals linked with the stages in the farming year. The dancers move in short steps, their heads high, backs straight, and bodies rigid.

Sardinian bells

A nuraghic bronze statuette of a flute player shows the musician playing reed pipes, the instrument that later became known as the launeddas.

Canto a Tenores is unaccompanied four-part singing.

The singers wear typical Nuoro costume.

Organittu, *together with the guitar and accordion, are the main instruments used to accompany the popular Sardinian round dances.*

The four voices are: *sa boghe, sa contra, sa basso,* and *sa mesa boghe.*

MUSICAL INFLUENCES

For years Sardinian musicians have used their folk tradition and instruments to create experimental music. The most famous are the Tenores di Bitti, who have recorded for Peter Gabriel's Real World, and who have also worked with the famous jazz artist Ornette Coleman. The *launeddas* player Luigi Lai has worked together with Angelo Branduardi.. Paolo Fresu, one of Italy's top jazz musicians, is Sardinian, and often draws inspiration from the music of his native land. Fresu was the driving force behind *Sonos 'e memoria,* an interesting project that brought together the leading island musicians to perform live for the soundtrack of a black-and-white film on Sardinian life in the first half of the 20th century.

Cover for the Tenores di Bitti's album *Intonos*

Paolo Fresu

Sardinian rock groups *often adapt traditional music and instruments to a modern style, as well as developing new ideas.*

THE TENORES DI BITTI

The Tenores from Bitti are the most famous Canto a Tenores group. They have appeared with Peter Gabriel and Ornette Coleman, increasing awareness of Sardinian folk music.

THE MUSIC MUSEUM

Tadasuni, a village on the shores of Lake Omodeo, near Ghilarza, has a jewel in store for music-lovers. The **Museo degli Strumenti della Musica Popolare della Sardegna** (Museum of Sardinian Folk Music Instruments) houses over 300 instruments collected by the local parish priest, Don Giovanni Dore. He spent decades traveling around the island to gather the instruments, which for the most part feature typical island wind and reed instruments,

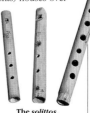

The *solittos*, a wind instrument

such as the *launeddas*. This ancient three-pipe wind instrument, made from seasoned cane, emits an uninterrupted sound (similar to the bagpipes). Other wind instruments on display in the museum include the *cornetts*, the *solittos*, the *bena doppia*, and *bena semplice*, all flutelike instruments made of cane. There are also drums, such as the *tumbarinu 'e gavoi*, the *moggiu*, and the *tumbarineddu*, made of cork, tin, or wood. The drum skin is traditionally made of stretched dog, donkey, or goat skin. Of these, the *trimpanu* was used to frighten horses and unseat the Carabinieri riders in times of civil unrest. There are also barrel organs, introduced in Sardinia in the mid-19th century.

🏛 **Museo degli Strumenti della Musica Popolare della Sardegna**
Via Adua 7, Tadasuni. 📞 0785-501 13.
⭕ *by appt only.*

The dance's name derives from the position of the dancers, who form a circle.

The dance takes place outside, during feasts and festivals.

Men and women hold hands.

Traditional costumes are still worn.

The Round Dance
This 19th-century print depicts a Sardinian round dance. The dance is not just found in Sardinia, and there are numerous local variations.

SARDINIA
THROUGH THE YEAR

SPRING IS BY FAR the best season to visit Sardinia. Perfumed flowers are in bloom in the maquis thickets, the woods and meadows are still green and, although the weather is warm enough for swimming as early as May, it has not reached the scorching temperatures of summer. Easter, with its colorful processions, marks the religious high point of the island. During the rest of the year, towns and villages organize festivals to commemorate the feast day of the local saint, and sanctuaries are enlivened by cel-

Mask from Mamoiada

ebrations and banquets. The summer is dedicated to activities along the island's stunning coast, such as swimming, sailing, and windsurfing. Inland, it can get stiflingly hot in summer, but the higher mountainous areas provide a cool retreat from the crowds and an ideal place for hiking. Grape harvesting begins in the autumn, and in early winter there is heavy snowfall on the Mount Gennargentu massif. At times snow can fall even on the lower areas covering the rocky landscape of the Supramonte.

Narcissus in bloom, a typical flower of the Mediterranean

SPRING

ONCE THE WARM spring weather sets in, the sheep and goats grazing on the hillsides will be moved to higher pastures. The aromatic plants and strongly scented flowers of the maquis are in full bloom, and bees abound. They produce the somewhat bitter honey used in many traditional Sardinian cakes.

In the flatlands and on the hills of the Anglona and Montiferru regions the fruit trees are in blossom, while in the countryside young artichokes are almost ready to be picked. These are shipped to vegetable markets on mainland Italy and are traditionally the first on the market.

MARCH AND APRIL

Holy Week and **Easter** *(Mar or Apr)* are a time of great religious celebrations, with colorful processions taking place throughout the island.

In Cagliari there is an important procession through the streets on Good Friday. A representation of the *Iscravamentu* and *Incontru* mystery plays is performed at Iglesias. At Oliena the costume procession known as *S'Incontru* takes place on Easter Sunday. *Su Concordu* in the town of Santu Lussurgiu features 15th-century psalms sung in Gregorian chant. On Holy Monday at Castelsardo, there is the *Luni Santu*, a religious feast of Spanish origin. The **Livestock Festival** *(Mar 25)* at Ollastra Simaxis, is in honor of St Mark.

Sagra del Riccio di Mare *(early Mar)*. A festival of the sea urchin in Alghero.

Festa Patronale *(2nd Sat after Easter)*. The island of Sant'Antioco celebrates its patron saint's feast day.

MAY

Sant'Efisio *(May 1-4)*, in Cagliari, offers a grand procession commemorating the end of the plague in 1656. The saint's statue is carried through the city and then taken to Nora on an ox-drawn cart. During this splendid display of religious feeling the faithful cast flowers into the street as the statue passes by.

San Francesco's feast day *(second Sun)*. Held at Lula, this is one of the most popular celebrations in the Baronie and Nuoro areas.

Festa dell'Annunziata *(third Sun)*, at Bitti. A pastoral celebration of the Annunciation.

San Bachisio *(May 29)*. This feast day consists of three days of *Ballu Tundu* (round dance) in the squares of Onanì.

The *S'Incontru* procession in the streets of Oliena on Easter Day

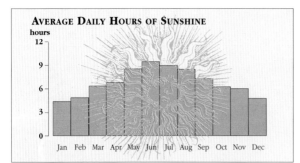

AVERAGE DAILY HOURS OF SUNSHINE

hours

12 — 9 — 6 — 3 — 0 —

Jan Feb Mar Apr May Jun Jul Aug Sep Oct Nov Dec

Sunshine Chart
Summer is the sunniest as well as the hottest time, and June has the maximum hours of sunshine daily. The least sunny month is January, but the weather varies a great deal between inland and coastal regions, and in general, coastal areas will be brighter.

The Ardia horse race in front of the Sant'Antine sanctuary at Sedilo

Cavalcata Sarda *(Ascension Day)*. Although this is a fairly new tradition, the "Sardinian Horseride" has become one of the island's major folk festivals. Handicraft stands and general festivities fill the streets of Sassari's old town center. People from all over the island crowd into the town on horseback or dressed in colorful costumes to hear traditional songs and poetry from the different towns and regions of the island.

SUMMER

THE HIGH TEMPERATURES and stunning coastline draw locals and visitors alike to the seashore during the summer months. The coastline is filled with swimmers and windsurfers, and yachts and sailboats from all over Europe dock at the small harbors. For snorkelers and scuba divers there are underwater beds of posidonia to explore. Sailing, windsurf, and scuba-diving clubs organize lessons throughout the summer months *(see pp198–9)*.

JUNE

Horse Festival *(Jun 1-3)* Santu Lussurgiu holds an important agricultural festival with a handicrafts exhibition.
Sagra delle Ciliegie *(first Sun of month)*. Festival celebrating the cherry harvest at Villacidro, Bonarcado and Burcei.
Handicrafts Fair *(Jun 11)*. The streets of Villanova Monteleone teem with stalls.

The cooler temperatures on the slopes of Gennargentu make it excellent for hikers, and the climb down the gorges of Su Gorroppu is also popular.

This is the period of rural festivals, when small religious sanctuaries hidden among the valleys and hills come to life with pilgrimages and feasting.
Pani, Pisci, Pezza e Piricchittus *(Jun–Sep)*, meaning bread, fish, pizza, and almond pastry, is a food festival held in the restaurants of Quartu. Cagliari offers a program of music, theater, and film. At San Gavino Monreale there are concerts and other cultural events as well as sports activities at night.

JULY

Ardia *(Jul 5-8)*. This characteristic rural festival is held at San Costantino a Sedilo in front of the Santu Antine sanctuary. A lively horse race accompanies celebrations honouring the saint.
Sagra del Torrone *(second Sun of month)*. At Tonara, at the foot of the Gennargentu mountains, the festivities end with the preparation of the famous nougat *(torrone)*.
Sagra delle Pesche *(Jul 17)*, is a peach festival held at San Sperate on the feast day of the town's patron saint.
Estate Musicale *(Jul–Aug)* at Alghero, with concerts in the Chiostro di San Francesco.
International Folklore Festival *(end of Jul)*, held in Tempio Pausania, during the summer Carnival.
Carpet Fair *(two weeks in Jul or Aug)* at Mogoro. This is one of the leading displays of Sardinian handicrafts, in particular carpets, tapestry, and handmade furniture.
Music in Antas Valley *(Jul–Aug)*. Classical music concerts held in the splendid setting of the Temple of Antas at Fluminimaggiore *(see p68)*.

Advanced sailing lessons off the Costa Smeralda

AVERAGE MONTHLY RAINFALL

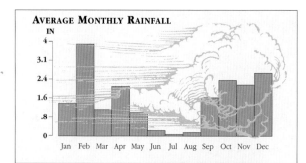

IN	
4	
3.1	
2.4	
1.6	
.8	
0	

Jan Feb Mar Apr May Jun Jul Aug Sep Oct Nov Dec

Rainfall Chart

In Sardinia most of the rainfall occurs in the autumn and winter. The rainfall is heavier in the mountainous regions of the interior, with precipitation as high as 1,000 mm (39 inches) per year. The driest season is during the summer months, particularly in the coastal regions.

AUGUST

Mauretanian Wedding *(Aug 1–15)* at Santadi. A ceremony dating back to the ancient traditions of the North Africans who inhabited the Sulcis region in Roman times.
Dieci Giorni Sulcitani *(Aug 1–15)* in Sant'Antioco. This consists of ten evenings of traditional local entertainment, including plays in dialect, Sardinian poetry, traditional folk dances, and local choral music.
Carpet Show *(first Sun of month)*. Traditional handmade carpets and blankets are exhibited at Aggius.
Madonna della Neve feast day *(first Sun of Aug)*. The hardships of winter are exorcised in the Tascusì sanctuary at Desulo.
Sagra del Vino *(Aug 4)*. Wine festival at Jerzu with costume parades, dances, traditional songs, and Cannonau wine.
Vernaccia Wine Festival *(Aug 6)*. Festival of the local wine at Baratili San Pietro, near Oristano.
Sagra del Pomodoro *(Aug 11)*. The tomato festival offers tomato-based dishes served

A drummer playing at the Time in Jazz festival at Berchidda

outdoors at Zeddiano. There is also an exhibition of local farm produce.
Faradda di Candelieri *(Aug 14)*. Candles *(candelieri)*, weighing between 200–300 kg (440–660 lbs) are carried by members of the ancient guilds in Sassari. Each candle is decorated with the coat of arms of the guild and its patron saint.
Time in Jazz *(the week incorporating Ferragosto)*. Berchidda hosts an annual jazz festival.
Processione del Redentore *(29 Aug)*. Nuoro hosts one of Sardinia's most popular celebrations with a procession

through the streets in honor of Christ the Redeemer, and performances of local folklore.
Launeddas Festival *(fourth Sun)* at San Vito. This festival features performances by leading musicians of the traditional triple-piped wind instrument *(see p90)*. The music is accompanied by the *Ballu Tundu*, a circular dance.
Rassegna di Musica Leggera *(Aug–Sep)*. Performances of popular music and theater in Piazza Peglia, Carloforte.
Regata Vela Latina *(end of Sep)*. A regatta for traditional Sardinian fishing boats.
Mostra del Tappeto *(mid-Aug–late Sep)*. A carpet fair held at Nule.

AUTUMN

IT IS STILL POSSIBLE to swim in the sea into September, but the air becomes cooler in the evening. October is grape harvest time, and autumn marks the beginning of the hunting season. The favorite game is wild boar, a tasty meat used in the strongly flavored Sardinian cuisine. The chestnut harvest in the mountains often ends with lively festivals.

SEPTEMBER

Pilgrimage to the Madonna di Gonare Sanctuary *(Sep 8, 16)*. Departures to this hilltop church alternate between the centers of Sarule *(see p103)* and Orani.
Fiera del Bestiame *(third Sun of month)* at Serri. A livestock fair on the day of Santa Lucia.
Santa Cosma *(Sep 27)*. The *Mamuthones (see p102)* parade through the streets of Mamoiada in sheepskins.

Traditional costumes worn for the Madonna della Neve festival at Desulo

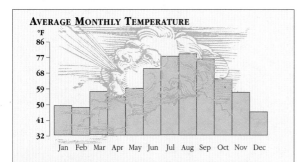

AVERAGE MONTHLY TEMPERATURE

°F
86
77
68
59
50
41
32

Jan Feb Mar Apr May Jun Jul Aug Sep Oct Nov Dec

Temperature Chart
The summer months between June and September are hot and dry, with temperatures above 20° C (68° F), and at times reaching 30° C (86° F). In winter the temperatures are mild, rarely dipping below 5° C (41° F). January generally has sunny days and cold nights.

Masked figures (Boes) with cowbells during carnival at Ottana

OCTOBER

Santa Vitalia Festival *(first Mon of month).* A festival dedicated to agriculture held at Serrenti, with stalls selling local handicrafts.
Sagra delle Castagne e delle Nocciole *(fourth Sun).* Festival to celebrate the ripening and the harvest of chestnuts and hazelnuts at Aritzo. There is also a handicrafts fair.

NOVEMBER

Festa della Madonna dello Schiavo *(Nov 15).* A statue of the Madonna is worshiped as it passes through the town of Carloforte. The statue is said to have been sculpted by citizens from Carloforte, who had been kidnapped by pirates and held in Tunis.
Santa Caterina *(Nov 25).* The saint's feast day is celebrated in Abbasanta.

WINTER

WINTER IS A FAIRLY cold season throughout the island, and snow covers the mountainous interior. Livestock

is returned to its lower winter pastures and pens, and the chill wind puts an end to fishing activity along the coast. As well as **Christmas**, which is very important in Sardinia, there are many other feast days and local festivals in the Carnival period before Lent.

DECEMBER

Sagra delle Salsicce *(first Sun of month)* held at Siligo. After the pig slaughter, preparation, and curing of the meat, the sausage festival is an opportunity to taste the year's new delicacies.
Christmas is celebrated at home with presents and by preparing traditional sweets.

JANUARY AND FEBRUARY

Feast of Sant'Antonio Abate *(Jan 16-17)* is celebrated at Fluminimaggiore *(see p68)* with huge bonfires in the various quarters of the town.
Carnival *(the ten days before Shrove Tuesday),* is extremely popular in Sardinia, especially in the small villages of the Barbagia region. Masked and costumed figures parade on Shrove Tuesday and the last

Sunday of Lent. At Mamoiada, the *Mamuthones,* men dressed in sheepskins with heavy bells around their necks, are run out of town by the *Issocadores (see p102).* Similar festivals during carnival are the *Thurpos* at Orotelli, and the *Merdules* and *Boes* at Ottana *(see p101).* At *Sa Sartiglia* in Oristano, masked horsemen spear a silver star hanging from a tree. There are cakes and free wine at Iglesias *(see p68),* and food is served in the main square at Perfugas. At Tempio Pausania an effigy of "King George" is burned, and at Santu Lussurgiu *(see p128)* there is the *Sa Carrela 'e Nanti* horse race.
Processo a Su Conte *(Ash Wednesday).* At Ovodda the stuffed figure of "Su Conte" is tried in the main square and burned at the stake.

Snow-covered mountains of the Gennargentu in winter

THE HISTORY OF SARDINIA

T HE ORIGINS of Sardinian history go back thousands of years. The first people to settle are thought to have reached the island by crossing over a natural causeway that once linked Tuscany and Sardinia, perhaps between 450,000 and 150,000 years ago. A succession of different cultures led up to the rise of the nuraghic civilization. These tribes of shepherds and warriors lived in round stone dwellings called nuraghi, defended by walled fortresses, and their occupation left exceptional megalithic ruins across the island. Of the 7,000 nuraghi left in Sardinia, some are in an excellent state of preservation: the Su Nuraxi settlement at Barùmini, the Santu Antine complex, and the nuraghi at Losa.

The Macomer Venus in the Museo Archeologico in Cagliari

The Phoenicians arrived in 1000 BC, settling along the coastline at Tharros, Nora, Bithia, and Cagliari; after winning the Punic Wars, the Romans occupied the island. Roman dominion lasted 700 years despite strong resistance from Sardinians, and evidence can still be seen in the many ruins. When the Roman Empire fell, Sardinia again fell prey to various conquerors. For centuries the Vandals, Byzantines, and Arabs fought for possession of the strategic harbors, until the maritime republics of Pisa and Genoa made their appearance on Sardinian waters. A golden age of Sardinian Romanesque architecture was introduced, which gave way to Gothic when the House of Aragon conquered the island. After 400 years of Spanish rule, control of the island passed to Austria, which ceded it to the House of Savoy in 1718. The Kingdom of Sardinia survived up to the unification of Italy. A long period of neglect was ended only after World War II, with the reclamation of the malarial marshes. The plan's success opened up possibilities for a tourist industry and the development of an autonomous, modern Sardinia.

Calaris, **modern-day Cagliari, in a print dating from 1590**

◁ **The Roman Temple of Antas at Fluminimaggiore, built over a 6th–5th century BC Phoenician temple**

Prehistoric Sardinia

LTHOUGH SOME stone tools found at Perfugas show that Sardinia was inhabited from the Paleolithic period (150,000 years ago), it was only around 9000 BC that the island began to be settled by populations from Asia Minor, the African coasts, the Iberian peninsula, and Liguria. The fertile, mineral-rich land and the obsidian mines at Monte Arci were a major factor in the island's prosperity. By around 3000 BC the Sardinians had grouped into tribes. They lived in villages with thatched-roof huts and buried their dead in rock-cut tombs called *domus de janas* (house of fairies). By about 1800 BC this rural society had evolved into the warrior nuraghic civilization, which built thousands of circular stone towers *(nuraghi)* across the island. Many of these remarkable prehistoric constructions are still visible.

Bronze figure from Teti-Abini

Necklace with Tusk
This ornament was found in a tomb dating from 2000–1800 BC, the bell-shaped pottery era.

Earthenware
These jugs and vases were everyday objects used to store water and grain.

The motifs on the prow have more to do with the land than the sea.

Monte d'Accoddi ruins
These traces reveal the ruins of a tiered, terraced construction, probably a temple, dating from the 3rd millennium BC. It looked remarkably similar to the famous ziggurat temples of Mesopotamia and the Aztec pyramids.

TIMELINE

6000 BC Sardinian peoples make tools and weapons from the obsidian found at Monte Arci

Obsidian arrowhead

A typical example of domus de janas

6000 BC		4000 BC

Boar tusk, an ornament from the early Neolithic period

4000–3000 BC The age of the Bonu Ighinu culture – small communities living by raising sheep and goats. Distinctive, high quality gry pottery with incised decoration is produced

Bronze Artifacts from Abini

These spears were part of a hoard of 100 kg (220 lb) of objects hidden in large clay vessels, perhaps to conceal them from the Roman invaders.

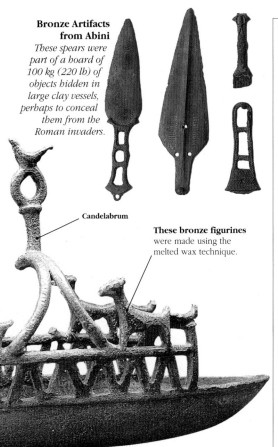

Candelabrum

These bronze figurines were made using the melted wax technique.

Ex Voto with Deer Motif

This ex voto lamp in the shape of a ship was one of 70 or so found at Is Argiolas near Bultei. It dates from the 8th–7th centuries BC and is now in the Museo Archeologico Nazionale in Cagliari. In the nuraghic age, Sardinians had a love-hate relationship with the sea, which ended with the arrival of the Carthaginians, Romans, and later conquerors, who forced the local inhabitants to live in the interior.

Where to See Prehistoric Sardinia

Prenuraghic ruins include a ziggurat at Monte d'Accoddi and rock-cut tombs *(domus de janas)* at Pranu Muteddu (Goni). Nuraghic villages survive at Su Nuraxi *(see pp64–5)*, Serra Òrrios *(see p84)*, Tiscali *(see pp104–5)*, and Abini. Burial chambers, or "Tombs of Giants," can be seen at places such as Sa Ena 'e Thomes, and holy wells can be visited at Santa Cristina (Paulilàtino) and Santa Vittoria (Serri).

The nuraghic village of Serra Òrrios *is one of the best preserved in Sardinia. It consisted of about 70 dwellings (see p84).*

The Montessu necropolis *houses domus de janas of the Ozieri prenuraghic era.*

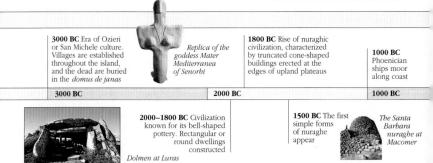

3000 BC Era of Ozieri or San Michele culture. Villages are established throughout the island, and the dead are buried in the *domus de janas*

Replica of the goddess Mater Mediterranea of Senorbi

1800 BC Rise of nuraghic civilization, characterized by truncated cone-shaped buildings erected at the edges of upland plateaus

1000 BC Phoenician ships moor along coast

3000 BC	2000 BC	1000 BC

2000–1800 BC Civilization known for its bell-shaped pottery. Rectangular or round dwellings constructed

Dolmen at Luras

1500 BC The first simple forms of nuraghe appear

The Santa Barbara nuraghe at Macomer

The Phoenicians, Carthaginians, and Romans

AROUND 1000 BC Phoenician ships began to use the inlets of the Sardinian coasts as harbors. When commerce intensified about 200 years later, they founded the cities of Nora, Sulcis, Tharros, Olbia, and later on Bithia and Karalis (today's Cagliari). But good relationships with the local chiefs soon waned. After a brief period of peace, the nuraghic populations attacked the Phoenician settlements that, in 509 BC, asked Carthage for help. In 238 BC the Carthaginians, defeated in the first Punic War, ceded Sardinia to the Romans, who made it their province. For over a century the Sardinians put up fierce resistance, a situation that ended in 215 BC with the battle of Cornus. The Romans never succeeded in subduing the entire island, and rebellion in the interior continued for years. However, Roman civilization gave the island a network of roads as well as baths, temples, aqueducts, and amphitheaters.

Oil jar, 2nd century BC

Gold Bracelet
Decorated with palmettes, lotus flowers, and scarab beetle, this bracelet came from Tharros (pp132–3).

This shape of nose is typical of the Phoenicians.

Glass Vase and Perfume Bottle
In Roman times glass was used to make ornamental vessels as well as practical objects like cups, bowls, and bottles. Numerous glass pieces have been found in burial grounds, and examples can be seen in the Museo Archeologico Nazionale in Cagliari (p58).

Lines on the face imitate tattoos.

Carthaginian Necklace
Carthaginian jewelry was often quite elaborate, as shown by this necklace with pendants carrying human and animal symbols.

GRINNING MASK

This mask dates from the 4th century BC, when the island was under Carthaginian rule. Masks like these were used to ward off evil, to protect children, or insure the sleep of the dead. This mask was found in the settlement beneath the modern town of San Sperate.

TIMELINE

900 BC Nuraghic villages, bronze figures, and stone sculptures

Phoenician ship

500–400 BC Sardinians flee to Barbagia after losing battles against Carthaginians

900 BC	750 BC		500 BC

730–700 BC First Phoenician harbors built: the future Nora, Tharros, Bithia, and Karalis

ca. 550 BC The Carthaginians arrive and found the first Punic cities

509 BC The nuraghic peoples attack the coastal cities, who ask Carthage for help

Statue of J. Caesar Drusus(13 BC–AD 23)
The portrait of the Roman consul, son of the emperor Tiberius, was found at Sant'Antioco (see p72), along with other busts from the early Empire.

The incisions show lotuses and rosettes.

Punic Inscription
This inscription was engraved on the base of the pedestal of a 4th-century BC statuette, found in the Temple of Antas.

The nose-ring is shaped like a leech.

WHERE TO SEE PUNIC–ROMAN SARDINIA

The best preserved Punic-Roman cities are Nora *(see p89)* and Tharros *(see pp132–3)*. The ruins at Sulki, present-day Sant'Antioco *(see p72)*, are entirely Punic. Roman ruins include the amphitheater in Cagliari *(see p54)*, near the Villa of Tigellio *(see p58)*, and baths at Fordongianus *(see p137)*.

***Roman amphitheater at Cagliari**, 2nd century AD.*

***The Roman theater at Nora** is still used for summer cultural events.*

Glass Bowl with the Figure of Christ
This beautiful early Christian piece was found inside a tomb near Ittiri. Christ is depicted in the role of both legislator and emperor.

238 BC The Carthaginians lose the first Punic War

227 BC Sardinia, together with Corsica, becomes Roman province

Mosaic found at Nora

AD 200–300 Full of disease, Sardinia becomes a deportation site

250 BC | **0** | **AD 250**

Temple of Antas dedicated to Sardus Pater

27 BC Sardinia is divided from Corsica and becomes a senatorial province

AD 66 Roman Sardinia becomes an imperial province and is occupied by legions

The Middle Ages, from the Vandals to the Aragonese

The Castello quarter, Cagliari
Built during the era of Pisan rule, the fortified Castello quarter in Cagliari was the heart of the city until the 1800s.

Arborea's coat of arms

IN AD 456 the Vandals conquered Sardinia. Shortly afterward, liberated by Byzantium, the island became one of the seven African provinces of the Eastern Roman Empire. The subsequent power vacuum, aggravated by Arab invasions, gave rise to the four autonomous *giudicati*, or principalities, of Torres, Gallura, Arborea, and Cagliari. Around AD 1000 the Pisans and Genoese, after fierce campaigns against the Arabs, took over parts of the island. The long relationship with Aragon was formalized in 1295, when Pope Boniface VIII signed the papal bull naming James II of Aragon as King of Corsica and Sardinia. On June 12, 1323 the Infante Alfonso landed in Sardinia with his army.

Eleonora of Arborea
This remarkable woman inherited Arborea from her father, Mariano IV, in 1383. After two wars against the Aragonese, Eleonora gained control of most of Sardinia in 1394. Known as the Giudica, she remains a symbol of Sardinian independence.

Papal coat of arms

66. B
detto
eletto
polo r

Benedetto Caetani was the real name of Pope Boniface.

Barison I's seal
In 1038 the Pisans, after wresting Sardinia from the Arabs, helped Barison I of Arborea take possession of its four giudicati (principalities).

BONIFACE VIII
In 1295, Pope Boniface VIII (depicted here while celebrating the Jubilee of 1300) signed the papal bull giving control of the *Regnum Sardiniae et Corsicae* to James II of Aragon, in exchange for relinquishing Sicily. The Aragonese proceeded to annex Sardinia, ignoring the agreement.

TIMELINE

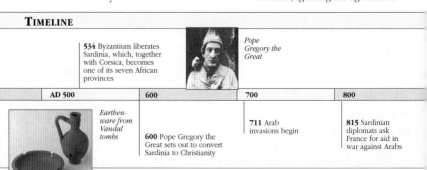

534 Byzantium liberates Sardinia, which, together with Corsica, becomes one of its seven African provinces

Pope Gregory the Great

AD 500	600	700	800

Earthenware from Vandal tombs

600 Pope Gregory the Great sets out to convert Sardinia to Christianity

711 Arab invasions begin

815 Sardinian diplomats ask France for aid in war against Arabs

Capo Falcone
This tower was part of the defense system that finally put an end to barbarian raids on Sardinia in the 16th century.

Pope Boniface VIII

WHERE TO SEE MEDIEVAL SARDINIA

The medieval conquerors often infiltrated the interior, influencing local architecture. San Saturnino in Cagliari *(see p59)* and San Gavino at Porto Torres *(see p120)* are two of the earliest medieval churches in Sardinia. Evidence of artistic contact with the mainland can be seen in the Romanesque churches of Logudoro *(see pp156–7)*, the cathedral of Oristano *(see pp134–5)*, and the cathedral of Santa Maria in Cagliari *(see p55)*. Some castles remain: the Rocca at Castelsardo *(see p164)* and the Castello complex in Cagliari *(see pp56–7)*.

Santissima Trinità di Saccargia *is Pisan Romanesque (see pp158–9).*

Boniface VIII, despite this serene pose, was a highly controversial pope.

Alghero city walls
The massive walls and their towers date from the 14th-century period of Catalan rule.

The Castello Malaspina *dominates the town of Bosa (see pp126–7).*

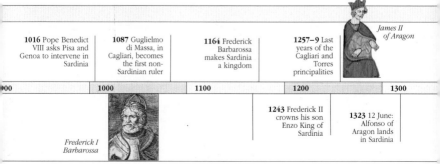

1016 Pope Benedict VIII asks Pisa and Genoa to intervene in Sardinia

1087 Guglielmo di Massa, in Cagliari, becomes the first non-Sardinian ruler

1164 Frederick Barbarossa makes Sardinia a kingdom

1257–9 Last years of the Cagliari and Torres principalities

James II of Aragon

900 **1000** **1100** **1200** **1300**

1243 Frederick II crowns his son Enzo King of Sardinia

1323 12 June: Alfonso of Aragon lands in Sardinia

Frederick I Barbarossa

Spanish Rule

Aragonese coat of arms

THE SPANISH CONQUEST of Sardinia was slow: the rulers of Arborea waged a lengthy war against the invaders; there were determined revolts in Alghero; and in 1355 the Spanish crown was forced to grant a form of parliament to the six largest cities. The Aragonese took power definitively only in 1409, when the principality of Arborea was eliminated after the bloody battle of Sanluri and replaced by the marquisate of Oristano. Spanish domination of Sardinia was strengthened in 1479 with the marriage of Ferdinand of Aragon and Isabella I of Castile and Leon. The Spanish era also saw the founding of the first universities: Sassari in 1562, and Cagliari in 1620. Following the Peace of Utrecht in 1714, the island was ceded to Austria which then, in the Treaty of London, passed it over to King Vittorio Amedeo II of the House of Savoy.

Vittorio Amedeo II of Savoy
Vittorio Amedeo became king in 1718 when Austria gave Sardinia to him in exchange for Sicily. The Cagliari parliament swore allegiance to the new king on August 2, 1720.

VICTOR AMÉDÉE.

The upper part shows scenes from the life of St. Peter; below are the saints with St. Peter in the center.

Decorated border

Four Moors Coat of Arms
Of Catalan origin, the coat of arms with four Moors first appeared in Sardinia after the arrival of Alfonso of Aragon in 1323. It has become one of the symbols of the island.

The Four Evangelists are depicted in the elaborately bordered predella. Sardinian artists put their own stamp on the Catalan *retablo* style.

TIMELINE

	1409 Battle of Sanluri; end of Arborea as a principality		**1541** On his way to Tunis, Charles V stops at Alghero
1355 Sardinian parliament established			
1350	**1400**		**1500**
1402 *Anno de Sa Mortagia Manna*, the year of the great plague	*Ferdinand of Aragon and Isabella of Castile*	**1509–1520** Repeated Arab pirate raids on Sardinia	

Alghero Cathedral
The interior of the cathedral of Santa Maria, begun in the 16th century, is a splendid example of the Catalan Gothic style in Sardinia.

WHERE TO SEE SPANISH SARDINIA

The first Spanish building in Sardinia was the Gothic-Aragonese chapel in the cathedral in Cagliari *(see p55)*, followed by San Francesco in Iglesias, San Giorgio in Perfugas, and San Francesco and the cathedral in Alghero *(see p118)*. The cathedral in Sassari was built in the style known as "Colonial Baroque." Baroque influence is also evident in Àles cathedral, and a notable school of *retablo* painting developed. There are 15th- and 16th-century paintings in the Art Gallery in Cagliari.

THE ST. PETER *RETABLO*

The *retablo* is a religious panel painting that was very often used as an altarpiece. It was one of the most important artistic genres in 16th-century Sardinia under Spanish rule. This work, *Madonna and Child with Saints Peter, Paul and George of Suelli*, is by Pietro and Michele Cavaro (1533–5). It is now in the church of San Giorgio at Suelli (Cagliari). The elaborate frame and wealth of decorative elements reveal its Flemish derivation.

Retablos often combined painting, sculpture, and carved decoration.

This Aragonese house at Fordongianus was built in the 15th–16th centuries.

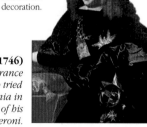

Philip V (1683–1746)
Forced to relinquish France and Sardinia, Philip tried to reconquer Sardinia in 1717 with the help of his chief minister Alberoni.

San Francesco in Alghero (14th century) was rebuilt in the Gothic-Aragonese style.

Charles V

1620 Under Philip III the University of Cagliari is founded

1688 Discontent and uprisings: the Spanish viceroy is assassinated

1600

1700

Cardinal Alberoni, Philip V's chief minister

1717 Philip V of Spain tries to reconquer Sardinia and Naples

1718 Treaty of London: Sardinia ceded to the House of Savoy

The Kingdom of Sardinia

ONE OF THE FIRST acts of the Savoyard government was to reinstate the island's universities. However, a serious economic and social crisis led to unrest and the spread of banditry. After the Revolution of 1789, France made vain attempts to conquer Sardinia, but, by 1795, the island was overwhelmed by revolutionary fervor of its own and a "Sardinian revolution" broke out in Cagliari. In 1799 the Savoys took refuge on the island after losing their other territories to Napoleon. In 1847, in Cagliari and Sassari, huge crowds persuaded the Savoys to link the kingdom of Sardinia with Piedmont in *"fusione perfetta."* In 1861 both became part of the Kingdom of Italy.

The Harbor at Cagliari
The port was developed after the arrival of the Savoy rulers. Together with Porto Torres it became the island's principal harbor.

The University of Cagliari
The university was founded as part of a cultural reorganization and development policy adopted by Carlo Emanuele III (1730–73), who set up a committee for Sardinian affairs in Turin.

Carlo Emanuele IV
King of Sardinia from 1796 to 1802, Carlo Emanuele took refuge there after losing his mainland territories to Napoleon in 1798. His brother Vittorio Emanuele I became King of Savoy.

THE ABSOLUTIST VICEROY

Carlo Felice, seen here receiving the keys of Cagliari, was viceroy of Sardinia from 1799 to 1821, when he became king. Unchallenged, he nonetheless governed the island as an absolute monarch.

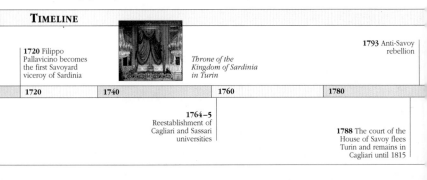

TIMELINE

1720 Filippo Pallavicino becomes the first Savoyard viceroy of Sardinia

Throne of the Kingdom of Sardinia in Turin

1793 Anti-Savoy rebellion

1720	1740	1760	1780

1764–5 Reestablishment of Cagliari and Sassari universities

1788 The court of the House of Savoy flees Turin and remains in Cagliari until 1815

Memorial Tablet
This tablet, embedded in Palazzo Viceregio in Cagliari, was dedicated to Carlo Felice by Vittorio Emanuele I, his brother, who abdicated in his favor in 1821.

Giuseppe Garibaldi
After years in exile because of his republican ideas, Garibaldi came to Caprera in 1857. He settled there permanently after conquering the Kingdom of Two Sicilies for the House of Savoy with his army of 1,000 volunteer soldiers, known as the Redshirts.

WHERE TO SEE SAVOYARD SARDINIA

Important Savoy buildings are the theaters in Cagliari, Sassari, and Alghero, the provincial administration buildings, and Cagliari Town Hall *(see p58)*. Many of Sardinia's railroad lines were laid down in this era. Statues of prominent Savoy figures, like the one of Garibaldi at Caprera, were erected everywhere. The Villa Aymerich at Làconi was one of many country houses to be rebuilt.

The Galleria Comunale d'Arte di Cagliari*, the capital's art gallery.*

Monument to Carlo Emanuele III *at Carloforte, the town he founded.*

House of Savoy Coat of Arms
Dating back to the 11th century, the dynasty first ruled Savoy and Piedmont, then the Kingdom of Sardinia, and finally the Kingdom of Italy.

Vittorio Amedeo III, king of Sardinia (1773–89)

1847 Sardinia and Piedmont join forces

1857 Garibaldi settles on Caprera and then buys part of the island

800	1820	1840	1860

1826 Alberto La Marmora's *Voyage to Sardinia* published

Tomb of Carlo Emanuele IV of Savoy, Cagliari

Alberto La Marmora

1861 Sardinia, together with Piedmont, becomes part of Kingdom of Italy

Sardinia and a United Italy

Ashes,
by Grazia
Deledda

INDUSTRIALIZATION in Sardinia began to make progress after unification: in 1871 the first railroad line was built, and the mines in Sulcis and Iglesiente became fully operational. The first daily newspapers were founded, and Nuoro became the center of a cultural movement that included the Nobel Prize-winning novelist Grazia Deledda. In World War I the heroism of the Brigata Sassari brigade emerged as a symbol of the island's new confidence and led to the foundation of the Partito Sardo d'Azione political party in 1921. Between the wars the mining industry continued to develop, and the town of Carbonia was founded in 1938. A wide-ranging program of land reclamation and artificial lakes – such as Lake Omodeo, created by a dam on the Tirso river – was carried out, significantly altering the health of previously malarial areas. On January 31, 1948 the island became an autonomous region of Italy.

The Monteponi mine
A 19th-century print shows the huge plant at this important Sardinian lead and zinc mine.

The crowd consisted of the social groups suffering most from the high cost of living.

Carbonia
In 1938 Mussolini himself inaugurated the newly built town of Carbonia (see p71). The town was meant to become the leading mining center in Sardinia.

Brigata Sassari
The brigade consisted entirely of Sardinians. They distinguished themselves in World War I by their heroism, winning two gold medals of honor.

Emilio Lussu (1890–1975) *This author recorded his World War I experiences in the Brigata Sassari in* Un anno sull'altopiano *(One Year on the Plateau).*

TIMELINE

1871 Writer Grazia Deledda is born		**1889–1899** Arrival of army task force to combat rampant banditry in Sardinia	**1897** First-ever special restrictive laws passed in Sardinia

1870	1880	1890	1900

Quintino Sella, Minister of Finance in 1862, 1865, 1869–73

1889 The first daily newspaper in Sardinia, *Unione Sarda,* is founded

1891 Political writer Antonio Gramsci born in Ales

Antonio Gramsci

The Cagliari-Arbatax Railroad
As part of a unified Italy, Sardinia embarked on a program of modernization. The first railroad lines were laid in 1871; by 1881 Cagliari and Sassari were linked by rail. The line connecting Cagliari and Arbatax passes through lovely scenery and is now an attractive tourist route (see pp92–3).

The strikers attacking the customs and excise office to protest against the bread tax.

The Dam on the Tirso River
This dam, 70 m (230 ft) high, with a 40-m (130-ft) drop, was begun in 1918, creating Lake Omodeo. At 20 km (12 miles) long, it was the largest artificial lake in Europe at that time.

The Cabras Marsh
The marsh, extending over 49 acres, is one example of the wide-ranging land reclamation programs carried out in Sardinia. These public works freed the island from malaria, paving the way for the development of a tourist industry.

THE STRIKE IN CAGLIARI
At the turn of the century, social conflict and tensions were so strong in Sardinia that the first special restrictive laws were enacted. The unrest of miners at the Buggerru mine on September 3, 1904 led to the first general strike in Italy. In 1906, distress at the high cost of living led to a wave of riots in Cagliari, which were brutally repressed; ten people died, and many others were injured.

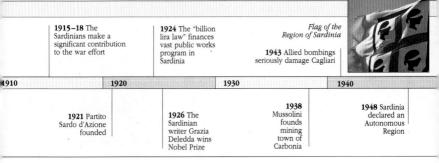

1915–18 The Sardinians make a significant contribution to the war effort

1924 The "billion lira law" finances vast public works program in Sardinia

Flag of the Region of Sardinia

1943 Allied bombings seriously damage Cagliari

1910 | 1920 | 1930 | 1940

1921 Partito Sardo d'Azione founded

1926 The Sardinian writer Grazia Deledda wins Nobel Prize

1938 Mussolini founds mining town of Carbonia

1948 Sardinia declared an Autonomous Region

Modern Sardinia

**Burgee of the
Costa Smeralda
Yacht Club**

THE RECLAMATION OF Sardinia's coastal marshes was crucial to the modern development of the island. Sardinia's lovely coastline, abandoned and shunned for millennia, could now be developed and resorts built. New luxury villas and vacation villages sprang up, and the Costa Smeralda, or Emerald Coast, became world-famous as an exclusive vacation spot. Reclaimed land could also be used for agriculture for the first time, and market gardens and orchards could be planted. The economy has started to shift as a result. Sheep-rearing is on the decline, while industry and services are developing, sometimes adversely affecting the environment. Sardinia today appears to be at a crossroads: modern life competing with the most precious resource: unspoiled nature and habitat diversity.

1972 The first mines are abandoned, signaling the decline of the Sardinian mining industry

1971 The Cagliari soccer team of star striker Gigi Riva wins the Italian championship for the first time

1962 Antonio Segni, a Christian Democrat from Sassari, is elected President of the Italian Republic

1950	1960	1970

1950	1960	1970

1956 Sardinia starts receiving television broadcasts from RAI, the Italian state TV

1970 Pope Paul VI visits Sardinia

1962 Creation of the Costa Smeralda syndicate, promoted by Karim Aga Khan (left), which triggers development in the Costa Smeralda and a consequent tourist boom in north-eastern Sardinia. That same year a law is passed with the aim of stimulating all business sectors

1953 First island kidnapping at Orgosolo, marking the beginning of one of Sardinia's most serious postwar problems, one that has fortunately decreased in recent years. Vittorio de Seta's film on Sardinian banditry was awarded a prize at the 1961 Venice Film Festival

1971 Industrial workers outnumber farmers for the first time

1972 Enrico Berlinguer from Sassari (center) elected secretary of the Italian Communist Party, a post he holds until his death (1983), promoting a "third way to socialism" and the "historic compromise" between Communists and Christian Democrats

1950 No Sardinian cases of malaria, for the first time. The American Rockefeller Foundation's public health program eliminates the *Anopheles maculipennis* mosquito, which transmits the illness

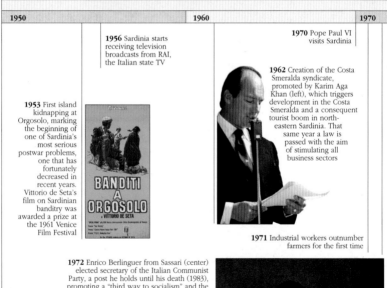

1977 *Padre Padrone*, the film directed by Paolo and Vittorio Taviani and based on the novel by Gavino Ledda, wins the Palme d'Or at the Cannes Film Festival. The work presents a hard, realistic picture of a Sardinia torn between pastoral tradition and modern ideas

1989 Fires, mostly cases of arson, kill ten tourists on the northeastern coast

1980 The Caprera National Park is founded

Today Together with tourism, the livestock industry (cattle breeding, dairies, tanning) is the leading force in the island's present-day economy

1979 Revolt of terrorists in maximum security prison on island of Asinara

1990 Sardinia struck by a terrible drought

1980   1990

1980   1990

1974 The oil crisis in the Middle East damages the Sardinian petrochemical industry

1995 The mining industry crisis worsens; the Sulcis coal mines are put up for sale

1979 Cases of kidnapping increase: well-known Italian singer/songwriter Fabrizio De André and his wife, Dori Ghezzi, kidnapped

1985 Francesco Cossiga from Sassari, former Prime Minister and Home Secretary, is elected President of the Italian Republic

Today The island's marinas, especially those at Porto Cervo, are rated among the best in the entire Mediterranean

SFIDA ITALIANA AMERICA'S CUP 1983

1983 The first Italian participation in the America's Cup, with the yacht *Azzurra*, is promoted by the Costa Smeralda Yacht Club

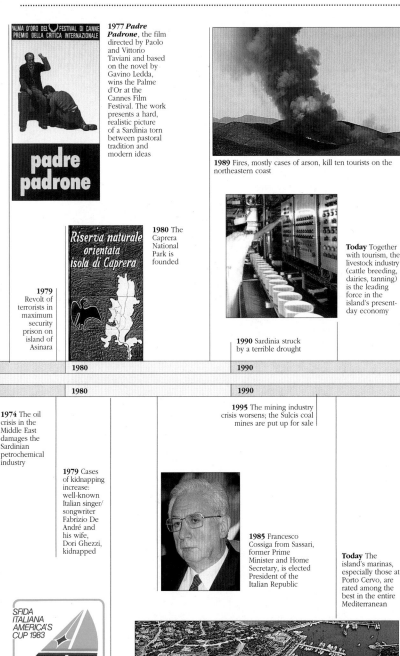

SARDINIA
AREA BY AREA

Sardinia at a Glance

FAMOUS MOSTLY FOR ITS SEA and coastline, Sardinia also abounds in spectacular natural scenery and numerous archaeological ruins. Prehistoric nuraghi are scattered throughout the island, from Su Nuraxi to Orroli, Santu Antine, and Silanus. Besides the Costa Smeralda, northern Sardinia is dotted with Romanesque churches in the Logudoro and Gallura countryside. In the Barbagia region and the eastern coast, which are dominated by the large Gennargentu National Park *(see pp82–3)*, the maquis vegetation reigns in the isolated valleys and on inaccessible hilltops. The south and west have interesting Punic ruins (Nora, Sant'Antioco, Tharros), as well as a relatively wild and undiscovered western coastline.

Ardara's Romanesque church, Santa Maria del Regno *(see p156)*

Flamingos wintering in the marshes around Oristano *(see pp134–5)*

THE WESTERN COAST

Oristano

The impressive ruins of Tharros *(see pp132–3)*

The rugged coast near Buggerru *(see p68)*

0 km   20

0 miles   20

CAGLIARI AND THE SOUTH

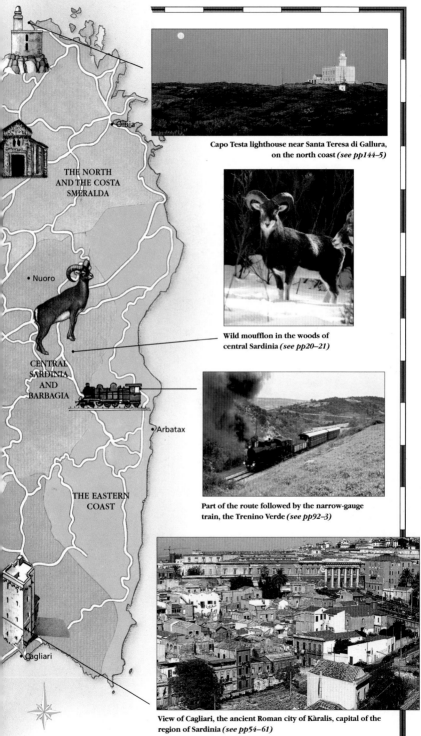

Capo Testa lighthouse near Santa Teresa di Gallura, on the north coast *(see pp144–5)*

Wild moufflon in the woods of central Sardinia *(see pp20–21)*

Part of the route followed by the narrow-gauge train, the Trenino Verde *(see pp92–3)*

View of Cagliari, the ancient Roman city of Kàralis, capital of the region of Sardinia *(see pp54–61)*

THE NORTH
AND THE COSTA
SMERALDA

CENTRAL
SARDINIA
AND
BARBAGIA

THE EASTERN
COAST

• Nuoro

• Olbia

• Arbatax

• Cagliari

CAGLIARI AND THE SOUTH

S OUTHERN SARDINIA *has a varied landscape with tall sand dunes along the coast, marshland where pink flamingos build their nests, and abundant maquis where the rare Sardinian deer still survive. It is also an area of interesting prehistoric sites, such as Nora and Su Nuraxi, and it was once the mining heartland of the island.*

The mining history of the area dates back to 5000 BC, when the island's inhabitants discovered how to extract and smelt copper and silver. The Phoenicians used the area as a base for trade and shipped local ores across the Mediterranean. In the Middle Ages the Pisans brought new wealth to the region with expansion of the silver mines. During the Fascist era, Mussolini exploited the island's coal in an attempt to make Italy self-sufficient.

Today, after years of decline, the industrial buildings of the Sulcis and Iglesiente areas are being converted into tourist attractions with mines and museums to visit. The area's natural beauty merges with the 19th-century mining buildings, which look like Gothic castles among the maquis.

The island's capital, Cagliari, was founded by Phoenician sailors, but it was the Aragonese who left the most enduring mark. The Spanish fortification, or Castello district, still dominates today's city.

North of Cagliari lies the Campidano plain, bordered by prickly pears and eucalyptus. This has long been Sardinia's "bread-basket," but farm labor now combines with factory work, especially around Cagliari.

In the uplands to the east are the ruins of Sardinia's largest prehistoric site, Su Nuraxi, chosen for its vantage point over the surrounding plains.

The islands of San Pietro and Sant'Antioco are separate from the mainland culturally as well as geographically: the towns of Calasetta and Carloforte are inhabited by the descendants of Ligurian coral fishermen who were held hostage in North Africa by Muslim pirates and, once freed, were offered a home on the islands. Today, their dialect, cuisine, and traditions remain little changed.

Volcanic rock framing Goloritzé bay

◁ Cagliari's waterfront with the arcaded Via Roma and the Castello district extending along the skyline

Exploring Cagliari and the South

THE SOUTHWESTERN COAST is one of the most unspoiled on the island, with undisturbed coves and beaches. Few roads run along the coast, so the best way to explore is by sea or on foot. Inland, the wild maquis of the rugged Iglesiente and Sulcis terrain contrasts with the derelict 19th-century industrial buildings of this former mining area. In the north, excavations at Su Nuraxi have revealed a complex nuraghic settlement. Cagliari offers the city's sights and a wildlife sanctuary in the salt flats and is also a good base for the ancient site of Nora.

18th-century walls at Carloforte on the island of San Pietro

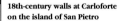
Map labels

Oristano ⑤

THE PISCINAS DUNES ⑧

GÙSPINI ⑨

ARBUS ⑩

N126

FLUMINIMAGGIORE

TEMPLE OF ANTAS ⑪

BUGGERRU ⑫

N130

SILIQUA

Cixerri

COSTA DI MASUA ⑭

IGLESIAS ⑬

MAR DI SARDEGNA

SULCIS

CARBONIA ⑯

N126

TRATALIAS ⑲

Lago di Monte Pranu

ISLAND OF SAN PIETRO ⑮

CALASETTA ⑰

SANT'ANTIOCO ⑱

ISLAND OF SANT'ANTIOCO

GOLFO DI PALMAS

KEY

▬▬	Highway
▬▬	Major road
═══	Minor road
═══	Scenic route
──	River

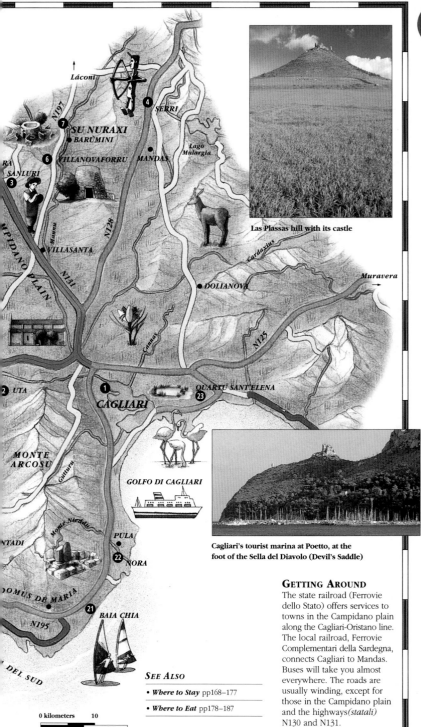

Las Plassas hill with its castle

Muravera →

Cagliari's tourist marina at Poetto, at the foot of the Sella del Diavolo (Devil's Saddle)

GETTING AROUND

The state railroad (Ferrovie dello Stato) offers services to towns in the Campidano plain along the Cagliari-Oristano line. The local railroad, Ferrovie Complementari della Sardegna, connects Cagliari to Mandas. Buses will take you almost everywhere. The roads are usually winding, except for those in the Campidano plain and the highways *(statali)* N130 and N131.

SEE ALSO

0 kilometers   10

0 miles   10

Cagliari ●

Lion on a pulpit in the Cathedral

T HE CITY'S SHELTERED position, tucked into the Golfo di Cagliari, has long made Cagliari an important harbor. The Phoenicians chose the eastern shore of Santa Gilla lagoon in the 8th–6th centuries BC, as a stopover for trade ships en route between the Lebanon and the Iberian peninsula. Kàralis ("rocky city") soon became one of the leading Mediterranean centers of trade. The city's present appearance was the work of the Pisans, who developed the Aragonese Castello district. Local inhabitants, who could enter the city only during the day, lived in the walled villages of Stampace and Villanova. These fortifications were demolished in 1862, and the areas are now part of the city. Modern-day Cagliari, capital of the region, is flanked on three sides by sea and marshes and has only expanded northward.

Sala della Giunta, Palazzo Comunale

Arcaded 19th-century buildings on Via Roma

Exploring Cagliari

For those arriving by sea, the elegant boulevard of Via Roma, parallel to the dock and lined with 19th-century buildings and long arcades, is the first view of the city. During the day crowds throng along this busy shopping street, stopping at the cafés to relax and chat. Stretching out behind are the narrow streets and run-down alleys of the old Marina district. Formerly inhabited by fishermen and merchants, this area is now filled with traditional trattorias and rustic taverns as well as shops selling antiques and local handicrafts. Heading northeast from Via Roma, Largo Carlo Felice is a wide, tree-lined avenue dating from the mid-1800s, with a statue of Carlo Felice, the viceroy of Sardinia (see pp40–41).

City's coat of arms

🏛 Palazzo Comunale

Via Roma. 🄲 070-67 71.
⏱ ask porter.
At the corner of Via Roma and Largo Carlo Felice is the Palazzo Comunale (town hall). Built in the early 20th century in Neo-Gothic style, the building was restored after World War II. Its facade is decorated with double lancet windows and turrets. Paintings by Filippo Figari and Giovanni Marghinotti hang in the Sala della Rappresentanza, and in the Sala della Giunta there is an interesting triptych of *I Consiglieri* (Councillors).

🏛 Bastione San Remy

Terrazza Umberto I.
Built in the late 19th century over the Spanish ramparts, the bastions can be reached from Piazza Costituzione up a stairway that leads to a wide terrace, Terrazza Umberto I. From here, there is a magnificent view of the waterfront to the surrounding marshes. Every Sunday morning a lively flea market fills the terrace. The covered passageway on the middle level is used for exhibits and cultural events.

🏛 Roman Amphitheater

Viale Fra Ignazio. 🄲 070-65 21 30.
⏱ May–Sep: 9am–1pm, 5–7pm daily.
Oct–Apr: 9am–1pm, 2:30–5pm daily.
Northwest of the city center is the most significant evidence of Roman Cagliari. The 2nd-century AD amphitheater was hewn entirely out of the rock, in the style of Greek theaters. Circus acts with wild beasts were performed here as well as *naumachiae*, popular recreations of famous naval battles. A canal system made it possible to fill the arena with water. Much of the brick masonry collapsed during the Middle Ages, and tons of stone were taken from the tiers to build the Castello district. Still visible are the *cavea*, the pit that held the wild beasts, the corridors behind the tiers, and underground passageways as well as some of the tiers where the spectators sat.

The ruins of the 2nd-century AD Roman amphitheater

🌿 Orto Botanico

Viale Fra Ignazio 13. 📞 070-67 51.
⭕ 8am–1:30pm daily. 🎟

South of the amphitheater, the Botanic Gardens extend over an area of about 12 acres. Founded in 1865, the gardens contain more than 500 species of tropical plants from America, Africa, Asia, and the islands of the Pacific as well as the most characteristic plants from the Mediterranean.

The Orto Botanico is full of small caves such as the Grotta Gennari, which is used to cultivate ferns because of its ideal temperature and high levels of humidity. There are also remains of Roman tunnels, constructed to improve the water supply to the gardens, a Roman gallery, and a well in the shape of a demijohn.

🏛 Cathedral

Piazza Palazzo.
⭕ 8am–noon, 4–7pm daily.
Museo Capitolare 📞 070-66 38 37. ⭕ by appt.

Cagliari's Cathedral of Santa Maria was built by the Pisans in the 11th and 12th centuries. Gradually transformed over the centuries, particularly with 17th-century additions, today's facade is

The Baroque marble interior of the Cathedral of Santa Maria

Holy water basin detail

the result of radical restoration in the 1930s, which reinstated the original Romanesque style. Four lions guarding the entrance date from this period. The church retains much Baroque decoration as well as some original detail. Near the entrance are two pulpits by Mastro Guglielmo, sculpted in 1162 for the cathedral of Pisa and donated to Cagliari by the Tuscan city. A marble basin for holy water is decorated with the image of an angel. A crypt under the altar houses the tombs of the princes of

the House of Savoy. In the chapterhouse paintings include a *Flagellation of Christ* by Guido Reni. The **Museo Capitolare** (Treasury) displays precious church items such as chalices and amphoras as well as a large gilded silver cross.

VISITORS' CHECKLIST

Road map C6. 🏛 *176,236.*
ℹ️ *Piazza Matteotti 9 (070-66 92 55); Piazza Deffenu 9 (070-65 48 11 or 070-65 16 98).*
🚆 *Sun am, Terrazza Umberto I (antiques); Sun, Sant'Elia district (general).* 🎉 *May 1: Sant'Efisio Feast Day.*

CAGLIARI TOWN CENTER

Bastione San Remy ④
Cathedral ⑤
Cittadella dei Musei ⑥
Exma ⑧
Orto Botanico ②
Roman Amphitheater ①
San Saturnino ⑨
Torre dell'Elefante ⑦
Villa di Tigellio ③

KEY

▨ Street-by-Street *see pp56–7*

🚉 Train station

⚓ Ferry boarding point

🅿 Parking

ℹ️ Tourist information

➕ Hospital

✝ Church

0 meters 350
0 yards 350

Street-by-Street: Castello

Torre dell'Elefante detail

THE CASTELLO DISTRICT, the oldest part of Cagliari, was built by the Pisans and Aragonese. Positioned at the top of a hill and protected by ancient city walls, it consisted of aristocratic mansions and the city's cathedral. With time its function as a center of power waned, and the elegant buildings gradually deteriorated. At the center of the district is Piazza Palazzo with the Palazzo Arcivescovile (Archbishop's Palace) and the cathedral. Surrounding the ancient citadel, imposing watchtowers dominate the entrance gates, and parts of the fortifications have been transformed into a museum complex and an esplanade.

★ Cathedral
Santa Maria Cathedral, rebuilt several times, combines Pisan, Aragonese, and Baroque features. The multicolored marble interior has fine sculptures. (See p55).

★ Cittadella dei Musei
This modern complex, converted from the former Savoyard arsenal, houses the city's most important museums. (See p58).

Palazzo Arcivescovile

PIAZZA
ARSENALE

VIA MARTINI

PIA
PAL

VIA DEI G

Torre di San Pancrazio
The northern gate of the Castello district was built in 1305 by Giovanni Capula. It is dressed on three sides with limestone ashlar, while the inner face is open, exposing the stairs and wooden balconies of the interior.

Via La Marmora
A number of craft workshops and antique shops line the characteristic Via La Marmora.

★ Bastione San Remy
In the early 1900s the Spanish defensive walls were transformed into the bastions of San Remy, opening out onto a wide esplanade with spectacular views.

Porta dei Leoni
The gate that leads into the lower Marina district owes its name to the two Romanesque lions' heads (leoni) above the arch.

BASTIONE
SAN REMY

VIA CANNELLE

VIA LA MARMORA

PIAZZA
CARLO
ALBERTO

VIA VIVALDI

...ESI

VIA UNIVERSITÀ

Palazzo Boyl
Overlooking the bastions of San Remy, this palazzo was built in 1840. It incorporates the remains of the Torre dell'Aquila (Eagle's Tower), one of the large Pisan towers that stood over the entrance gates of the ancient city.

Torre dell'Elefante
The "Elephant's Tower" was built by local architect Giovanni Capula in 1307. The mechanism for opening the gates is still visible, and an elephant statue, after which the tower was named, can be seen on the facade.

KEY

--- Suggested route

0 meters   50

0 yards   50

STAR SIGHTS

★ **Cittadella dei Musei**

★ **Bastione San Remy**

★ **Cathedral**

Cittadella dei Musei, the modern complex in the Castello district

Cittadella dei Musei

Piazza Arsenale.

At the northern end of the Castello district is the modern museum complex, the Cittadella dei Musei. Fashioned from the former royal arsenal that had been built on the site of the Spanish citadel, the complex houses the Museo Archeologico Nazionale, the Museo Civico d'Arte Orientale Stefano Cardu, and the Pinacoteca Nazionale. A terrace offers fine views of the city.

🏛 Museo Archeologico Nazionale

Cittadella dei Musei. 📞 070-65 59 11. ◯ 9am–7pm Tue–Sun. 🖾

The National Archaeological Museum is devoted to the history of Sardinia. The ground floor exhibits are arranged in chronological order, from the Neolithic era to the Middle Ages. In the Neolithic hall are fine alabaster statues of female divinities, including one in the shape of a cross from Senorbì. Objects from the late Bronze Age include axes with raised edges. There is an interesting collection of nuraghic bronze figurines (see pp32–3), found in the Tempio di Teti at Abini. Some of these hold votive swords decorated with the head of a deer, a tribal chief, or a warrior. In the third hall is a statuette of a musician playing the Sardinian flute, the launeddas (see p90).

The Phoenician and Roman periods are represented by objects found mostly at sites around Cagliari, Tharros, and Nora. These include jewelry and amulets, small colored glass heads, and terra-cotta votive statuettes. Among the loveliest pieces of jewelry are an embossed golden bracelet and gold earrings from Tharros.

The Early Christian pieces, such as jugs, lamps, and gold jewelry, give an insight into the island's medieval culture, and influences from Byzantine, Vandal, and Moorish invaders.

🏛 Museo Civico d'Arte Orientale Stefano Cardu

Cittadella dei Musei. 📞 070-49 07 27. ◯ 9am–7pm Tue–Sun. 🖾

The Museum of Oriental Art, reopened in late 1996, has on exhibit most of the 1,300 objects donated to the city in 1917 by Stefano Cardu, a Sardinian who served at the court of the King of Siam. The collection includes imperial gold and silver objects, ivory statues, and vases, mostly dating from the 11th century.

🏛 Pinacoteca Nazionale

Cittadella dei Musei. 📞 070-67 01 57. ◯ 9am–7:30pm daily. 🖾

The entrance to the three-story National Gallery is on the upper floor. Here, 15th- and 16th-century paintings include a collection of Catalan and Sardinian altarpieces, such

as the *Annunciation* by Juan Mates (1391–1431), *Sant'Eligio* by the Master of Sanluri (early 16th century), and *Nostra Signora della Neve* (1568) by Michele Cavaro.

The middle floor houses a collection of 17th- and 18th-century paintings as well as a display of typical Sardinian costumes and objects. The lower floor features a painting by the Stampace school, *Chiesa di San Francesco*, which was damaged by fire in 1871.

🏛 Galleria Comunale d'Arte

Giardini Pubblici, Viale Regina Elena. 📞 070-49 07 27. ◯ 9am–1pm, 5–8pm (Oct–Apr) Tue–Sun. 🖾

On the avenue east of the Castello district, the Municipal Art Gallery has a collection of significant works by Sardinian artists from the late 19th century to the 1970s. On the ground floor are works by Francesco Ciusa. The first floor features contemporary art.

⛩ Necropoli Tuvixeddu

Via Falzarego. ◯ Mar–Sep: 8am–sunset.

The hundreds of underground burial chambers of the Punic necropolis, west of the Botanical Gardens, are overgrown with brambles. The funerary paintings on the tombs, however, are worth a visit, especially the *Tomba del Guerriero* (Warrior's Tomb) and the *Tomba dell'Ureo*.

⛩ Grotta della Vipera

Viale Sant'Avendrace. ◯ Apr–Sep: 9am–1pm, 5–8pm Tue–Sun; Oct–Mar: call Cagliari tourist information.

One of the tombs in the necropolis is that of Atilia Pomptilla, wife of Cassius Philippus, exiled here in the 1st century AD. Two snakes adorn the facade of the "viper's cave," and on the walls are inscriptions in Greek and Latin.

Marble sarcophagus (4th century AD) from the Archaeological Museum

The early Christian church dedicated to San Saturnino, patron saint of Cagliari

⋔ Subterranean Cagliari

Viale Fra Ignazio. 📞 070-66 30 52.
🕐 by appt. 📷

Northeast of the city center, in the area below the Roman amphitheater, the hospita,l and the Orto Botanico, there are underground chambers and passageways cut out of the rock by the Phoenicians. The most spectacular of these is the vast chamber named after King Vittorio Emanuele II. From the Casa di Riposo in Viale Fra Ignazio, visitors descend via a dingy stairway into an eerie chamber. The walls, around 2,500 sq m (26,900 sq ft), are covered with thick facing to protect them from the humidity.

The Phoenician underground chamber, "Vittorio Emanuele II"

⌖ Villa di Tigellio

Via Tigellio. 🌑 to the public.

Situated southeast of the Botanical Gardens, Villa di Tigellio is a group of three aristocratic Roman villas and baths dating from the Imperial era. The *tablinum*, the room used to receive guests, opens onto the central atrium.

⌖ Exma

Via San Lucifero. 📞 070-66 63 99.
🕐 9am–1pm, 5pm–midnight (Oct–Apr: 9am–8pm) by appt only. 📷

On the eastern side of the Castello district stands the former municipal slaughterhouse, built in the mid-19th century and closed in 1964. The dark red building, decorated with sculpted heads of cows, has been restructured to house the city's arts center.

The center's cultural calendar offers temporary exhibitions of photography, painting, and sculpture as well as courses for children and adults. Classical music concerts are held in the courtyard in the summer and in the auditorium in the winter.

There are plans to make this the permanent home of the graphic arts section of the Galleria Comunale d'Arte.

A cow's head on the Exma building

🔓 San Saturnino

Piazza San Cosimo. 📞 070-201 01.
🕐 10am–noon, pm by appt only Mon–Sat. 🌑 public hols.

East of the Exma building is the church of San Saturnino, also known as Santi Cosma e Damiano. Reopened after 18 years of restoration and still not completely refurbished, this simple church is one of the oldest Christian buildings on the island. It was begun in the 5th century to commemorate the martyrdom of Saturno, the city's patron saint.

In the Middle Ages, San Saturnino, together with its adjacent monastery, became an important religious and cultural center. The Greek cross plan of the church was enlarged in the 11th century by French Victorine friars from Marseille, who built three aisles with barrel vaults. Inside, a marble ex voto holds the oldest representation of San Saturno.

Glass windows have been placed in the sturdy tufa construction to prevent further damage and decay from humidity and air, and this has given the church a rather modern appearance. Nonetheless, it is still a fascinating place to visit.

The Marshes and Salt Flats

A yellow-bellied toad from the marshes

A NETWORK OF MARSHES and lakes extends around the outskirts of Cagliari, particularly along the western shore of the bay. The vast lagoon of the Santa Gilla marsh stretches over 9,800 acres, including the ancient Macchiareddu salt flats. These saltworks are now the only ones in operation in the area. After years of neglect and environmental deterioration, the marshy areas around Cagliari have finally become preserves, and the area once again has a rich and varied fauna. To the east of the city, the Molentargius marsh is a favorite refuge for migratory birds. At least 170 species have been identified there, which is one-third of the entire bird population of Europe. Between August and March, flamingos attract dozens of naturalists. Since 1993 these beautiful birds have begun once again to nest along the banks of the Molentargius marsh.

A Naturalist's Paradise
In autumn the marshes are filled with migratory birds and are a favorite with bird-watchers.

The Saltworks
Of the numerous saltworks that once operated around Cagliari, only those in the Macchiareddu industrial area are still active.

Macchiareddu Salt Flat

N130

N131

Fishing port of Giorgino

GOLFO DI CAGLIARI

N195   Stagno di Santa Gilla

Nesting Grounds
In recent years, flamingos have begun to use the marshes as a nesting ground again.

WILDLIFE OF THE MARSHLANDS

Many migratory and endemic bird species populate the marshes around Cagliari. These feed upon the small creatures, such as the brine shrimp *Artemia salina*, which thrive in the salt-rich water. As well as the colony of flamingos, which sometimes exceeds 10,000, you will also see many other species of water birds such as blackwinged stilts, avocets, cormorants, and teals. The waters of Macchiareddu salt flats, on the other hand, are populated by mallards, coots, and pintail ducks, which hunt peacefully among the islets and inlets.

Flamingo   **Blackwinged Stilt**   **Avocet**

Cormorant   **Teal**   **Cat's-tail flowers**

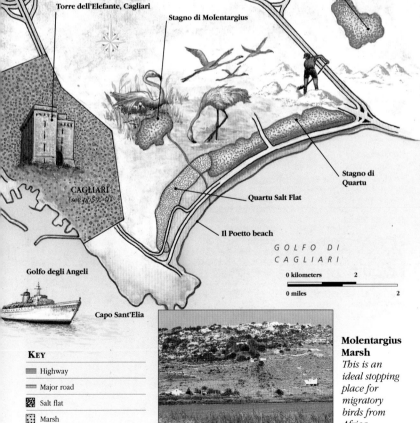

31D

N554

Torre dell'Elefante, Cagliari

Stagno di Molentargius

Stagno di Simbirizzi

N125

CAGLIARI
(see pp.54–9)

Stagno di Quartu

Quartu Salt Flat

Il Poetto beach

GOLFO DI CAGLIARI

Golfo degli Angeli

0 kilometers   2
0 miles   2

Capo Sant'Elia

KEY

▨ Highway	
▭ Major road	
▨ Salt flat	
⊞ Marsh	

Molentargius Marsh
This is an ideal stopping place for migratory birds from Africa.

The Romanesque church of Santa Maria at Uta

Uta ❷

Road map C6. ☗ 6,599. ⊟ ⊟
ⓘ Via Umberto I (070-96 83 36).
☗ Aug 26-31: Santa Lucia.

THE FLOURISHING agricultural town of Uta is situated at the edge of the Campidano plain, a vast fertile corridor that stretches northward from Cagliari to Oristano. On the outskirts of town is the simple church of **Santa Maria**, built in 1140 by French Victorine friars from Marseille. The church facade is made of light-colored stone, with blocks of a darker hue and is decorated with blind arches and a small bell gable. Sculptures of human heads, deer, calves, and geometric patterns adorn the arches.

ENVIRONS: The village of **San Sperate**, 8 km (5 miles) northeast of Uta, is a living museum with murals, and sculptures by local artist Pinuccio Sciola.

🏠 **Santa Maria**
Via Santa Maria. ☏ 070-96 90 59.
◯ 8am–12:30pm, 3–6:30pm daily.

Sanluri ❸

Road map C5. ☗ 8,645. ⊟ ⊟
ⓘ Piazza Mazzini 4 (070-937 05 05).
☗ Aug 10: San Lorenzo.

AN IMPORTANT TOWN in the Campidano plain, Sanluri developed around the 14th-century castle of Eleonora d'Arborea (see p36). This stronghold changed hands several times before it was taken by the Aragonese in 1709. The massive square structure has towers on its four corners and an ornate wrought-iron gate.

Today the castle is owned by the Villasanta family and houses the **Museo Risorgimentale Duca d'Aosta**. The historical exhibits include fine furniture such as a 16th-century bed. A sculpture of San Michele (St. Michael) stands in the entrance hall. On the upper floor is the **Museo della Ceroplastica** featuring 16th-century miniature wax sculptures.

In the restored 16th-century Convento dei Cappuccini, on a hill overlooking the town, the **Museo Storico Etnografico** displays a collection of tools and archaeological finds.

Wax statue in Sanluri's Museo della Ceroplastica

🏛 **Museo Risorgimentale Duca d'Aosta**
Castello di Eleonora d'Arborea.
☏ 070-930 71 05. ◯ Jul–Sep: 4:30–8pm Tue, Wed, Fri; Oct–Dec & Mar–Jun: 9:30am–1pm, 3pm–sunset first & third Sun of month, Easter Mon, Apr 25, May 1. 🖼

🏛 **Museo Storico Etnografico**
Via San Rocco 6. ☏ 070-930 71 07.
◯ 9am–noon, 4–6pm Mon, Wed, Fri by appt only.

Serri ❹

Road map C4. ☗ 802. ⊟ ⊟
ⓘ Via Municipio 1 (0782-80 60 81).
☗ Third Sun of Sep: Santa Lucia.

THIS SHEEP-FARMING center lies on the edge of a rocky plateau dominating the Trexenta hills. Right on the spur of the promontory is the **Santuario Nuragico di Santa Vittoria**, one of Sardinia's most fascinating nuraghic sites. The archaeological ruins here have yielded some important bronze votive statuettes, now housed in the Museo Archeologico Nazionale in Cagliari (see p58). Pilgrims came here to worship the God of Water at the sacred well. The temple well, which is in an excellent state of preservation, is reached by 13 amazingly precise basalt steps. A five-minute walk from the entrance takes you to the *Recinto delle Feste* (festivities area). This elliptical building has a porticoed courtyard surrounded by rooms for the pilgrims. This is possibly a predecessor of the rural sanctuaries (*cumbessias* or *muristeni*) found today in Sardinia's country churches.

🏠 **Santuario Nuragico di Santa Vittoria**
7 km (4 miles) NW. ☏ 0782-80 60 81.
◯ May–Sep: 10am–8pm daily; Oct–Apr: ask at town hall.

A modern mural in the village of San Sperate

The 16th-century parish church of the Beata Vergine Assunta at Sàrdara

Sàrdara ❺

Road map C5. 4,492.
22 Sep: Santa Maria is Acquas.

Situated at the northern edge of the Campidano plain, the town of Sàrdara lay on the border between the medieval principalities of Arborea and Cagliari *(see pp36–7)*. Stone houses from this period, with large arched doorways, have been preserved in the district around **San Gregorio**. This Romanesque church was built in the 6th century. Its tall, narrow facade, however, shows the initial influence of Gothic architecture. On the western outskirts of town is the 16th-century parish church of **Beata Vergine Assunta**, interesting for its sculpted columns and arches, and its vault patterned with stars.

Not far from the Assunta are the remains of a nuraghic well-temple. This underground chamber, from the 9th–10th centuries BC, has uneven walls of basalt and limestone and an open domed ceiling. Also

known as the *Funtana de is Dolus* (fountain of pain), worshipers came here to take the curative spring waters. The source of the temple water was an ancient underground well, and a stone canal carried the mineral water from the sacred spring to the temple. Decorated earthenware votive objects found in the temple are now kept in the Museo Archeologico Nazionale in Cagliari *(see p58)*.

Sàrdara is also famous for its carpet-weaving and woolen and cotton tapestries. These are colorfully embroidered with traditional animal and floral decorative motifs.

Environs: Ruins of the medieval **Castello di Monreale**, a fortification of the principality of Arborea, stand on a hill 1 km (half a mile) southwest of town. A little farther west are the remains of the **Aquae Neapolitanae**, Roman baths, and nearby is the Gothic church of **Santa Maria is Acquas**, where a festival takes place in September.

Villanovaforru ❻

Road map C5. 727.
Piazza Costituzione (070-930 00 00). Jul 15: Santa Marina.

This small agricultural center was founded in the 17th century by the Spanish and has retained much of its original layout. Many houses have kept their decorative features and character. Today, the Monte Granatico building (formerly a granary), in the town's central square, houses a small but well-run **Museo Archeologico**. Finds from the nearby nuraghic site of Genna Maria are on display here, including bronze, iron, and ceramic objects from the 9th century BC on the ground floor. On the first floor are votive objects dedicated to Demeter and Persephone from the Roman era.

Environs: On the road to Collinas, 1 km (half a mile) west of the town, is the nuraghic village of **Genna Maria**. Discovered in 1977, the site, which is still being excavated, is on a prominent hilltop. This nuraghe has a typical design *(see pp36–7)*. Thick walls with three towers form a triangle that encloses a central tower and courtyard with a well. Another wall with six corner towers surrounds the entire village area.

🏛 Museo Archeologico
Piazza Costituzione. ☎ 070-930 00 50. ◯ 9am–1pm, 3:30–5:30pm (May–Sep: 6:30pm) Tue–Sun. combined ticket with Genna Maria.
⋔ Genna Maria
1 km (half a mile) W. ☎ 070-930 00 48. ◯ 9:30am–1pm, 3:30–7pm (Oct–Mar: 6pm) Tue–Sun.

The Saffron of Sardinia

Stigma

The production of Sardinian saffron, prized throughout Europe, is based around San Gavino in the Campidano plain. Saffron is obtained by drying the dark red stigma of *Crocus sativus*, a purple flower that carpets the barren fields in autumn. The harvest, however, is very brief because the stigmas must be collected the day the flower comes into bloom. Saffron, once considered as precious as gold, was used to make dyes for fabrics and rugs, as a coloring agent for candies and as a spice for savory dishes. It is still used in cooking *(see p180)*.

Crocus flowers

Su Nuraxi ❼

EXCAVATIONS EAST OF BARÙMINI have brought to light the largest nuraghic fortress in Sardinia, Su Nuraxi. The original settlement dates from 1500 BC, during the Middle Bronze Age. Built on a hill, the 19 m (62 ft) high fortress occupied an excellent vantage point, with clear views over the surrounding plains. In the 7th century BC, with the threat of Phoenician invasion, the central section of the fortress, consisting of a tower connected to four external nuraghi, was further protected by a thick outer wall with turrets and a sentinel's walkway. The village gradually developed outside the main fortifications with single- and multiroom dwellings, including a flour mill and bakery. The area was inhabited for almost 2,000 years although, after the Carthaginian conquest, the upper parts of the fort were demolished, and the site lost its strategic importance.

Single Dwellings
The oldest living quarters were circular with a single room.

Defenses
In order to defend themselves from Carthaginian invasions, the Nuraghic inhabitants built an outer bulwark. This consisted of seven towers connected by a wall with a walkway for sentinel patrols.

The circular assembly hall was built against the outer wall. During meetings the elders sat on a long stone bench that ran along the inside of the wall. Objects found here are held in Cagliari's archaeological museum *(see p58)*.

Multiroom Dwellings
These living areas were made up of seven square or trapezoidal rooms that opened onto a courtyard or vestibule, often with a well.

Northeastern Tower
The outer corner towers of the fortress were pierced by a double row of radially arranged fissures through which light could penetrate.

Building Techniques
Huge irregular blocks of stone, laid in "dovetail" fashion without mortar, were used to build the nuraghi. The inner walls of the towers were often reinforced by another wall of stone.

The outer wall was added in the 7th century BC.

The "keep," or central section, was the highest part and the center of military operations.

The four main towers were connected by a central courtyard.

Sentinel's walkway

The Village
The dwellings were built outside the fortress walls between the 8th–6th centuries BC. There were about 200 circular houses with roofs made from wooden beams and branches.

The Piscinas Dunes ➑

THE HILLS OF SAND at Piscinas and Is Arenas ("the sands" in Sardinian) are "moving" dunes, sometimes as much as 50 m (164 ft) high, which rise up around the estuary of the Piscinas River. Wind erosion by the mistral, the cold north wind that blows in from France, continually changes the landscape, while strongly rooted pioneer plants work their way across the sand. The robust roots of marram grass *(Ammophila arenaria)* gradually stabilize the dune slopes, which are then covered by other salt-resistant plants such as juniper and mastic trees. This unique ecological niche is also the habitat for many animals, and footprints of foxes, wild cats, partridges and rabbits are a common sight on the sand. Remains of the 19th-century mines, once the mainstay of the Sulcis regional economy, are also still visible.

Piscinas beach
The sandy beach at Piscinas is 9 km (5 miles) long. Exposed to the strong mistral wind in winter, the shape of the beach is continually changing.

Marine turtles
The isolated position of Piscinas makes it an ideal spot for the loggerhead turtles to lay their eggs.

The Sardinian partridge favors sunny habitats. It was introduced from North Africa by the Romans.

The sand, shaped by the wind, is an ever-changing landscape.

Tracks of wild animals can often be seen in the sand, particularly in the morning.

Le Dune Hotel
This hotel overlooking the sea shore occupies an old restructured mine building (see p174).

The wild lily, though slim and delicate, manages to bloom and survive even in arid environments.

Mine railroad

A section of the 19th-century narrow-gauge railroad, once used to transport material from the mines to the sea, has been reopened near the beach.

Marram grass
This strongly rooted, perennial plant, Ammophila arenaria, *is typical of sandy environments.*

Wild rabbits are a common sight on the dunes. You may also come across other small animals such as foxes and lizards.

The sand dunes
Areas of the dunes are covered in thick maquis vegetation.

San Nicola di Mira, at Gùspini

Gùspini ❾

Road map B5. 🏠 13,283. 🚌
🛈 Via Don Minzoni 10 (070-97 16 82). 🎭 Aug 15-31: Santa Maria.

OVERLOOKING the flat and fertile Campidano plain, Gùspini is surrounded by olive groves and backed by the gradually rising foothills of Monte Arcuentu. The town's lovely 16th-century church of **San Nicola di Mira**, in the main square, has a large rose window and is the hub of local life. The feast day of Santa Maria is celebrated with a procession and a horse race.

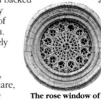

The rose window of San Nicola di Mira

The **Montevecchio mine**, 8 km (5 miles) west, was one of the largest in Europe until the 1950s. Despite its dilapidated state, the miners' houses, headquarters, church, school, and hospital are worth a visit. In the summer there are guided tours of the mine and the office building as well as an exhibition on the lives of the miners.

🏭 Montevecchio mine
8 km (5 miles) W of Gùspini. 📞 0368-53 89 97. 🕐 Jun–Oct: 9:30am–1pm, 3–8pm daily. 🎫 📷 compulsory.

Arbus ❿

Road map B5. 🏠 7,570. 🚌 🛈 Via Repubblica 132 (070-975 87 88).
🎭 Jun 13: Sant'Antonio; Aug 21: Santo Lussorio Palio (horse race).

GRANITE HOUSES characterize the village of Arbus, set on the slopes of Monte Linas. Arbus is known for the production of traditional knives with curved blades, *arrasoias*, made by local craftsmen.

Southwest down the N126 for 7 km (4 miles), then due west across a winding mountain road, is the mining village of **Ingurtosu**, built by the French firm Pertusola. Once home to over 1,000 mine workers, the houses, office building and church are now abandoned. The pine forest surrounding the run-down buildings was planted by the mine workers.

A dirt road runs among the old mines, abandoned buildings, and former dumping area as far as Naracauli, where there are ruins of a more modern mine complex built shortly after World War I. A train once transported the extracted lead and zinc to the sea, where it was loaded onto ships. Certain sections of the narrow-gauge track and some train cars can be seen on the Piscinas beach.

Stretching northward from the dune beach of Piscinas is a maquis-covered coast aptly called the Costa Verde. A quiet, scenic road follows the coastline, offering spectacular views of the sea. The road goes as far as the resort of Marina di Arbus, with easy access to sandy beaches.

The large tanks at the Montevecchio mine

Temple of Antas ⓫

Road map B5. 🚗 to Fluminimaggiore.
ℹ️ Via Cavour 17, Fluminimaggiore
(0781-58 09 90).

Fᴵᴿˢᵀ ᴰᴵˢᶜᴼᵛᴱᴿᴱᴰ in 1966, the ancient Temple of Antas is believed to have been a sacred nuraghic site. It was adopted by the Carthaginians in the 4th century BC and dedicated to Sid Addir Babài. A century later the Carthaginians re-structured the temple with an atrium and a central chamber. Egyptian and Ionic decoration adorned the temple.

In the 3rd century AD, the Romans rebuilt the temple using some of the existing material, such as the Ionic capitals of the columns. This temple was dedicated to the god and "creator of Sardinians," Sardus Pater (perhaps a cor-ruption of the Carthaginian name). Although only six columns remain standing, the temple's isolated position amid the wild maquis makes it an enchanting location.

ENVIRONS: Set in the fertile valley of the Mannu River , 9 km (5 miles) north, is the small agricultural village of **Fluminimaggiore**, founded in the 18th century. Turning west toward the sea for 9 km (5 miles), the road proceeds to **Portixeddu beach**, protected by sand dunes. The headland of Capo Pecora offers stunning views of the sea and coast.

The old mining community of Buggerru, now a tourist resort

Buggerru ⓬

Road map B5. 🏚 1,469. 🚗
ℹ️ Via Roma 41 (0781-545 22).

Sᴵᵀᵁᴬᵀᴱᴰ ᴵᴺ ᴬ ᵛᴬᴸᴸᴱʸ opening out onto the sea, Buggerru was founded in the mid-18th century in an area rich in mineral deposits. It soon became a flourishing mining town with a small theater where opera singers used to perform, and the headquarters of the French *Société Anonyme des Mines des Malfidano*. The mines have now closed, and the town is surrounded by slag heaps. In the lower part of the town, a sculpture by Pinuccio Sciola *(see p62)* is dedicated to the miners who died in the strikes of 1904.

Today, the town has been reclaimed as a harbor for pleasure boats, the only one between Carloforte and Oristano. The docks, where boats were once loaded with local minerals for export, now serve as a port for visitors to the wild western coast of the island and its long stretches of sandy, sheltered beaches. To the south is the long and secluded **Cala Domestica**, a rocky bay overlooked by a Spanish watchtower.

Iglesias ⓭

Road map B5. 🏚 29,960. 🚗 🚉
ℹ️ Biblioteca Comunale, Via Gramsci
(0781-417 95). 🎭 Easter Week.

Iɢʟᴇsɪᴀs, or Villa Ecclesiae, was founded in the 13th century by Count Ugolino della Gherardesca (mentioned in Dante's *Inferno* XXXIII). The Pisans had conquered the area in 1257 and reopened mines abandoned in Roman times. Silver was extracted, and the city had the right to mint

---

TEMPLE OF ANTAS

This plan shows how the later Roman temple incorporated the 3rd-century BC Carthaginian temple. The rectangular plan and six columns of the pronaos, the enclosed portico leading to the temple chamber, are still visible. An architrave above the entrance supported a triangular pediment and steps led up to the temple.

The columns, 8 m (26 ft) high, were made of smooth limestone blocks placed on bases about 1 m (3 ft) wide.

The capitals were in the Ionic style but are atypical, lacking the abacus and volutes.

The Roman temple was built over the Carthaginian temple.

Pronaos

Columns

Steps

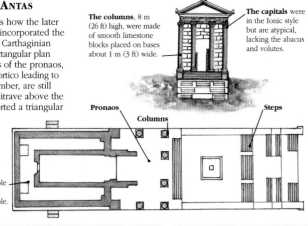

The Easter procession during
Holy Week at Iglesias

its own coins. In the mid-19th
century more mines were
opened, and Iglesias grew into
an important mining center.

Today, the ruins of the mine
buildings, most of which have
been abandoned, create a
striking contrast with the well-
preserved historic center. The
elegant pedestrian shopping
street, Corso Matteotti, leads
to Piazza del Municipio and
the Palazzo
Vescovile (Bishop's
Palace), built in
1785. On the west
side is the 19th-
century Palazzo
del Comune (Town
Hall) and opposite
is the cathedral of
Santa Chiara.
Completed in the
late 17th century,
the cathedral has
a Romanesque
facade dating
from 1288.

The narrow, winding streets
around the cathedral are lined
with two-story buildings
adorned with wrought-iron
balconies. **San Francesco**
on Via Don Minzoni was built
between the 14th and 16th
centuries and has side chapels
dedicated to noble families.
Half an hour's walk from
Piazza Sella is the **Castello
di Salvaterra**, built in 1284
as part of the city's medieval
defensive walls. A part of
these walls is also visible in
Via Eleonora d'Arborea.

During Easter week, holy
processions and performances
of mystery plays take place in
the town (see p26).

**Romanesque portal of
Santa Chiara, Iglesias**

THE SULCIS MINES

The history of Sardinia's mines is
inextricably linked with the island's
economic development. Ancient
rock formations, particularly in the
southwestern region of the island
known as Sulcis, have left rich
mineral deposits of silver, copper,
lead, iron, and zinc. Nuraghic
people are known to have had
metalworking skills, and there is
evidence of Phoenician and Roman

**Entrance to an
abandoned mine**

mines. In the short-lived boom of 19th-century industrialization, the mines stood like citadels in a predominantly
agricultural country. Today, the dream of prosperity through
mining is vanishing, and all that remains is a rich heritage
of mining architecture and culture.

The area around Iglesias is the mining heart of Sardinia,
and the landscape descending to the sea has been deeply
scarred by mine working. At Monteponi the industrial
plants, mine shafts and miners' houses look as though they
were only recently abandoned, while at Masua, tunnels and
tracks are still visible. At Buggerru, the Malfidano mine,
exploited for eight centuries, opens onto the waterfront.

ENVIRONS: At Case Marganai,
10 km (6 miles) northeast of
Iglesias, the **Linasia Botanical
Gardens** extend over an area
of 9 sq km (3 sq miles) with
examples of plants
from the maquis.
The **Museo Casa
Natura** here has a
collection of local
plants and pieces
from mine shafts.

Guided tours
of local mines are
organized by the
**Associazione
Minatori** (Miners'
Association). One
tour takes in the
lead and zinc
Monteponi mine,
with the elegant Bellavista
building and Sella shaft.
Another tour begins at the
San Giovanni mine and ends
at the abandoned village of
Seddas Moddizzis. This
includes the Santa Barbara
mine shaft whose crenellated
walls make it look like a
medieval castle.

🌿 **Linasia Botanical Gardens**
Località Marganai. 📞 0781-200 61.
🕐 Oct–Apr: 9:30am–1pm Sat & Sun;
May–Sep: 9am–noon, 4:30–7pm Tue,
Thu, Sat & Sun. 🏛 **Museo Casa
Natura** as above.
⛏ **Associazione Minatori**
Località Nicolay, Monteponi.
📞 0781-49 14 10. 🖥

Costa di Masua ⑭

Road map B5. 🅸 (0781-545 22).

THE CORNICHE ROAD between
Fontanamare and Masua,
12 km (7 miles) north,
follows a wild and splendid
coastline. At Masua, the little
beach of Porto Flavia is overlooked by pillars of eroded
limestone and, offshore, the
unmistakable profile of Pan
di Zucchero ("sugarloaf")
island. This sheer rock rises
132 m (433 ft) from the sea.
At Nebida you can see the
abandoned mines of the
industrial archaeological area.

A panoramic path along the
coast leads to the abandoned
remains of La Marmora mine
buildings and shafts.

**The island of Pan di Zucchero
jutting out from the sea**

Island of San Pietro ⑮

NAMED AFTER THE APOSTLE PETER, who is said to have taken refuge here during a storm, the island of San Pietro was virtually uninhabited until 1736, when Carlo Emanuele III offered it to a community of Ligurian coral fishermen whose ancestors had been exiled to the island of Tabarca, off the Tunisian coast. San Pietro's Ligurian origins can be seen in the architecture, dialect, and cuisine, which bears traces of North African influences. The rugged coast, inhabited by the rare Eleonora's falcon, has coves that can be reached only by sea. The island is covered in thick maquis vegetation.

La Punta
Houses that once belonged to the tuna fishermen are being converted into vacation homes.

Cala Fico
Walls of silver rock on one side and brown rock on the other enclose this sheltered inlet.

Cala Vinagra

Montagna di Ravenna

Carloforte

Capo Sandalo
The westernmost point of the island, dominated by a lighthouse, is frequently exposed to the mistral wind.

Eleonora's falcon, so named because Eleonora d'Arborea *(see p36)* was the only one allowed to hunt it, is protected in this preserve. The conservation area has observation points and marked trails.

Monte di Gasparro

La Caletta

Stagno della Vinagna

0 kilometers   2
0 miles   2

Salt flats on the outskirts of Carloforte attract a large number of migratory birds.

La Caletta
Protected from rough seas by Punta Spalmatore, the sheltered bay of La Caletta has a white, sandy beach.

KEY

▬▬	Major road
──	Minor road
▦	Salt flat
──	River

Carbonia's Piazza Roma, a typical example of Fascist architecture

Isola
Piana

Carloforte
*The only town on the island,
Carloforte overlooks the port,
with alleys and stairways
descending to the water.
The center of social life is
Piazza Carlo Emanuele III.
The San Pietro feast day
procession of boats is also
worth watching.*

Punta delle Colonne
*The name, Cape of Columns,
refers to the trachytic stacks
that jut out from the sea.*

Carbonia ⑯

Road map B6. 33,046.
Piazza Marmilla (0781-67 16 27).

CARBONIA, LOCATED in the
mining region of Sulcis,
was founded by Mussolini in
1936, during the international
embargo imposed against
Italy because of the Abyssinian
campaign. The town, which
took only two years to build,
has retained its Fascist town
planning and architectural
conception, with imposing
buildings and broad streets
that converge at the central
Piazza Roma. The town's most
important public buildings are
found here, including the
Town Hall, the Torre Civica
tower, and parish church of
San Ponziano, with a trachyte
bell tower that is a copy of
the one on the cathedral in
Aquileia in northeast Italy.
    Villa Sulcis, the former
residence of the director of
the mines, has become the
Museo Archeologico. On
display are earthenware and
bronze statuettes, jewels from
local *domus de janas*, and
finds from the archaeological
sites at Monte Sirai.

ENVIRONS: West of Carbonia
along the N126, a marked
road leads to the imposing
hill occupied by the Monte
Sirai archaeological site. The
stunning view alone is worth
the visit, as you can see the
islands of Sant'Antioco and
San Pietro. The fortified
Acropolis of Monte Sirai
was built by the Phoenicians
in the 4th century BC to
defend Sulki (present-day
Sant'Antioco). The outer wall,
4 m (13 ft) thick, protected
the acropolis and the surrounding garrison town,
which could house 500 foot
soldiers and 100 mounted
soldiers. The ruins of this

ancient military camp were
discovered in 1963, and
excavation is still under way.
    The necropolis, northwest
of the main citadel, has a
Phoenician section with
common graves as well as an
area of Punic tombs with a
dozen hypogea (underground
burial chambers).

🏛 **Museo Archeologico**
Villa Sulcis, Via Napoli 4. 0781-
640 44. 9am–1pm, 3–7pm daily.
⋔ **Acropolis of Monte Sirai**
3 km (2 miles) S of Carbonia.
9am–noon, 2–7pm Tue–Sun.

**Underground burial chambers in
the necropolis of Monte Sirai**

Calasetta ⑰

Road map B6. 2,731.
Piazza Municipio 10 (0781-885 34).

THE SECOND LARGEST village on
the island of Sant'Antioco
(see p72) and a trading port
for Carloforte, Calasetta was
founded in 1769 to house the
Ligurian fishermen arriving
from the Tunisian island of
Tabarca. The straight streets
with their two-story houses
lead to the main square. Here,
the parish church has a bell
tower of Arab derivation. The
road heading south along the
western coast offers a
panoramic view of alternating
cliffs, coves, and beaches.

Urns that held the ashes of babies in the Tophet outside Sant'Antioco

Sant'Antioco

Road map B6. 12,197.
Via Nazionale 175 (078-820 31).
Jun 29: San Pietro.

Sant'Antioco is the main town on the island of the same name. The island is connected to Sardinia by a causeway, and remains of a Roman bridge are still visible from the road. The *faraglioni*, two large menhirs, stand on one side. According to legend these are the petrified figures of a nun and a monk, turned to stone as they tried to elope.

The town was founded by the Phoenicians in the 8th century BC and named Sulki. It soon became a major port in the Mediterranean, due to the trade in minerals, including gold, extracted from the area. Ptolemy, the Greek astronomer, gave it the name of *insula plumbaria* (island of lead). The Carthaginians used the port during the second Punic War *(see p34)*, but this alliance was harshly punished by the victorious Romans. Under the Roman Empire the town flourished, until continuous pirate raids during the Middle Ages led to its gradual decline.

The picturesque town cener climbs away from the sea, and its characteristic houses have small wrought-iron balconies. The main street, **Corso Vittorio Emanuele**, is shaded by an avenue of trees. Above the town is the church of **Sant'Antioco**, built in the 6th century with a Greek cross plan and central dome, but modified in the 11th century.

According to tradition the remains of the island's patron saint, Sant'Antioco, are buried in the catacombs, reached via the transept. The body of the martyr is said to have floated here after he was killed by the Romans in Africa. Some catacombs are open to the public. The chambers are less than 2 m (6 ft) high and some are decorated with frescoes.

In nearby Via Regina Margherita, the Monte Granatico building is now occupied by the **Antiquarium**. This museum contains Phoenician and Roman earthenware, jewels, and other objects found in the area, including urns from the nearby Tophet necropolis.

The **Museo Etnografico** is housed in a former wine-making plant. The large central hall contains kitchen equipment used to make cheese and cultivate grapevines. The weaving section

has spindles and looms on display, once used for the processing of wool and *byssus*, a fine filament taken from the *Pinna nobilis*, the largest bivalve mollusk in the Mediterranean. Under the arcade outside, original wine-making equipment and implements used for raising livestock are on display.

Dominating the town is the red stone **Castello Sabaudo**, rebuilt by the Aragonese in the 16th century. Just outside town, on a cliff overlooking the sea, the bleak **Tophet** is a Phoenician sanctuary and necropolis. This burial ground was used for the ashes of stillborn babies, or those who died shortly after birth. Nearby is the Carthaginian **Necropolis** with about 40 underground family tombs.

Fresco in the catacombs of Sant'Antioco

This area was later used by the Romans for the ashes of their dead. The tombs occupy the upper part of town and were used as catacombs during the Early Christian period.

Sant'Antioco
Via Necropoli. 0781-830 44.
Catacombs 9am–noon, 3–6pm
Mon–Sat, 10–11am, 4–8pm Sun &
public hols; Oct–Mar by appt only.

Cala Domestica, north of Sant'Antioco *(see p68)*

🏛 **Antiquarium**
Via Regina Margherita 113. 📞 *0781-835 90.* ⏰ *9:30am–1pm, 3:30–6pm daily.* 🎟 *combined ticket with Museo Etnografico, Tophet, and Necropolis.*
🎟
🏛 **Museo Etnografico**
Via·Necropoli. 📞 *0781-84 10 89.* ⏰ *9:30am–1pm, 3:30–6pm daily.* 🎟 *combined ticket.*
⛪ **Tophet and Necropolis**
Via Castello. ℹ *Archeotur (0781-835 90).* ⏰ *9:30am–1pm, 3:30–6pm daily.* 🎟 *combined ticket.*

Tratalias ⓳

Road map B6. 🏔 *1,182.* 🚌

THIS VILLAGE in the Sulcis region was the seat of the diocese until 1413. The facade of the Pisan Romanesque cathedral of **Santa Maria**, consecrated in 1213, is divided horizontally by a row of little arches surmounted by a rose window. The tympanum is curious, in that the last section of a stairway juts out from it.

The sides and apse are decorated with pilasters and blind arches. Inside, the three naves are separated by large, octagonal pillars. An altarpiece from 1596 depicts St. John the Baptist and St. John the Evangelist with the Madonna and Child.

Cathedral of Santa Maria, Tratalias

Santadi ⓴

Road map C6. 🏔 *4,014.* 🚌 ℹ *Via Vittorio Veneto 1 (0781-94 10 00).* 🎉 *first Sun in Aug: Matrimonio Mauritano.*

BUILT ON THE BANKS of the River Mannu, Santadi's old town sits on the higher, north side. Some traditional architecture made from rough volcanic rock is still visible in the medieval center. Evidence that the area has been inhabited since the nuraghic age can be seen in the copper, bronze, gold, and earthenware objects found here, which are now on display in the Museo Archeologico in Cagliari *(see p58)*. Local tools and furniture can be seen at the **Museo Etnografico Sa Domu Antigua**. The shop here sells typical Sulcis handicrafts.

ENVIRONS: On a plateau southwest of the town is the 7th-century BC Phoenician fortress, **Pani Loriga**. Continuing south for 5 km (3 miles) are two caves, the **Grotta Is Zuddas**, with splendid formations of stalagmites and stalactites, and the **Grotta Pirosu**, where archaeological finds such as a votive lamp and a Cypriot-style tripod were found.

The necropolis at Montessu

North of Villaperuccio, the **Montessu Necropolis** has typical *domus de janas (see p33)* tombs, some of which still have traces of the original yellow and red wall facing. Other tombs were probably used for worship.

The August festival, Matrimonio Mauritano (Mauretanian Wedding), is a ceremony that may have started with the North Africans who settled here during the Roman age.

🏛 **Museo Etnografico Sa Domu Antigua**
Via Mazzini 37. 📞 *0781-95 59 83.* ⏰ *9am–12:30pm, 3–7:30pm daily.*
🦇 **Grotta Is Zuddas and Pirosu**
Benatzu. ℹ *Cooperativa Monte Meana (0781-95 57 41).* ⏰ *noon & 4pm Mon–Fri; 9:30am–noon, 2:30–5pm Sun.* 🎟
⛪ **Montessu Necropolis**
Località Peruccio. ℹ *0781-84 10 89.* ⏰ *9am–1pm, 3–7pm daily.* 🎟 🎟

MONTE ARCOSU

The mountains in the Sulcis region are covered with forests of cork oak, holm oak, strawberry trees, and heather, from which the granite peaks seem to emerge. This area extends for about 17,300 acres, interrupted only by a rough road that connects Santadi and Capoterra along the Mannu and Gutturu Mannu river valleys. There are plans to make the area into a National Park: the World Wildlife Fund for Nature (WWF) has purchased 741 acres of land on the slopes of Monte Arcosu to protect the Sardinian deer, which roamed the entire island until 1900 but is now restricted to a few isolated areas. Other forest mammals include fallow deer, wild cats, boar, and martens. Among the birds found here are the golden eagle, peregrine falcon, and goshawk. This nature preserve is open all year, and

Stag in the Monte Arcosu preserve

visitors can stay overnight in shelters. There are well-marked nature trails as well as unmarked wild walks, although an official WWF guide is obligatory in some areas. The Cagliari-based Cooperativa Quadrifoglio *(070-96 87 14)* has information regarding accommodations and trekking. To reach the preserve, take the road east from Santadi along the Gutturu river.

The sheltered beach at Baia Chia

Baia Chia ㉑

Road map C6. **[i]** *Via Provinciale 41, Domus de Maria (070-923 02 41).*

THE SOUTHERN COAST (Costa del Sud) is an area of high sand dunes and white beaches that extend as far as the Capo Spartivento headland. Junipers grow in the sand, and the marshland is frequented by egrets, purple herons, grebes, and other migratory aquatic birds. The area is slated to become the center of a regional nature preserve.

Along the coastal road, the hamlet of Chia is a popular tourist destination set among orchards and fig trees. A rough road leads to the sheltered bay of Chia, flanked on one side by the 17th-century **Torre di Chia**, and on the other by red cliffs covered with maquis vegetation.

At the foot of the tower you can visit the remains of Phoenician **Bithia**. This ancient city, mentioned in the writings of Ptolemy and Pliny the Elder, had been covered by the sea for centuries and has not yet been completely excavated.

Remains of a Punic and Roman necropolis are visible, as are the ruins of a temple probably dedicated to the god Bes. Earthenware pots and amphorae from the 7th century BC have been discovered in the sand, and traces of Roman wall paintings and mosaics decorate porticoed houses. Ancient Punic fortifications can be seen near the base of the watchtower, and an elliptical cistern has also been found.

⋔ Bithia
Domus de Maria, Località Chia.
◯ *at all times.*

ENVIRONS: Along the coast as far as the promontory of Capo Spartivento, where there are spectacular views, is a series of bays, dunes, and pine forests that can be reached on foot.

The Roman theater at Nora

Nora ㉒

Road map C6. **[i]** *070-920 91 38.* **◯** *9am–sunset daily.*

FOUNDED UNDER Carthaginian rule in the 9th–8th centuries BC, the ancient city of Nora was built on a spit of land jutting out to sea. The town became the island's most important city, a role it continued to enjoy under the Romans. In AD 238, Nora became the capital of the Roman province of Sardinia.

Repeated Saracen raids and the lack of fertile land finally forced the inhabitants to abandon the city in the Middle Ages, and the three ports were gradually covered up by the encroaching sea.

The ruins of the ancient city extend as far as the headland of Capo di Pula, covered with

The promontory of Capo Spartivento overlooking the southern coastline

maquis and dominated by the Spanish **Torre del Coltelazzo**.

An impressive vestige of the Carthaginian city is the raised Temple of Tanit, the goddess of fertility. Little else remains of the Punic period, although rich findings in the tombs testify to active trading.

The Roman city is well represented. Left of the entrance are the 4th-century Terme di Levante, Roman baths decorated with mosaics. Nearby is a 2nd-century AD theater and the large rectangular Forum behind it. South of the theater, the mosaics in the *frigidarium* and *caldarium* of the baths are decorated with white, black, and ocher tesserae. Paved roads and the city's extensive sewage system are also still visible.

Many finds, including Punic inscriptions in which the name of the island of Sardinia is first mentioned, are kept in Cagliari's Museo Archeologico Nazionale *(see p58)*.

Some earthenware objects found at the site are on display in the small **Museo Civico Archeologico**.

The nearby Romanesque church of **Sant'Efisio**, built by French Victorine monks in the 11th century, is the site of an annual procession from Cagliari *(see p26)*.

🏛 **Museo Civico Archeologico**
Corso Vittorio Emanuele 67.
📞 070-920 96 10.
🕐 9am–7pm. 🌐

Golden pen found at Nora

The popular resort of Poetto, between Quartu Sant'Elena and Cagliari

Quartu Sant'Elena ㉓

Road map C6. 🏠 *65,610.*
🚌 🚊 *Cagliari.* ✈ *Elmas.* ℹ *070-860 12 37.* 🎉 *Sep 14: Sant'Elena.*

SITUATED ON THE OUTSKIRTS of Cagliari, Quartu Sant'Elena has grown to become one of the island's largest cities. It lies at the edge of the salt flats and marsh of the same name, which are favorite breeding and nesting grounds for flamingos.

The medieval church of **Sant'Agata** stands in the town's main square, Piazza Azuni. From here Via Porcu leads to the **Casa Museo Sa Dom 'e Farra**, literally "the house of flour." This large country house, converted into a museum, features over 14,000 traditional farm and domestic tools and equipment collected over the years by Gianni Musiu, a former shepherd. Each of the museum's rooms is dedicated to different farm activities: from saddles and leather harnesses to wagons and blacksmiths' bellows. One of the more curious objects is the snow-cooled icebox. Gathered in the Barbagia region, the snow was taken to Cagliari on muleback and kept cold in underground, straw-lined containers.

The farmstead consisted of the owner's home and living quarters for farm laborers. Other rooms around a large courtyard were used for various domestic and farm activities such as milling, breadmaking, and tool repair.

A bus ride southwest of Quartu Sant'Elena brings you to the beach resort of Poetto, a favorite with local people.

🏛 **Casa Museo Sa Dom 'e Farra**
Via Eligiu Porcu 143. 🕐 *9am–1pm, 4–8pm daily.*

FORESTA DEI SETTE FRATELLI

The Forest of the Seven Brothers was named after the seven peaks that can be seen from Cagliari and which tower over the holm oak forests and maquis. Run by the *Azienda Foreste Demaniali (070-279 91),* the forest covers an area of more than 9,800 acres, replanted with pine, eucalyptus, and cypress trees, and reaching an altitude of 1,023 m (3,355 ft). It is also one of the few areas inhabited by the rare Sardinian deer, now almost extinct. The mountain has many mule trails, once used by coal merchants; one of these footpaths begins at the forest headquarters at Campu Omo on the N125. To drive into the mountains take a right turn past the Arcu 'e Tidu pass on the N125.

Densely wooded **Foresta dei Sette Fratelli**, which extends over seven hills

THE EASTERN COAST

M ILE AFTER MILE OF PASTURES AND ROCKS *characterize the interior of eastern Sardinia, falling away to inaccessible cliffs on the coast, refuge for the rare monk seal. The coastline of the Golfo di Orosei is now part of the Parco Nazionale del Gennargentu, a vast nature preserve founded to protect golden eagles and moufflon.*

There are no towns of any great size along the Eastern coast, but there are some good seaside resorts around Arbatax and Villasimius. Except for a few stretches, the road runs inland, so that most of the beaches can be reached only after walking a long way or by driving on dirt roads. The largest towns are Orosei, Muravera, and Dorgali, also situated in the interior at a certain distance from the coast. The historical reasons for this go back to the endemic malaria that afflicted the island until after World War II and, before that, the constant pirate raids that plagued the coasts for centuries. This area is still unknown Sardinia, the interior the domain of shepherds and their flocks, and the southeast yet to be discovered by tourism. Until recently the region of Sarrabus was isolated because of the absence of negotiable roads. The only way of reaching it was by a narrow-gauge railroad from Cagliari, which followed the contours of the valleys. It is still in operation and offers a delightful opportunity to take a trip back into the past. Sarrabus today attracts visitors who prefer to stray from the beaten track. Farther north, the Ogliastra region, with its sandy beaches varying from pearly gray to a startling reddish color, has rugged mountains and hills where time seems to have stood still, and where pastoral life has not been invaded by the 20th century and strong traditions survive. The Baronie region has the towns of Siniscola and Orosei, with good public transportation and a fast modern highway, making the area more accessible.

The alluvial plain around Posada, seen from the Castello della Fava

◁ Steep limestone cliffs on the Golfo di Orosei

Exploring the Eastern Coast

SPLENDID NATURAL scenery and prehistoric
archaeological sites around Dorgali and
Orroli are the main attractions of the Eastern
Coast. The cliffs along the coast are steep,
and the most secluded coves in the Golfo di
Orosei (Cala Sisine, Cala Luna, Cala Golo-
ritze) are most easily reached by boat. The
alternative is a lengthy walk, best tackled in
hiking boots. The countryside is marvelous
however, and the trek rewarding. The main road
winding through the region is the Orientale Sarda.
There is a proposal – supported by the local people
but vehemently opposed by environmentalists – to
widen this road into a fast access highway.

A glimpse of the Golfo di Orosei, near Baunei

SIGHTS AT A GLANCE

Arbatax ❷
Barì Sardo ❶❺
Dorgali ❺
Gairo ❶❹
Galtellì ❽
*Gennargentu National
Park pp82–3* ❹
Jerzu ❶❸
Lanusei ❶❷
Muravera ❶❻
Orosei ❼
Orroli ❶❽

Perdasdefogu ❶❾
Posada ❶❶
Santa Maria Navarrese ❸
Siniscola ❶⓿
Villasimius ❶❼

Tours
Codula di Luna ❻
Monte Albo Tour ❾
The Orientale Sarda Road ❶
A Trip on the Trenino Verde pp92–3 ⓴

0 kilometers   10

0 miles   10

KEY

▬▬	Highway
▬▬	Major road
▬▬	Minor road
▬▬	Scenic route
──	River

Panoramic view of the foothills of Mount Gennargentu

Rocky outcrops of reddish granite at Arbatax

O DI
SEI

NTALE SARDA ROAD

③ **SANTA MARIA**
   NAVARRESE

② **ARBATAX**

ARGENTU
NAL PARK
LANUSEI
⑫

⑮ **BARÌ SARDO**

⑬ **JERZU**

OGU ⑲

A TRIP ON THE
TRENINO VERDE

umendosa

⑯ **MURAVERA**

Cagliari

COSTA
REI

⑰ **VILLASIMIUS**

Pisan tower at Orosei

GETTING AROUND

The Orientale Sarda road (N125) is winding and slow. The road leading to the interior from Tortolì to Nuoro is faster, thanks to the tunnel that avoids the Arcu Correboi pass and goes directly from the Barbagia to Ogliastra. There is also a north-south bus service. The Ogliastra plain (Tortolì and Arbatax) is connected to Cagliari by the Ferrovie Complementari della Sardegna narrow-gauge train; the trip takes about eight hours. It isn't quick, but the line goes through wonderful scenery.

One of the rocky coves on the Eastern Coast near Cala Luna

The Orientale Sarda Road ❶

Along the eastern peaks of the Gennargentu National Park *(see pp82–3)*, the N125, or the "Eastern Sardinian" route, connects Olbia to Cagliari. The most spectacular stretch is between Dorgali and Baunei, 63 km (39 miles) of winding road hewn out of the rock by Piedmontese coal merchants during the mid-1800s. These "foreigners" carved a road through the remote mountain valleys and felled trees that were sent to the mainland. The deforestation that resulted has proved irreversible.

Flumineddu River Valley ②
This stretch of the N125 road goes through rugged terrain with cliffs and a fine view of the Flumineddu river valley under the peaks of Monte Tiscali. There are many places where you can stop to enjoy the wonderful scenery.

Genna Silana Pass ③
This is the highest point of the tour at 1,017 m (3,336 ft). Stop here to get a dramatic view of the Gorroppu ravine. A trail from Pischina Urtaddalà descends to the Flumineddu riverbed.

Urzulei ④
Built on different levels on the slopes of Punta Is Gruttas, Urzulei was once an isolated town difficult to reach. The stone church of San Giorgio di Suelli dates from the 15th century.

Dorgali

GROTTA DEL BUE MARINO

GOLFO DI OROSEI

N125 (Orientale Sarda)

Flumineddu

Codula di Luna

Codula di Sisine

GENNARGENTU NATIONAL PARK

KEY

▬ Major road

▬ Minor road

— River

Baunei ⑤
The white houses of this mountain village stand out under the limestone crags.

0 kilometers   5

0 miles   5

TIPS FOR DRIVERS

Length 63 km (39 miles).
Stopping-off points: at Dorgali,
Genna Silana, San Pietro, and Santa
Maria Navarrese there are cafés and
restaurants. Allow a full day to take
into account the winding roads
and opportunities to stop.

Cala Gonone ①

A 400-m (1,300-ft) tunnel
cut out of the limestone
rock leads to the popular
seaside resort of Cala
Gonone. A winding road,
with fabulous views of the
sea, white rocks, and the
maquis, continues to the
Grotta del Bue Marino where
there have been sightings of
the rare monk seal *(see p17)*.

San Pietro ⑥

A rough track with
precipitous hairpin
bends climbs to a
wooded plateau where
wild pigs graze. At the
end is the Golgo ravine,
295 m (967 ft) deep. A
little further along is the
18th-century church of
San Pietro. Shepherds
still make offerings here,
and a rural festival takes
place from June 28-29.

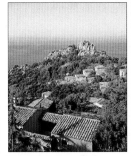

**The vacation resort of Cala
Moresca, at Arbatax**

Arbatax ❷

Road map D4. 🏘 *1,100.* 🚂 🚌 🚢
ℹ *Tortolì (0782-62 28 24).* 🎭 *Jul
12-15: Madonna di Stella Maris.*

THE SMALL TOWN of Arbatax
lies on the northern tip of
the Bellavista promontory, a
red porphyry cliff that
plunges into the
sea. The port,
guarded by a
Spanish tower, is
the terminal for
the narrow-gauge
trains arriving
from Cagliari.
Ferries from
Cagliari, Olbia
and the Italian
mainland also
dock here.
   This stretch
of coast has
clear, clean
water, and
enticing coves
such as **Cala Moresca**, south
of Arbatax. Several tourist
resorts now cover this small
promontory, such as the
popular *Vacanze Club* village,
built to resemble a typical
Mediterranean village. The
solid wood doors and
wrought-iron grilles on the

**The Aragonese tower at Santa
Maria Navarrese**

windows were taken from the
abandoned village of Gairo
(see p89). Farther south is
Porto Frailis, also protected
by a Spanish tower, and the
long, sandy Orrì beach. From
Arbatax trails lead up to the
lighthouse high on the
Bellavista promontory.

Santa Maria
Navarrese ❸

Road map D4. 🏘 *1,430.* 🚂 🚌
ℹ *Piazza di Navarra (0782-61 50
65).* 🎭 *Aug 15: Festa dell'Assunta.*

THIS SEASIDE resort was
named after the lovely
country church around which
it developed. It is said that
this three-aisle construction,
with a semicircular apse, was
built in the 11th century by
the daughter of the king of
Navarra after she had been
saved from a shipwreck.
   In the church courtyard
is a gigantic wild olive
tree that is
reputed to be
over a thousand
years old.
   The beautiful
beach at Santa
Maria Navarrese
is bordered by
a pine forest
and protected
by a Spanish
watchtower.
Opposite this
is the huge
Agugliastra (or
Sa Pedra Longa) rock, a slim
limestone pinnacle that rises
up 128 m (420 ft) from the
sea. Boat services from the
little port of Santa Maria
Navarrese will take visitors to
this rock as well as to Cala
Luna, Cala Sisine, and Cala
Goloritzè, farther up the coast.

The rocky Ogliastra island viewed from Capo Bellavista

Gennargentu National Park ❹

Peonies in flower

THIS LARGE PARK EXTENDS OVER 146,000 acres of some of the wildest, most mountainous landscape in Sardinia and includes the island's highest peak, Punta La Marmora. Established in 1989, most of the park, except for the island of Asinara, lies in the province of Nuoro. There are 14 towns in this protected area but few paved roads, and the steep-sided valleys and bare peaks give the area an isolated air. The unspoiled nature of the park makes it fascinating for hikers, geologists, and naturalists alike. The climb up the granite peak of Punta La Marmora (1,834 m, 6,015 ft) is rewarding, and the limestone desert of Supramonte is one of Italy's spectacular sights. Monte Tiscali hides the prehistoric rock village of Tiscali *(see pp104–5)*, and the ravines of Su Gorroppu and the Su Gologone spring are not to be missed. The coast to the east, home to the endangered monk seal, is one of Europe's loveliest.

The Wild Cat
Larger than the domestic cat, the wild cat lives on Gennargentu and Supramonte.

The Mount Gennargentu Massif
In winter the barren peaks and the lower slopes, carpeted in oak and chestnut trees, are sometimes covered by snow.

Bearded vulture

Moufflon

Shelter

ONNI

N128

DÉSULO

Marten

ARITZO

Punta La Marmora

SEU

Griffon vulture

0 kilometers   15

0 miles   15

THE HIGHEST PEAK IN SARDINIA: PUNTA LA MARMORA

The massif of Gennargentu, whose name means "door of silver," reaches its peak in Punta La Marmora which, at 1,834 m (6,015 ft) above sea level, is the highest point on the island. The landscape here is quite barren and wild. The sky is populated by raptors circling around in search of prey and with a little luck you might be able to see, in the distance, small groups of moufflons, or mountain sheep.

Hikers on the top of Punta La Marmora

The Crests of Supramonte
The peaks rise to the east of Gennargentu, and their slopes descend toward the sea.

Visitors' Checklist

Road map D4. ■ *EPT Nuoro, Piazza Italia 19 (0784-323 07 or 300 83); WWF Nuoro, Piazza Santa Maria della Neve 8 (0784-328 88); Pro Loco Dorgali, Via La Marmora 181 (0784-96 243); Desulo Town Hall (0784-61 92 11).*

Shelter

DORGALI

GOSOLO

Flumendosa

N125

Codula di Luna

The Monk Seal
The monk seal (Monachus albiventer), *thought to be extinct, has been sighted in recent years in the Golfo di Orosei. Tourism is blamed for the fall in its population.*

URZULEI

N125

BAUNEI

Key

▬ Major road

▬ Minor road

▬ River

N389

Lago Alto del Flumendosa

ARZANA

N198

Eagle

Wild Boar

Tips for Travelers

Ascending Punta La Marmora
From Desulo, follow the road to Fonni for about 5 km (3 miles) until you come to the S'Arcu de Tascusì pass, then take the asphalt road on the left until you reach a fork. Follow the dirt road on the left for 100 m (328 ft) and then take the right-hand road leading to the Girgini vacation farm. Skirt around it by keeping to the left. In a little less than 4 km (2 miles), take the right-hand fork and continue for 5 km (3 miles) until you reach the control cabin for an aqueduct. Leave your car here and follow the road on the right on foot until you reach the end, then proceed up the valley floor on the left until you reach the crest. From here bear right and continue up to the summit (an hour and a half on foot).

Su Gorroppu
This wild gorge, with its steep sides, can be scaled only by expert climbers.

Displays of exhibits at the Museo Archeologico in Dorgali

Dorgali ❺

Road map D3. 🏘 *8,114.*
🛈 *Pro Loco (0784-933 87).*
🎭 *Jan 16-17: Sant'Antonio Abate.*

THE CHARMING TOWN OF Dorgali lies on a ridge that descends from Monte Bardia and is 30 km (19 miles) from Nuoro and a little less than 10 km (6 miles) from the sea at Cala Gonone. Dorgali is predominantly an agricultural center and is also important

Santa Caterina parish church in the center of Dorgali

for locally produced crafts such as leather, ceramics, and filigree jewelry as well as carpet-weaving.

In the old part of town the buildings are made of dark volcanic stone. These include several churches: Madonna d'Itria, San Lussorio, and the Maddalena. The central square, Piazza Vittorio Emanuele, is dominated by the facade of the parish church, Santa Caterina, home to a large carved altar.

Dorgali's **Museo Archeologico** contains an important collection of objects from nuraghic sites, as well as finds from sites dating back to Punic and Roman times. Some of the most important nuraghic pieces come from the nearby site of **Serra Òrrios**. The museum also provides information on visits to the rock village of Tiscali, another major nuraghic site *(see pp104–5)*. The town is

known for its wine, and the local wine-making cooperative and the local dairy can be visited.

Nuraghic dwelling at Serra Òrrios

🏛 **Museo Archeologico di Dorgali**
Scuola Elementare, Via La Marmora.
📞 *0784-961 13.* ◗ *Apr–Oct 10am–1pm, 4–7pm.*
⌂ **Serra Òrrios**
🛈 *0784-933 87.* ◗ *May–Sep 10am–1pm, 4–7pm.* 🎟 🖼

THE NURAGHIC VILLAGE OF SERRA ÒRRIOS

At Serra Òrrios – about 10 km (6 miles) to the north-west of Dorgali and 23 km (14 miles) east of Nuoro – lies one of Sardinia's best preserved nuraghic villages, which dates from the 12th–10th centuries BC. The 70 round dwellings, each with a central hearth, are arranged in at least six groups around large central spaces with a well. Small places of worship have also been found in the village.

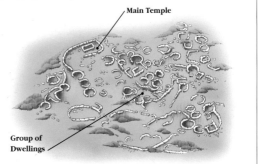

Main Temple

Group of Dwellings

Codula di Luna ❻

A THREE-HOUR WALK down the "Codula Illune," or Valley of the Moon, will take you from the Supramonte to the sea. The path is straightforward to follow, although there is little shade from the sun in summer. The track runs through aromatic maquis scrub, and passes shepherds' huts on the way, as well as the entrances to enormous caves, many of which have not yet been fully explored.

The beautiful, secluded beach of Cala Luna, backed by a small lake

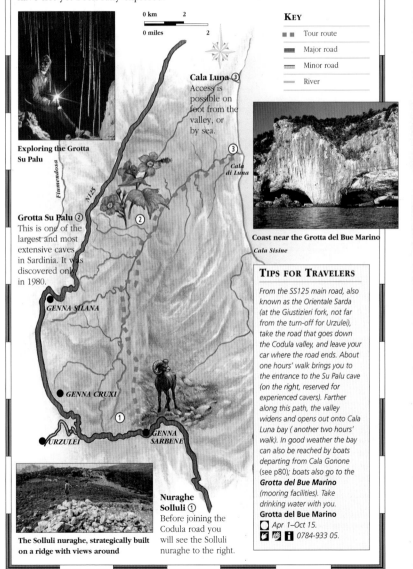

Exploring the Grotta Su Palu

Grotta Su Palu ②
This is one of the largest and most extensive caves in Sardinia. It was discovered only in 1980.

Cala Luna ③
Access is possible on foot from the valley, or by sea.

KEY

▪▪ Tour route
▬ Major road
▭ Minor road
— River

Coast near the Grotta del Bue Marino

The Solluli nuraghe, strategically built on a ridge with views around

Nuraghe Solluli ①
Before joining the Codula road you will see the Solluli nuraghe to the right.

TIPS FOR TRAVELERS

From the SS125 main road, also known as the Orientale Sarda (at the Giustizieri fork, not far from the turn-off for Urzulei), take the road that goes down the Codula valley, and leave your car where the road ends. About one hours' walk brings you to the entrance to the Su Palu cave (on the right, reserved for experienced cavers). Farther along this path, the valley widens and opens out onto Cala Luna bay (another two hours' walk). In good weather the bay can also be reached by boats departing from Cala Gonone (see p80); boats also go to the **Grotta del Bue Marino** *(mooring facilities). Take drinking water with you.*
Grotta del Bue Marino
☐ *Apr 1–Oct 15.*
📷 ♿ ℹ *0784-933 05.*

The Chiesa delle Anime at Orosei

Orosei ❼

Road map D3. 🏘 *5,502.* 🚗
ℹ *Piazza del Popolo 54 (0784-985 90).*
🎭 *Easter Week, Jul 26, San Giacomo.*

THE HISTORIC CAPITAL of the Baronia region is situated about 5 km (3 miles) inland, and has a bustling, well-kept historic center with churches, archways, and small, white-washed stone buildings over-looking flowered courtyards.

The town of Orosei was probably founded in the early Middle Ages, and its golden age occurred under Pisan domination, when it was ruled by the barons of the Guiso family. Orosei developed into an important harbor with moorings alongside the Cedrino River. After yielding to Aragonese rule, the town began to decline as a result of malarial disease, repeated pirate raids, and the gradual silting up of the river.

The portal of Santa Maria 'e Mare

A labyrinth of alleys leads to the central Piazza del Popolo, where three churches stand. At the top of a flight of steps is **San Giacomo Maggiore** with an 18th-century facade and terra-cotta tiled domes. Opposite is the **Chiesa del Rosario**, with a Baroque facade, and the **Chiesa delle Anime**, founded by the brotherhood of monks that participates in the Easter Week ceremonies.

Sant'Antonio Abate, once an isolated rural sanctuary, is now surrounded by the expanding town. Local handicrafts are on display in the Pisan tower inside the precincts of Sant'Antonio. The 17th-century Sanctuary of the Madonna del Rimedio, also once isolated, is now part of the outskirts and is surrounded by *cumbessias*, the houses used by pilgrims each September.

Monte Albo Tour ❾

THE MASSIVE WHITE limestone ridge that gave this mountain its name (*albo* means white) extends like a bastion between the Barbagia and Baronia regions. There are magnificent panoramic views from the maquis-covered slopes of the mountain. The area is destined to become a preserve to protect 650 plant species as well as moufflons, wild boar, and raptors. Part of this tour follows a narrow road along the base of the limestone cliffs.

Lodè ②
This small town amid olive trees and maquis is the home of the Annunziata sanctuary, with its whitewashed, red-roofed *cumbessias*. On May 22-23 the sanctuary becomes a pilgrimage site.

Bitti ③
This lively town *(see p100)* lies in lovely countryside surrounded by clusters of oak and wild olive trees.

The Annunziata Sanctuary, Lodè

KEY

▬▬ Tour route

═ Other roads

— River

0 kilometers　　4

0 miles　　　　4

ENVIRONS: Near the mouth of the Cedrino River is **Santa Maria 'e Mare**, founded in the 13th century by Pisan merchants. The church is full of ex votos, and on the last Sunday in May it is the focus of a pilgrimage, when a statue of the Madonna is taken down the river on a boat, followed by a flotilla of boats.

At the mouth of the estuary the river divides in two. The northern part flows into an artificial canal; the southern half feeds the Su Petrosu marsh. This is where to find coots, moorhens, mallards, and purple gallinules. The shallows are home to avocets, stilts, gray herons, and egrets.

Galtellì ⓧ

Road map D3. 👣 2,366. 🚉 🛈
Piazza del Popolo 54, Orosei (0784-985 90). 🎭 *Jan 16-17, Sant'Antonio Abate.*

LYING ON THE SLOPES of Monte Tuttavista, Galtellì was the most important town in the region in the Middle Ages. Until 1496 it was the bishopric, as can be seen in Romanesque San Pietro, the former cathedral built in the 12th century. After this era the town began to decline thanks to the ravages of malaria and frequent pirate raids, but traces of its glorious past have been preserved in the parish church of Santissimo Crocifisso, which contains fine 16th- and 17th-century wooden statues.

The historic center of Galtellì is still pretty, with its whitewashed buildings and small, well-kept houses.

ENVIRONS: One of the most interesting sights in this area is Monte Tuttavista. A dirt road and then a path take you to Sa Pedra Istampada ("the perforated rock"), a wind-sculpted arch 30 m (98 ft) high. There are splendid views from the summit.

Near the village of La Traversa, 12 km (8 miles) from Galtellì, is the Tomba di Giganti (giants' tomb) of **Sa Ena 'e Thomes**, a very impressive prehistoric monument with a 3-m (10 ft) stele hewn out of a single block of granite.

The Sa Ena 'e Thomes "giants' tomb" near La Traversa

Sant'Anna ①
This pass is 624 m (2,050 ft) above sea level, and offers splendid scenic views. The road winds up among cliffs, euphorbia bushes, and cluster pines.

TIPS FOR TRAVELERS

Length: 76 km (47 miles).
This tour takes about two hours by car, but allow half a day to include the stops.
Stopping-off points: the Sant'Anna roadman's house and the town of Bitti (see p100).

View of Monte Albo

Lula ④
This town in Barbagia has a famous sanctuary, dedicated to St. Francis. Thousands of worshipers participate in the saint's feast day celebrations from May 1-10, events described by Grazia Deledda in *Elias Portolu*.

The road leading up Monte Albo ⑤
The 20 km (12 miles) of this hillside road run along the northern slope of the mountain through pastures and maquis. On the right are steep limestone walls streaked with pink.

Siniscola

Road map D2. 👥 *10,056.* 🚉
ℹ️ *Via Monfalcone 17 (0784-87 75
25).* 🎪 *Aug 18: Sant'Elena.*

SET AT THE FOOT of Monte
Albo, the once agricultural
town of Siniscola was an
important trading center in
the 14th century under the
principality of Gallura *(see
p36).* Since then, the town has
grown in a haphazard manner
around the medieval center.
On the lively main street,
Via Sassari, the 18th-century
parish church of **San Giovanni
Battista** is decorated with a
fresco representing the life of
St. John the Baptist. The town
is also well known for its
local pottery studios.

ENVIRONS: A straight road
northeast from
Siniscola leads to
La Caletta, a small
tourist port with a
wide sandy beach,
4 km (2 miles)
long. Heading
southward, the
N125 passes the
fishing village
of **Santa Lucia**.
Probably founded
by emigrants
from the island
of Ponza, the
village is guarded
by a Spanish
watchtower.
Today Santa Lucia is a popular
summer resort, with a pine
forest that extends behind
the beach. Continuing southward, a long walk along the
shore will take you to the

The church at Santa Lucia

white sand dunes and juniper
bushes of **Capo Comino** (also
accessible from the N125).

The headland of Capo
Comino consists of rounded
rocks and pebble beaches
and is overlooked by a lighthouse. A two-hour walk along
the seashore and pine forest
will take you to **Berchida
beach**, where there is a
huge rock called *S'incollu
de sa Marchesa*
(The Marquise's
Throat). Eels
and gray mullet
populate an
area of marsh-
land here.

An alternative
excursion is to
take the rough
track that turns
right from the
N125 after the
Berchida
River and
winds through
the maquis until it reaches a
splendid beach with white
sand and clear sea. On the
way, the road passes the
remains of the nuraghic
settlement of Conca Umosa.

Spanish tower at Santa Lucia

Posada ⓫

Road map D2. 👥 *1,646.* 🚉

PERCHED ON TOP of a lime-
stone bank covered with
euphorbia and mastic trees,
this village is dominated by
the ruins of **Castello della
Fava**. The castle was built in
the 12th century by the rulers
of Gallura, who were later
conquered by the principality
of Arborea before passing
under Aragonese dominion
(see p36). In the Carthaginian
era this place was known as
the colony of Feronia.

The town retains its
medieval character, with
alleyways connected by steep
stairways, arches, and tiny
squares. The gray stone
houses have been preserved,
and the castle has also had a
face-lift. Wooden steps lead to
the top of the castle's square
tower where there is a
panoramic view of the sea,
the mouth of the Posada River
and the surrounding plain
covered with fruit orchards.

ENVIRONS: Inland, 9 km
(5 miles) west of Posada, is
the artificial lake of Posada.
The pine forests and fine views
make this a popular spot.

Lanusei ⓬

Road map D4. 👥 *6,387.* 🚌 🚉 🚉
🎪 *Jul 22: Santa Maria Maddalena.*

THIS LARGE, austere-looking
town, situated on a hillside
at 600 m (1,926 ft), overlooks
the plain that descends to the

The white sand dunes at Capo Comino

The village of Posada and the Castello della Fava

sea. It was once a health retreat due to its excellent climate, high altitude, and the many hiking trails in the surrounding forest. The town was built on various levels and still has some aristocratic buildings of interest.

Jerzu ⑬

Road map D4. 🏛 *3,561.* 🚫
🎉 *Jun 13: Sant'Antonio; Jul 25: San Giacomo; Aug 4: Sagra del Vino.*

T ALL, SHARP pinnacles of rock, known locally as *tacchi* (high heels), are an impressive sight as they emerge from the maquis on the mountainous approach to Jerzu. This modern town is built on several levels up the hillside with houses of two stories or more overlooking the main street. Steep

Wine labels from Jerzu

side streets in the lower quarter lead to older houses with many original features.

Jerzu's economy is based mainly on viticulture: small vineyards cling to the steep slopes around the town. The area produces about 11,000 tons of grapes from which the local wine cooperative makes the good red wine Cannonau DOC, one of the most famous in Sardinia.

The most important holiday is the feast day of Sant'Antonio da Padova, on June 13. One of the town's churches is dedicated to the saint.

ENVIRONS: At Ulassai, 7 km (4 miles) northwest of Jerzu, is the limestone **Grotta Su Màrmuri**, (*Il Marmo*, "the marble," in Italian). Steps descend to reveal spectacular pools and stalagmites.

🏞 **Grotta Su Màrmuri**
ℹ *Via Dante 69 (0782-798 05).*

Gairo ⑭

Road map D4. 🏛 *1,902.* 🚫 🚫
🎉 *third Sun in Sep: Nostra Signora del Buoncammino.*

G AIRO SANT'ELENA lies in the Pardu River valley, a deep ravine with impressive limestone walls. The present-day village was built after 1951, when Gairo Vecchio had to be evacuated after excessive rain that autumn caused a series of landslides. All that remains of the abandoned village are gutted houses without doors and windows. The entire area has spectacular scenery, though.

ENVIRONS: On the coast, the bay of Gairo is protected by a headland covered with maquis. From here you can go to Coccorocci, the only black sand beach in Sardinia. The coast road runs along the seashore, which is characterized by sandy inlets and cliffs of pink rock.

Barì Sardo ⑮

Road map D4. 🏛 *4,054.* 🚫
🎉 *Aug 29: San Giovanni Battista; Sep 8: Nostra Signora di Monserrato.*

T HIS AGRICULTURAL center is set in fertile countryside filled with vineyards and orchards. The name of the town is derived from the Sardinian word for marshes, *abbari*. In the oldest part of town, around the district of San Leonardo to the southwest, original stone houses are still visible. Here, the parish church, **Beata Vergine del Monserrato**, has a Rococo bell tower dated 1813. The town is also known for its textiles: tapestries, rugs and linen cushions, and bedcovers.

ENVIRONS: On the coast, east of Barì Sardo, **Torre di Barì** is a pleasant seaside resort that developed around the 17th-century Spanish tower built to defend the town from pirates. It has a sandy beach and small pine forest. The festivities for San Giovanni Battista, known here as *Su Nenneri*, are unusual. In a ritual to encourage a good harvest, grain and vegetable seedlings are cast into the sea.

The vineyards at Jerzu produce Cannonau, Sardinia's best-known wine

The basalt rock promontory at Capo Ferrato, south of Muravera

Muravera ⑯

Road map D5. 🏔 *4,478.* ℹ️ *Via Europa 22 (070-993 07 60).* 🎉 *Aug 14-15: l'Assunta.*

MURAVERA LIES at the mouth of the Flumendosa River, in the middle of an area of fruit orchards. It is a modern tourist town, catering to the resort complexes that have grown up along the coast. In ancient times this was the Phoenician city of Sarcapos. Today, the only building of historical interest is the church of **San Nicola**, off the main street, which has kept its original 15th-century chapels.

ENVIRONS: Muravera is an ideal starting point for trips along the coast and into the valleys of the interior. To the east, the beach around **Porto Corallo** is long and sandy, interrupted by small rocky

headlands. Near this tourist port is another **Spanish tower** that, in 1812, was used as a stronghold in one of the rare victories of the Sardinians over the Muslim pirates.

Northward, 11 km (7 miles) along the N125, also known as the Orientale Sarda road *(see p80)*, are the remains of the **Castello di Quirra** and the small Romanesque church of **San Nicola**, the only church in Sardinia built of brick.

To the south, the coast around **Capo Ferrato** is also beautiful, with basalt rocks, small white sandy coves, and pine trees. Past the headland of Capo Ferrato is the **Costa Rei**, a stretch of straight coastline with beaches and tourist villages. The seabed at the bay of **Cala Sinzias** farther to the south consists of long slabs of rock, giving the water a strikingly clean and transparent look.

Inland, the route toward Cagliari along the N125 offers spectacular scenery, with red rock among myrtle, juniper, and strawberry trees. A trip down the Flumendosa River valley, beyond San Vito, also offers spectacular scenery.

Castiadas is a hamlet behind the Costa Rei, set around a 19th-century prison amid vineyards and citrus trees. From the late 19th century to the 1950s the area was occupied by a prison farm, where prisoners worked on the land.

Villasimius ⑰

Road map D6. 🏔 *2,710.* ✈️ ℹ️ *Via Marconi 12 (070-79 15 46 14).* 🎉 *Jul: Madonna del Naufrago.*

WITH ITS HOTELS, residences, and second homes, this modern town is the leading seaside resort on the southeastern coast. Villasimius lies on the northern edge of a promontory that extends to **Capo Carbonara**. At the center of the headland is the **Notteri marsh**, separated from the sea by Simìus beach, a long stretch of sand. In the winter the marsh is a popular stopping-off point for migratory flamingos. On the tip of the promontory the lighthouse offers a sweeping view of the coast and the tiny islands of **Serpentara** and **Cavoli** in the distance. The stretch of water between the two islands is shallow and has

---

THE TOWN OF THE LAUNEDDAS

Northeast of Muravera is San Vito, an agricultural town that thrived in past centuries thanks to the silver mines on Monte Narba. In the center of town, the parish church with its twin bell towers over the facade is worth a visit. San Vito is known for its tradition of craftmanship, in particular the flutelike instrument, the *launeddas,* which was originally played by shepherds *(see p25).* Luigi Lai, Sardinia's most famous player of this ancient instrument, lives here and makes the instrument himself. Other crafts at San Vito include fine embroidery and basket-weaving with juniper twigs.

Luigi Lai, one of Sardinia's most famous *launeddas* players

The long beach separating the sea from Notteri marsh, south of Villasimius

witnessed many shipwrecks over the years. Off the island of Cavoli, at a depth of 10 m (33 ft), is the statue of the *Madonna dei Fondali* (Our Lady of the Sea Floor) by local sculptor Pinuccio Sciola. Excursions by glass-bottomed boat leave from the dock at Porto Giunco to view the submerged statue. This port is protected by the **Fortezza Vecchia**, a star-shaped fortress built in the 17th century. The sea around the headland is rich in fauna and flora and is popular with scuba divers.

Orroli ⑱

Road map C4. 🏘 *3,300.* 🚌
ℹ️ *Largo Aldo Moro (0782-84 70 06).* 🎉 *Jun 30: Santa Caterina.*

THE TOWN of Orroli lies in a hollow in the somewhat barren Pranemuru plateau, at the edge of the Flumendosa valley. The area is dotted with numerous archaeological sites, such as the necropolis of **Su Motti** where *domus de janas* tombs are cut out of the rock.

Other archaeological sites in the area include the ruins of the **Arrubiu Nuraghe**, 5 km (3 miles) southeast of Orroli. This complicated, pentagonal site is larger than the one at Su Nuraxi *(see pp64–5)*. The complex, made of red stone, was built around an 11th–10th-century BC central tower which, according to experts, was 27 m (88 ft) high. Five towers, probably dating from the 7th century BC, and connected by tall bastions, were built around the complex. An outer defensive wall was added in the 6th century BC. The ruins of the nuraghic village, consisting of round and rectangular dwellings, lie around the nuraghe.

Another interesting site is the nearby **Su Putzu** nuraghe, which has many dwellings in excellent condition.

🏛 **Su Motti**
4 km (2 miles) SE of Orroli. 📞 *0782-84 71 46.* 🕐 *at all times.*

🏛 **Arrubiu Nuraghe**
📞 *0782-84 77 83.* 🕐 *8:30am–1pm, 3–8:30pm (Oct–Apr: 9:30am–5pm).*

The Arrubiu Nuraghe near Orroli

Perdasdefogu ⑲

Road map D4 & D5. 🏘 *2,470.* 🚌
🎉 *Sep 12: San Salvatore.*

AN ISOLATED mountain village in the lower Ogliastra area, Perdasdefogu lies at the foot of the striking *tacchi*, vertical limestone walls that tower over the maquis *(see p89)*. The road that meanders northeast toward Jerzu is one of the most scenic in Sardinia. It runs along a plateau at the base of these dolomitic walls, offering a spectacular view of the sea and Perda Liana peaks in the distance. Along the way is the rural church of **Sant'-Antonio**, set in a meadow at the foot of Punta Coróngiu, one of the most impressive of the limestone *tacchi*.

View from the headland of Capo Carbonara, south of Villasimius

A Trip on the Trenino Verde ⑳

IT TAKES ALMOST FIVE hours to travel 160 km (99 miles) on the narrow-gauge *trenino verde* (little green train), but the reward is a trip back in time through some of the wildest landscapes in Sardinia. The route passes through the softly rolling hills of Trexenta, carpeted with almond and olive trees, to the rugged mountains of Barbagia di Seui, where the train runs along the foot of a magnificent *tònnero*, with a broad view of its vertical limestone walls. The route follows the craggy contours of the mountain, and there are so many bends that it is easy to lose your sense of direction. The train makes two hairpin turns through the town of Lanusei in order to get over a steep slope. The only drawback is the timetable: travelers cannot make the return trip on the same day.

Lake Alto Flumendosa, on the southern side of Gennargentu

Villanovatulo ⑥
This isolated shepherds' village has a view of the Flumendosa River basin. The walls of the houses have murals by Pinuccio Sciola.

The Trenino Verde
This picturesque train skirts the hillsides, well away from the road amid unspoiled scenery. As well as the timeless landscape, you can appreciate the atmosphere of a forgotten age.

Mandas ⑧
69 km (43 miles) from Cagliari, Mandas is the leading agricultural town in the area. The church of San Giacomo, with statues of San Gioacchino and Sant'-Anna, is worth a visit.

Orroli ⑦
Surrounded by oak forests, the town of Orroli lies on a basalt tableland crossed by the Flumendosa River. Watch for the Arrubiu nuraghe.

VISITORS' CHECKLIST

ℹ *Mandas (070-58 00 75),* **Train timetable** *mid-Apr–mid-Jun: from Arbatax, 2:30pm daily; from Mandas, 8:27am daily; mid-Jun–mid-Oct: from Arbatax, 7:50am, 2:30pm daily; from Mandas, 8:27am, 3:15pm daily; Jul 7– Aug 30: from Arbatax to Sadali, 9:10am return 5:30pm; from Mandas to Sadali, 8:30am return 7pm; mid-Oct–mid-Apr: private hire.*

Montarbu Forest ③
This is one of the best preserved forests in Sardinia, where moufflons live among ash, holm oak, and yew trees. A striking feature here are the *tònneri*, massive vertical limestone walls.

Lanusei ②
This village lies on the slope of a hill commanding a fine view of the sea *(see p88)*.

Tortolì ①
The capital of the Ogliastra region is 3 km (2 miles) from the sea, on the edge of a large marsh that attracts thousands of migratory birds in winter. Watch for the ruins of Castello di Medusa.

Sadali ⑤
Lying in the middle of a karstic plateau, Sadali boasts a 7-m (23-ft) waterfall fed by springs that flow into an underground chasm. There are numerous caves, such as Is Janas, 205 m (672 ft) long with an underground lake and impressive stalagmites and stalactites.

Interior of the Trenino Verde

Seui ④
The village of Seui, on the side of a steep valley, retains some traditional stone houses. The 17th-century Spanish prison is now occupied by the Civic Museum of Rural Culture with displays of traditional farm utensils and reconstructions of an 18th-century kitchen and bedroom.

0 kilometers   4

0 miles   4

KEY

▬▬ Train route

▬▬ Major road

▬▬ Minor road

▬ River

The train passing through Orroli

TIPS FOR TRAVELERS

Refreshments are not served on the train and the few stations en route are not equipped to offer restaurant facilities, so it is advisable to take along something to eat and drink. Going toward Mandas, the best views can be appreciated from the left-hand side of the train (and vice versa).

The "normal" train, called TL, is superior to the AT (single-unit rail diesel car), which is noisier and less comfortable.

CENTRAL SARDINIA, AND BARBAGIA

THE CENTRAL REGION OF SARDINIA *is the area that most vividly reflects the ancient character of the island. Rugged mountains are marked by shepherds' trails, and villages perch over steep valleys. The inhabitants of this isolated region are known as hardy and proud and have retained many aspects of their traditional way of life.*

The name Barbagia comes from the Latin word *barbària*, used by the Romans to designate the inaccessible regions of the interior inhabited by "barbarians" (any culture that did not share the values and beliefs of the Roman civilization). Inhabited since prehistoric times and rich in archaeological sites, such as the nuraghic village of Tiscali *(see pp104–5)*, the heart of Sardinia resisted Roman invasions for many centuries and preserved its nuraghic religious rites up to the advent of Christianity.

Getting to know this rugged land requires some effort, since the roads are slow and winding, road signs are sometimes missing, and many sights can be reached only by rough dirt tracks. The people, however, are often hospitable, and tradition is still an essential part of local life. The churches and villages come to life during the colorful folk festivals, the patron saints' feast days, and at religious festivities. At Mamoiada the *Mamuthones* lead the Mardi Gras processions wearing forbidding masks, cowbells, and sheepskins *(see p102)*.

The mountainous landscape dominates central Sardinia. Trekkers can enjoy hikes from the rocks of Supramonte di Oliena to the dense forests of holm oak on the slopes of Monte Novo San Giovanni *(see p107)* and the chestnut woods along the old railroad near Belvì *(see p109)*.

The local cuisine is flavored with herbs from the maquis, such as rosemary and thyme, and the crafts draw inspiration from pastoral life. Woven carpets, baskets, and pottery with traditional motifs can be seen in Nuoro's Museo Etnografico *(see p99)*.

A shepherd and his flock in the high summer pastures at Pietrino

◁ Wind-battered cork oak, a common sight in the Barbagia

Exploring Central Sardinia and Barbagia

Nuoro is the capital of Sardinia's interior region: to the east lies the Supramonte mountain range, with Oliena, Orgòsolo, and Dorgali at its feet, while to the west the valleys descend toward Lake Omodeo and Macomer. In this landscape of hills and steep limestone walls (the *tònneri* formations) are some of the most important towns in the region: Mamoiada, Bitti, and Sarule. To the south is the Gennargentu massif, carpeted with forests, on the slopes of which are typical mountain villages such as Gavoi and Fonni. Heading northeast and skirting the slopes of Monte Ortobene, which towers above the city of Nuoro, the road descends among almond trees and vineyards toward the Baronia region.

Barren slopes on the Gennargentu mountain range

Sights at a Glance

A mural painted on rocks near Orgòsolo

A dwelling in the nuraghic village of Tiscali

GETTING AROUND
Public transportation in the interior of Sardinia is slow and unreliable if it exists at all, and is not the best way to visit the area. If you have a car, the main roads are the N131 from Siniscola to Nuoro up to Lake Omodeo; the N125, the Orientale Sarda road, which skirts Supramonte and links Orosei to Arbatax, and the N389, which also goes to Arbatax from Nuoro, passing Gennargentu on the east. For sights such as Tiscali and Punta La Marmora, you have to hike up fairly steep paths.

A pleasant alternative mode of transportation is the little narrow-gauge train on the Cagliari-Sòrgono line *(see p109).*

SEE ALSO
- *Where to Stay* p175
- *Where to Eat* p185

KEY

▬▬▬	Highway
▬▬▬	Major road
▭▭▭	Minor road
▭▭▭	Scenic route
──	River

0 kilometers   80

0 miles   80

Nuoro

Nùgoro, as the locals still call their city, is one of Sardinia's most important centers. The city began to expand in the 14th century, but by the 18th century there was social unrest and riots erupted. In 1746 the Piedmontese prefect, De Viry, described the city as "a hotbed of bandits and murderers." A decree in 1868 that put an end to the common use of farmland culminated in a popular rebellion known as *Su Connottu*.

Traditional costume   At the turn of the 20th century Nuoro became the heart of the island's cultural life, producing political and social writers such as Grazia Deledda. The city became the provincial capital in 1926, and today it is the commercial heart of the Barbagia region.

Santa Maria della Neve

The huge granite blocks in Piazza Sebastiano Satta

Exploring Nuoro

The city is set in spectacular surroundings on a granite plateau beneath Monte Ortobene. Its isolated position and relatively recent exposure to tourism have helped to preserve local culture, traditions, and costumes.

The modern city retains many picturesque streets and buildings in the old center. Corso Garibaldi, once known as Bia Maiore, leads up to the quarter of San Pietro and the city's Neo-Classical cathedral, **Santa Maria della Neve** (1836). Near Corso Garibaldi is the whitewashed Piazza Sebastiano Satta, paved with large granite blocks in 1976.

Nuoro is the birthplace of some of Sardinia's most important men and women of letters, who at the end of the last century injected new life into the island's culture. Apart from Grazia Deledda, other native literary figures are politician and essayist Attilio Deffenu (1893–1918) and poet Sebastiano Satta (1867–1914).

⥦ Civico Museo Speleo-Archeologico

Via Leonardo da Vinci. [0784-300 83. ● *for restoration.*
This museum combines the collections of fossils and fossil plants of the *Gruppo Speleologico Nuorese*, with archaeological finds excavated over many years in the area. Exhibits range from Neolithic to medieval objects, including the skeletons of an ancient hare, *Prolagus sardus*, a giant otter, *Lontra gigante*, and a collection of cave finds. Also of interest are Bronze Age menhir statues from Làconi and nuraghic bronze statuettes. Finds from the Roman era include belt buckles and other everyday household objects.

⥦ Museo Deleddiano

Via Grazia Deledda 28. [0784-345 71. ● 9am–1pm, 3–7pm (Oct–Mar: 6pm) Tue–Sun. ● Sun pm. ⥦
Grazia Deledda's birthplace retains the atmosphere of a mid-19th-century Sardinian home. The house has been arranged according to her own description, set out in her novel *Cosima*, with objects marking the stages of her career. The courtyard leads to what was the kitchen garden (now a place for cultural events), while the upper floors are given over to displays of the covers of her books, programs for her plays, and a copy of the diploma for the Nobel Prize for Literature.

GRAZIA DELEDDA (1871–1936)

Grazia Deledda won the Nobel Prize for Literature in 1926 in recognition of her understanding portrayal of the power and passions in the primitive communities around her. Born in Nuoro in 1871, she has become a symbol of Sardinian culture and an example of the island's prolific artistic production. The eventful and difficult years of her early career are described in the auto-biographical novel *Cosima* (1937). Her world of fiction revolves around Barbagia, with its mysteries and strong sense of identity. Among her best-known novels are *Elias Portolu* (1900), *Cenere* (1903), and *Canne al Vento* (1913). She died in Rome in 1936.

The author Grazia Deledda

The whitewashed Museo Etnografico in Nuoro

VISITORS' CHECKLIST

Road map D3. 🚹 *37,929.*
🛈 *Ente Provinciale per il Turismo,
Piazza Italia 19 (0784-300 83).*
🎫 *19 Mar: San Giuseppe; 6 Aug:
San Salvatore; last Sun in Aug:
Processione del Redentore.*

solemn procession known as the *Processione del Redentore* in which representatives from almost every town in Sardinia take part *(see p28)*.

**Traditional costume from Desulo,
Museo delle Tradizioni Sarde**

🏛 Museo Etnografico

Via Antonio Mereu 56. 📞 *0784-24
29 00.* ⬜ *9am–1pm, 3–7pm (Apr–
Sep: 6pm) Tue–Sun.* ⬛ *Sun pm.* 🖼

The Museum of Sardinian life and popular traditions was designed in the 1960s by architect Antonio Simon Mossa. The aim of the project was to re-create a typical Sardinian village, with courtyards, alleys, and stairways, as a setting for artifacts, objects, and costumes representing Sardinian daily life.

On display in this popular ethnographic museum are traditional pieces of furniture, such as a 19th-century chest and cover and silver jewelry used to adorn aprons or handkerchiefs. Characteristic costumes worn daily or on special occasions by women are also shown, as are different types of traditional bread molds, looms, and hand-woven carpets. One room is dedicated to carnival masks and costumes.

The museum also has a library specializing in anthropological literature, an auditorium and an exhibition center. Every other October, the museum features a festival of ethnographic and anthropological films.

**Chest and cover in the
Museo Etnografico**

ENVIRONS:

🎑 Monte Ortobene

East of Nuoro.
Nuoro was founded on the granite slopes of this mountain, and the inhabitants have always held it in high regard. To reach its wooded areas, take the N129 Orosei road east out of the city. The road passes the church of **Nostra Signora della Solitudine**, where Grazia Deledda is buried. At the summit is a statue of the Redentore (Christ the Redeemer), that overlooks the city below, and next to it is the church of **Nostra Signora di Montenero**. On the last Sunday in August this church is the focus of the

🏛 Necropoli di Sas Concas

N128. 📞 *0784-24 29 00.* ⬜ *at all
times.*
To visit this necropolis, take the N131 15 km (9 miles) west out of Nuoro and then the N128 southward for 3 km (2 miles) toward Oniferi. The complex consists of a series of *domus de janas*, some decorated with bas-reliefs, such as the *Tomba dell'Emiciclo* (Tomb of the Hemicycle). The area is unattended, so a flashlight may be useful.

The Sagra del Redentore procession on Monte Ortobene

Su Tempiesu well-temple near Bitti

Bitti ❷

Road map D3. 🏠 *3,786.* ℹ *Town Hall (0784-41 51 24).* 📅 *Apr 23: San Giorgio.*

THIS PASTORAL village has recently become known thanks to the *Tenores de Bitti* musical group, whose interpretations of traditional Sardinian close-harmony songs have won them acclaim throughout Europe *(see pp24–5).* Experts say the local dialect is the one that most resembles Latin.

The 19th-century church of **San Giorgio Martire** stands in the central Piazza Giorgio Asproni. In the nearby parish home is a fine small collection of local archaeological finds.

ENVIRONS: Not far from Bitti on the road to Orune (watch out for the signs, which can be difficult to follow) is the **Su Tempiesu** well-temple. This consists of several chambers, made of large square basalt stones, and houses the sacred well. The well water was used

in nuraghic rituals. East of Bitti are five churches, Santo Stefano, Santa Maria, Santa Lucia, San Giorgio, and *Babbu Mannu* (Holy Ghost). All these churches hold religious festivities.

Bono ❸

Road map C3. 🏠 *4,045.* ℹ *Town Hall (079-79 02 19).* 📅 *Aug 31: San Raimondo Nonnato.*

SET AT THE FOOT of the Gocèano mountain range, Bono is an ideal starting point for trips to the wooded Monte Rasu and the Foresta di Burgos. In the center of town is the parish church of **San Michele Arcangelo**, which has been rebuilt several times over the years. Inside is a curious clock driven by the weight of four cannonballs, shot at the town during the 1796 siege, when the government troops were driven out by the city's inhabitants. This episode is re-enacted every year during the traditional festival held on August 31. On this day the largest pumpkin from the local kitchen gardens is awarded to the person who comes in last in the festival horse race as a facetious sign of recognition of the "valor" of the routed army. Until recently, this pumpkin was

rolled down the mountain to the valley to symbolize the government troops escaping from the local inhabitants.

In early September Bono plays host to the colorful *Fiera dei Prodotti Tipici Artigiani del Gocèano,* a fair featuring typical handicrafts from the Gocèano region.

ENVIRONS: From the Uccaidu pass, northwest of Bono, you can hike up the ridge to the summit of Monte Rasu at an altitude of 1,258 m (4,125 ft). From here there are magnificent sweeping views of the Foresta di Burgos and surrounding mountain range as well as most of Sardinia.

The countryside between Bono and Burgos

Burgos ❹

Road map C3. 🏠 *1,094.*

THE HAMLET of Burgos lies below a cone-shaped peak in the Gocèano mountains. The town was founded in 1353 by Mariano d'Arborea and is dominated by the ruins of

The village of Burgos, dominated by the 12th-century castle.

Small Giara horses in the Foresta di Burgos

Burgos Castle, built much earlier, in 1127. The castle was the scene of many battles between the Sardinian principalities and mainland colonists during the Middle Ages. It was from here that in 1478 Artaldo di Alagon's troops marched from the castle to the battle of Macomer, marking the end of Sardinian independence and the start of Aragonese dominion. Inside the outer defensive walls, more fortifications surround a restored tower. The entrance to the tower was once through a wooden stairway that could be raised in case of a siege.

ENVIRONS: The **Foresta di Burgos**, 5 km (3 miles) northwest of Burgos, is a well-kept forested area with holm oak and cork oak trees, cedars, conifers, and some chestnut trees. The area is also known for the small Sardinian Giara horses that graze in fenced-off pastures.

Ottana ❺

Road map C3. 🏠 2,609. 🚍 Town Hall (0784-758 30). 🎭 Carnevale.

O TTANA LIES IN the valley of the Tirso River, not far from the slopes of the Barbagia di Ollolai region.

In the Middle Ages the town was an important religious center. On the southern outskirts of town is the church of **San Nicola**, once the cathedral of the regional diocese. It was built in 1150 in austere Romanesque style, with black and purple trachyte ashlars showing strong Pisan influence. Inside is a 14th-century polyptych showing the Madonna flanked by the bishop of Ottana and Mariano d'Arborea, count of Gocèano. In the apse is a 16th-century wooden crucifix.

San Nicola, near Ottana

Almost abandoned in the 16th century due to an outbreak of malaria, Ottana was chosen in the 1970s as an industrial development site,

Typical masked figures dressed for the Carnival at Ottana

promoted by ENI, the National Hydrocarbon Corporation. The industries have not produced the expected profits, however, and the ecological problems are so serious the entire project is to be abandoned.

Carnival is a popular festival in Ottana, when locals dress in sheepskin and bells and wear bull-like masks *(see p29).*

Ollolai ❻

Road map C3. 🏠 1,760. 🚍 Town Hall (0784-514 99). 🎭 Aug 24: San Bartolomeo.

Asphodel, used in traditional basket-weaving at Ollolai

T HE VILLAGE of Ollolai was once the medieval administrative center of the Barbagia di Ollolai region, an area that included the northern part of Barbagia and still retains the name today. The town's decline began in 1490 after a terrible fire destroyed most of it; today it is a small hamlet.

Some original houses decorated with dark stone doorways are visible in the old center, and there are still a few craftsmen who weave the traditional asphodel baskets in their courtyards.

ENVIRONS: A short distance west of Ollolai is the church of **San Basilio**. A traditional rural religious festival is held here on September 1. A rough road climbs up to S'Asisorgiu peak to an altitude of 1,127 m (3,700 ft). From here there are splendid views of the surrounding mountain range and the summit is popularly known as "Sardinia's window."

Sarule seen from the nearby hills

Sarule ⑦

Road map C3. 🏘 *2,017.* ℹ *Town Hall (0784-760 17).* 🎪 *Sep 8: Madonna di Gonare.*

SARULE IS A VILLAGE of medieval origin that has preserved its tradition of carpet-weaving. Along the main street you can still see the workshops where these vividly colored carpets with stylized figures are woven on antique vertical looms and then sold on the premises.

Perched on a spur overlooking the village is the sanctuary of **Nostra Signora di Gonare**, one of the most sacred shrines in Sardinia. The church was built in the 13th century for the ruler of the principality, Gonario II di Torres, and by the 16th century it had already become a famous pilgrimage site. The sanctuary was enlarged in the 17th century with a dark stone exterior and austere buttresses.

To reach the sanctuary, a rough road heads east from Sarule and climbs up Monte Gonare for 4 km (2 miles). This granite rock mountain is interspersed with layers of limestone and outcrops of schist covered in vegetation. The mountain slopes are populated by many species of birds, including partridges, turtle doves, woodpeckers, shrikes, and various birds of prey. The forest has holm oaks and maples, while in the spring the undergrowth is enlivened by brightly colored cyclamen, peonies, and morning glory. The road ends at an open space with pilgrims' houses *(cumbessias)*, and a winding trail up the bluff through the holm oak forest leads to the sanctuary. From here there are marvelous views of Monte Ortobene towering over Nuoro, Monte Corrasi near Oliena, and the Gennargentu mountains in the distance.

From September 5-8 a lively festival takes place at the sanctuary for the Madonna di Gonare, to which pilgrims travel on foot from all of the neighboring villages. As well as religious festivities, a horse race is held, and the square resounds with poetry readings and sacred songs sung in traditional dialect.

The sanctuary of Nostra Signora di Gonare at Sarule

Mamoiada ⑧

Road map D3. 🏘 *2,618.* ℹ *Town Hall (0784-566 25).* 🎪 *Jan 17, Carnival Sun & Shrove Tue: Mamuthones procession.*

SOME OLD BUILDINGS, possibly of Aragonese origin, are still visible among the modern houses that line the main street of Mamoiada. In 1770 the town was mentioned by the Savoyard viceroy, Des Hayes, as a place of some interest with its many vineyards and an exceptional number of sheep. Flocks are still taken every summer to the slopes of Barbagia di Ollolai to graze.

TRADITIONAL FESTIVALS IN THE BARBAGIA

S'Incontru, the procession held in the streets of Oliena on Easter day, commemorates the Resurrection of Christ and his subsequent encounter with the Virgin Mary. On this occasion, and during the festivities in honor of San Lussorio on August 21, you can admire the colorful traditional costumes and watch the impressive procession of horsemen through the streets of the town.

The *S'Incontru* procession

At Mamoiada the lively celebrations on the night of Sant'Antonio Abate (January 17), Shrove Tuesday, and the last night of Carnival, all revolve around the figures of the *Mamuthones* and *Issohadores*. The former wear tragic masks and shepherds' garb, with sets of cow bells tied on their backs. The bells jangle in time with their rhythmic steps as they go through the village to the main square, where there is music and dancing all evening. The *Issohadores*, with their red waistcoats, are more colorful: they "capture" spectators and drag them inside the circles of the traditional round dance *(see p25).*

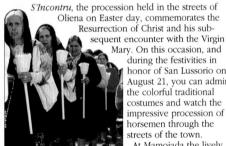

The carnival *Mamuthones* at Mamoiada

A typical street in the town of Oliena

Mamoiada is best known for the dark, forbidding masks of the *Mamuthones*, who appear in the village streets on the feast days of Sant'Antonio Abate (January 17), the Sunday of Carnival, and in particular on Shrove Tuesday during the Barbagia's most famous Carnival celebrations *(see p29)*.

ENVIRONS: About 5 km (3 miles) southwest of Mamoiada, along a secondary road toward Gavoi, is the **Santuario di San Cosimo**. This typical rural church has a central structure surrounded by *cumbessias*, lodgings for pilgrims to the sanctuary. The present-day church dates from the 17th century, and its main feature is the single nave. At the end of the nave, recent restoration has brought to light an Aragonese niche with columns and an architrave made of volcanic rock.

6 km (4 miles) farther south is the **Santuario della Madonna d'Itria**, an imposing church with *cumbessias*. Here, on the last Sunday of July, there is a horse race around the church, known as *Sa Carrela*.

Oliena ❾

Road map D3. 🏘 *7,732*. 🛈 *Town Hall (0784-28 75 23)*. 🎉 *Easter am: S'Incontru; Aug 21: San Lussorio*.

THE APPROACH to Oliena toward evening, along the northern road from Nuoro, is an unforgettable sight. The lights of the town shine at the foot of the steep white mass of Supramonte, which rises

eastward toward the Golfo di Orosei. The countryside is covered in vineyards, which yield the famous Sardinian wine Cannonau.

Some original houses, built around courtyards with external stairways and pergolas and brightly colored rooms, are still visible along the narrow streets and alleyways. There are also several religious buildings, such as the church of **Santa Croce**, said to be the oldest in the town. Rebuilt in the 17th century, it has a bell tower decorated with an unusual trident motif.

The **Jesuit College** on Corso Vittorio Emanuele II is a reminder of the arrival of this religious order in Oliena. From the beginning of the 17th century onward, the Jesuits encouraged the town's economy by promoting winemaking and silkworm breeding. Next door to the Jesuit college, the church of **Sant'Ignazio di Loyola** has wooden statues of Sant'Ignazio and San Francesco Saverio,

as well as an altarpiece depicting San Cristoforo.

Oliena, known for its good wine, is also famous for its jewelry, cakes, and the traditional costumes worn by the women: a black shawl, interwoven with silk and gold, and a light blue blouse.

There are two important festivals at Oliena that end with impressive processions: *San Lussorio* in August and *S'Incontru* on Easter morning.

ENVIRONS: South of Oliena, it is possible to take various hiking tours on the rugged and spectacular rocks of the **Supramonte di Oliena**. Starting from the Monte Maccione refuge, you can cross the chain and descend into the Lanaittu valley floor.

The **Su Gologone** natural springs are 8 km (5 miles) east of Oliena. The waters, which have cut channels through the mountain rock, are refreshingly cool in the summer and turn into an extremely cold, rushing torrent in winter. Su Gologone is the most important spring in Sardinia, with an average production of 300 liters (66 gallons) per second. It lies in a pleasant wooded area ideal for picnics in the shade.

For many years speleologists have been exploring the depths of the underground cave of **Grotta Sa Oche**, in the Supramonte mountains. Every year divers penetrate deeper underground into the Supramonte mountains to study the various aspects of this natural phenomenon.

The Su Gologone natural spring at the foot of Supramonte

Tiscali ❿

A LITTLE OVER A CENTURY AGO some woodcutters, traveling over the mountain range that dominates the Lanaittu valley, discovered a nuraghic settlement hidden in the depths of an enormous chasm in Monte Tiscali. The village of Tiscali, which had been inhabited up to the time of the Roman invasion, consists of a number of round dwellings with juniper-wood architraves around the doors and roofs. Years of neglect have led to the partial deterioration of the site, but it is still one of the most exciting nuraghic finds in Sardinia, particularly because of its unique position. The climb to Tiscali is tiring but not difficult.

The Path to the Village
Red and white markings on the rocks indicate the way to the village.

The chasm had no natural springs, so the inhabitants collected water that dripped down the walls of the rock.

Dwellings
Round nuraghic dwellings are still visible among the crumbling rocks and ruins.

Bronze Model
Cagliari's Museo Archeologico (see p58) has a model of the dwellings.

View of Monte di Tiscali
*Hidden inside this 518-m (1,700-ft) high mountain,
the nuraghic village of Tiscali was discovered in
the 19th century. Archaeological
excavations did not begin until
many years later.*

VISITORS' CHECKLIST

Road map D3. ☐ 9am–7pm
(Oct–May: 5pm). 🗺 ✇
🛈 Town Hall, Dorgali (0764-961
13) or Pro Loco, Dorgali (0784-
962 43). Monte Maccione refuge,
Oliena organizes tours and hikes.
☎ 0784-28 83 63.

Entrance to the Chasm
*The difficult terrain and steep walls were the best
defense for the inhabitants of Tiscali.*

The roofs were
made of juniper
wood.

GETTING THERE

*From Oliena take the road east
toward Dorgali. After about 5 km
(3 miles), take the right-hand turn
for Su Gologone. Just before the
hotel of the same name (see
p175), take the dirt road to the
left that goes to the Lanaittu
plain. Proceed along the floor of
the valley (keeping to the left)
until the road becomes too
difficult for vehicles. Clear red
and white markings on the rocks
or trees indicate the trail to the
chasm of Tiscali. The walk will
take you about an hour.*
  *It is possible to make other
trips in this area, although it is
advisable to go with a guide.
Places to head for include the
gigantic Gole di Su Gorroppu
ravines, parts of the caves of Su
Bentu, Sa Oche, or S'Elicas Artas,
or the climb down to the Codula
di Luna valley (see p85).*

The walls of the
dwellings were made
of limestone blocks.

THE NURAGHIC VILLAGE OF TISCALI
*This reconstruction of the nuraghic village shows how the
settlement might have looked. A crater opening allows natural
light in, and steps from the entrance made the descent easy.*

MURALS IN SARDINIA

Sardinian murals began to appear on walls at Orgòsolo in the 1960s and soon became a feature of many of the island's villages and towns. The most famous of these is San Sperate *(see p62)*, the home town of the artist Pinuccio Sciola. The themes of this particular artistic genre are satirical, political, or social. The styles vary greatly but are always characterized by bright colors. Even in the open

Mural at Orgòsolo

country you may come across faces, shapes, hands, and penetrating stares painted onto the boulders, rocks, or cliffs. The *Associazione Italiana Paesi Dipinti* (Italian Association of Painted Towns) was founded to preserve and publicize the towns with these murals and also to encourage creativity and cultural exchange between different regions.

Mural on a wall at San Sperate

A mural painted on rock near Orgòsolo

Orgòsolo ⓫

Road map D3. 👥 *4,741.* ℹ️ *Town Hall (0784-40 21 26).* 🎏 *first Sun of Jun: Sant'Anania; Aug 15: Festa dell'Assunta.*

THIS CHARACTERISTIC village in the interior of the island has been compared to an eagle's nest and a fortress, perched precariously on the mountainside. The villagers are known as rugged and hardy shepherds, proud of their lifestyle and traditions. Rampant banditry in the 1960s was documented in Vittorio De Seta's film *Bandits at Orgòsolo*, in which the hard life of the shepherds and their mistrust of the government is narrated with cool detachment. The passion of the locals for social and political issues is also visible in the hundreds of murals painted on the walls of houses and on the rocks around Orgòsolo. The images describe the harsh life of the shepherds, their struggles to keep their land and Sardinian traditions, as well as injustices committed in other parts of the world.

Simple low stone houses can be seen along the steep and narrow streets of the town and some original features are still visible on a few isolated houses. On Corso Repubblica, the church

of **San Pietro** still has its 15th-century bell tower. Traditional dress, a brightly colored apron embroidered with geometric patterns and a saffron-yellow headscarf, is still worn by some local women.

In summer two popular local festivals draw large crowds: the Assumption Day Festival on August 15 and Sant'Anania's feast day on the first Sunday of June.

ENVIRONS: Just outside Orgòsolo is the 17th-century church of **Sant'Anania**. The church was built where the saint's relics are said to have been found. Orgòsolo is an ideal starting point for excursions up to the surrounding Supramonte mountains, where open pastures are interspersed with dense forests of oak. A road leads to the **Funtana Bona**, 18 km (11 miles) south of Orgòsolo. These natural springs emerge at an altitude of 1,082 m (3,550 ft), at the foot of the limestone peak of **Monte Novo San Giovanni**, 1,316 m (4,316 ft) high. From here it is also possible to reach the shady **Foresta di Montes**, a forest of holm oak that stretches out to the south.

Sculpted detail on San Gavino, Gavoi

Gavoi ⓬

Road map C3. 👥 *3,050.* ℹ️ *Town Hall (0784-531 20).* 🎏 *last Sun of Jul: rural festival at Sanctuary of the Madonna d'Itria; second Sun after Easter: Sant'Antioco's feast day.*

FOR MANY CENTURIES this village was famous in Sardinia for the production of harnesses and bridles. Today its most characteristic product is cheese, including *fiore sardo* pecorino, made from sheep's milk *(see p181)*. The center of town is dominated by the pink facade of the 14th-century church of **San Gavino**, which overlooks the square of the same name. Some of Gavoi's oldest and most characteristic streets begin here. A stroll down these narrow alleys will reveal historic buildings with dark stone facades and balconies overflowing with flowers, such as the two-story building on Via San Gavino.

In the little church of **Sant'Antioco**, in the upper part of town, dozens of ex votos in gold and silver filigree are pinned to the wall. There is also a fine statue of the saint, whose feast day is celebrated the second Sunday after Easter.

View of the Lago di Gusana seen from Gavoi

Fonni ⑬

Road map D3. 👥 *4,543.* 🚉 *Town Hall (0784-570 22).* 🎉 *first Sun & Mon in Jun: Madonna dei Martiri feast day.*

FONNI IS ONE of the highest towns in Sardinia, lying at an altitude of 1,000 m (3,280 ft). Its economy relies on tradition and tourism, offering locally made produce, such as traditional candies as well as fabrics and rugs famous for their fine workmanship. Although recent construction has slightly diminished its charm, at first sight the town gives the impression of sprouting from the mountainside.

On the edge of town is the Franciscan **Madonna dei Martiri** complex, which dates from the 17th century. Inside

is a curious statue of the Virgin Mary made from pieces of ancient Roman sculptures.

The town's major festival is held in mid-June to celebrate the return of the shepherds and their flocks from the winter pastures.

On the road toward Gavoi, 4 km (2 miles) west of Fonni, is the **Lago di Gusana**, a large artificial lake. Its tranquil shores, surrounded by holm oaks, make it a popular spot.

Teti ⑭

Road map C4. 👥 *872.* 🚉 *Town Hall (0784-680 23).* 🎉 *third Sun in Sep: San Sebastiano.*

PERCHED ON the rocky mountains that dominate Lago di Cucchinadorza, the village of Teti distinguishes

itself by its small museum, the **Museo Archeologico Comprensoriale**. Run by a team of enterprising young local people, the museum illustrates with clarity and detail the history of the area's ancient nuraghic settlements (in particular the village of S'Urbale and the sacred precinct of Abini). The display cases contain pieces found during excavations, including everyday objects used by the nuraghic people. One hall has a reconstruction of a round dwelling dating from about 1000 BC.

Bronze statuettes found at Teti, Cagliari Museo Archeologico

Inside are spinning tools, pots, small axes, and granite mills. In the middle of the house is the area used as a fireplace.

The halls of the lower floor are used for temporary exhibitions on local culture and traditions, such as traditional costumes and handicrafts.

ENVIRONS: About one kilometer (half a mile) southwest of Teti is the entrance to the nuraghic archaeological site of **S'Urbale**. The village was inhabited from 1200 to 900 BC, and the ruins of nearly thirty prehistoric dwellings are still visible. The ancient nuraghic village of **Abini** is found 10 km (6 miles) to the north of Teti.

🏛 **Museo Archeologico Comprensoriale**
🎫 *0784-681 20.* ⏰ *9am–1pm, 3–6pm Tue–Sun.* 📷

FORESTA DI MONTES

At the foot of the rocky bluffs of Monte Novo San Giovanni and Monte Fumai, is the largest holm oak forest in Europe. Although many trees were destroyed in the past by fires – often started by shepherds in order to acquire more grazing land – the vast forest is once again increasing in size thanks to replanting, and today it attracts visitors

Monte Novo San Giovanni

from all over the island. Even in the heat of the summer, a walk through this area and the plateau around the Olai River is very enjoyable. The dense forest offers shade from the sun, and there is a chance to see asphodels in bloom, and perhaps even some sheep and pigs. The many trails around the Funtana Bona forest headquarters offer opportunities for hiking and mountain-biking.

The rural Sanctuary of San Mauro, near Sòrgono

Sòrgono ⑮

Road map C4. 🏘 2,082. ℹ *Town Hall (0784-601 17).* 🎉 *May 26: San Mauro feast day.*

The Pisan fountain at Sòrgono

SET IN A DENSELY cultivated area of orchards and vineyards, famous for producing Cannonau wine *(see p182)*, Sòrgono has been an important town since Roman times. Today it is the administrative center of the Mandrolisai area.

Two rather dilapidated sites in the town are worth a visit: the 17th-century **Casa Carta**, featuring a typical Aragonese window, and a medieval fountain of Pisan origin.

Just west of town is one of the most interesting and oldest rural sanctuaries in Sardinia, the **Santuario di San Mauro**. This imposing church is surrounded by the traditional *cumbessias*, the houses used by the pilgrims during their stay at the sanctuary. The building is a mixture of local architectural features and the characteristic Gothic-Aragonese style.

A fine stairway flanked by two stone lions leads to the gray trachyte facade, which has a beautiful carved Gothic rose window. Numerous inscriptions are recorded on the stones of the church, some many centuries old and others more recent, carved by pilgrims to commemorate their visits to the sanctuary.

The interior of San Mauro has a single vault and is interrupted only by an arch that leads into the presbytery. Here there is a Baroque altar and some statues.

Various buildings were added to the original church to accommodate pilgrims and offer them adequate dining facilities, in particular during the San Mauro feast day. One of Sardinia's most important livestock and horse fairs used to be held on this day on the grounds of the sanctuary.

Not far from the church are two other sites worth visiting: the **Tomba di Giganti di Funtana Morta** (Tomb of the Giants) and, on a hilltop overlooking the church, the **Talei Nuraghe**, built with large granite stones and partly into the surrounding rock.

Làconi ⑯

Road map C4. 🏘 2,426. ℹ *Town Hall (0782-86 90 20).*

THE TOWN of Làconi is built around a rocky spur of the Sarcidano mountain range, with panoramic views of the surrounding countryside. Another striking feature of the town is the ruins of **Castello Aymerich** in the park above the town. Only a single tower from the original fortress, built in 1053, remains. The rest of the castle includes later additions such as the 15th-century hall and the 17th-century portico. The magnificent park around the castle includes a botanical garden and waterfall, and today it is a popular destination for walks and picnics.

Once the seat of the local noble overlords, Làconi has preserved the Neo-Classical **Palazzo Aymerich**, built in the first half of the 19th century by architect Gaetano Cima from Cagliari. Near the 16th-century parish church is the birthplace and small museum of **Sant'Ignazio da Làconi**, a miracle worker who lived here in the second half of the 18th century. There is also a monument in his honor in the square.

ENVIRONS: The area around Làconi has many prehistoric remains. Among these are the anthropomorphic menhirs, single stones on which ancient sculptors carved human features. These can be seen at Perda Iddocca and Genna 'e Aidu, but it is advisable to be accompanied by a local guide.

The ruins of Castello Aymerich at Làconi

The Cagliari – Sòrgono Railroad ⑰

THE TRAIN RIDE BETWEEN CAGLIARI and Sòrgono is a slow approach to the foothills of the Gennargentu mountain range (the trip takes four-and-a-half hours, while you can cover the same distance by car in two hours). The narrow-gauge railroad nevertheless offers a scenic route through spectacular mountains and an insight into travel from another age. DH Lawrence described the trip in his book *Sea and Sardinia* (1921). In the first stretch, up to Mandas, the train goes over the rolling hills of Trexenta. It then climbs up to the road house at Ortuabis, an area of thick vegetation with a backdrop of mountain peaks, and on beyond Belvì through a wood of dense tree heathers.

Lush scenery *and waterfalls characterize the stretch between Làconi and Meana.*

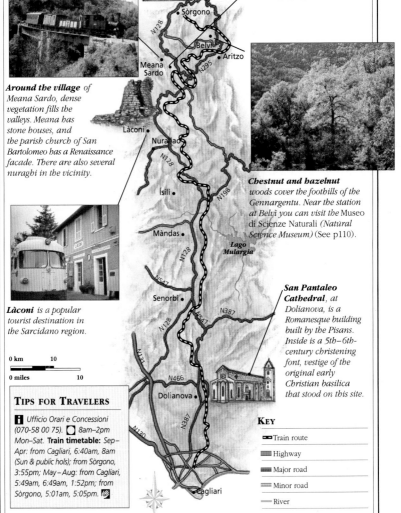

Around the village *of Meana Sardo, dense vegetation fills the valleys. Meana has stone houses, and the parish church of San Bartolomeo has a Renaissance facade. There are also several nuraghi in the vicinity.*

Làconi *is a popular tourist destination in the Sarcidano region.*

Chestnut and hazelnut *woods cover the foothills of the Gennargentu. Near the station at Belvì you can visit the* Museo di Scienze Naturali *(Natural Science Museum) (See p110).*

San Pantaleo Cathedral, *at Dolianova, is a Romanesque building built by the Pisans. Inside is a 5th–6th-century christening font, vestige of the original early Christian basilica that stood on this site.*

TIPS FOR TRAVELERS

ℹ️ *Ufficio Orari e Concessioni (070-58 00 75).* 🕐 *8am–2pm Mon–Sat.* **Train timetable:** *Sep–Apr: from Cagliari, 6:40am, 8am (Sun & public hols); from Sòrgono, 3:55pm; May–Aug: from Cagliari, 5:49am, 6:49am, 1:52pm; from Sòrgono, 5:01am, 5:05pm.*

0 km 10
0 miles 10

KEY

🚂 Train route
▬ Highway
▬ Major road
▬ Minor road
— River

Canoeing on the Flumendosa river near Aritzo

Aritzo ⑱

Road map C4. 🏘 1,633. 🛈 Pro Loco (0784-62 98 08). 🎉 second Sun in Aug: Sant'Isidoro.

THE SMALL TOWN of Aritzo was once famous for selling snow, at a very high price, packed in straw-lined boxes and transported throughout the island during the hot summer months. Under Aragonese rule, the town had the privilege of being governed by its own, locally elected inhabitants.

There are still many traces of the old town. Some houses retain typical stone facades and long, wooden balconies. Among the most important buildings are the **Casa degli Arangino** (in Neo-Gothic style) and the impressive 17th-century stone **Aritzo prison** on Via Maggiore.

The market for snow no longer exists, but the town has continued its tradition of making wooden furniture, such as hand-carved wedding chests. These are sold from the craftsmen's workshops.

The good climate, the high altitude, and panoramic views of the surrounding mountains make Aritzo a pleasant tourist destination in the summer. Rodeos are a popular attraction outside town and interesting walking tours and horseback rides take place

toward the Gennargentu massif and the upper Flumendosa River valley. Here canoeing on the river is a popular activity.

ENVIRONS:
Just north of Aritzo is the **Tacco di Texile**, a vertical limestone pinnacle, 975 m (3,200 ft) high, in the shape of a mushroom. From here there are spectacular views of the mountains of the Barbagia region.

During the Middle Ages, the humble saint Efisio lived in this area. For many years he preached to the local inhabitants and eventually converted them to Christianity.

Wedding chest made by Aritzo craftsmen

Belvì ⑲

Road map C4. 🏘 802. 🛈 Pro Loco (0784-62 92 16). 🎉 Aug 28: Sant'Agostino feast day.

THE VILLAGE of Belvì lies in a dominating position overlooking the Iscra River valley, which is full of fields of hazelnut trees and orchards.

In the past it must have been an important economic and trading center, as the surrounding mountain region, Barbagia di Belvì, has also adopted the name.

The narrow-gauge railroad that connects Cagliari and Sòrgono runs along the stretch of road near the village. The route goes through magnificent scenery as well as tackling a thousand tortuous bends and high viaducts *(see p109)*.

In the village, several old houses are still visible. One of these, on the main street, Via Roma, houses the **Museo di Scienze Naturali e Archeologiche** (Natural Science Museum). Founded in the 1980s by a group of enthusiasts (including a German naturalist who lived in Belvì for almost ten years) it has interesting paleontology and mineralogy departments as well as occasional exhibitions of its collection of typical Sardinian fauna and insects.

🏛 **Museo di Scienze Naturali e Archeologiche**
Via Roma 17. 📞 0784-62 92 16.
🕐 8–11am, 3–7pm daily. 🎫

The rodeo held near Aritzo

Overlooking Dèsulo

Dèsulo ⑳

Road map C4. 🏔 *3,153.* ℹ️ *Pro Loco (0784-61 98 87).* 🎭 *Second Sun of Pentecost, Corpus Domini.*

PERCHED AT AN altitude of 895 m (2,900 ft) on the slopes of Gennargentu, the village of Dèsulo was not converted to Christianity or ruled by outsiders until the 7th century. Unfortunately, un-regulated building development has had a devastating impact on the village and has almost eliminated the traditional schist houses. It is still quite common, however, to see villagers in traditional dress.

The local economy is based on sheep-raising and the ancient tradition of cultivating the chestnut groves and mountain pastures. Until quite recently, the inhabitants, skilled-in wood-carving, used to travel to the various markets and fairs throughout Sardinia to sell their handmade spoons, cutting boards, and other wooden objects as well as locally grown chestnuts.

The parish church of **Sant'Antonio Abate**, and other churches such as the **Madonna del Carmelo** and **San Sebastiano**, are worth a visit for a series of colorful wooden statues sculpted in the mid-1600s. But the main reason to visit this village is its natural scenery and the splendid views of the highest peak on the island. There are plans to give the area National Park status, incorporating it into the Gennargentu National Park. Dèsulo is a favorite destination for hikers eager to attempt the arduous climb up Gennargentu and Punta La Marmora *(see p82).* As groups of hikers and mountaineers become more common, a number of hotels and hostels catering to this new form of tourism have been built.

Tonara ㉑

Road map C4. 🏔 *2,538.* ℹ️ *Town Hall (0784-638 23).* 🎭 *second Sun in Aug: Sagra del Torrone.*

IN THE PAST the economy of Tonara was based largely on the chestnut and hazelnut groves that surround the town, and on other products typical of a mountain environment. Since tourism discovered this side of the mountain, the local production of cow-bells, *torrone* (nougat) and hand-woven rugs has become famous. During the local festivals in the town square, blacksmiths forge the celebrated Tonara bells by hammering

Chestnuts

the metal on specially shaped stone molds. The inhabitants will be more than willing to tell you how to arrange to see craftsmen at work and purchase traditional rugs. The atmosphere of a typical mountain village can still be seen in the shepherds' houses, which have not changed in over a century.

Tonara is another popular starting point for excursions to the Gennargentu massif. One of the most interesting is the tour to **Punta Mungianeddu** (1,467 m, 4,800 ft). A road climbs through holm oak and chestnut woods to reach the summit, from which there are magnificent views.

Stone used as a mold for making cowbells at Tonara

SARDINIAN NOUGAT

Nougat (*torrone* in Italian) is one of the most common candies in the culture and tradition of central Sardinia. Every local fair or festival will have stands selling the delicious, hard nougat made in Tonara, Dèsulo, or one of the other mountain villages. The main ingredients are almonds, walnuts, hazelnuts, various qualities of honey, and egg whites (in some cases the yolk is also used). Cooking – during which the mixture has to be stirred continuously – takes more than five hours. The different styles of nougat are created by variations in the type of honey, the flavor of the nuts, or number of eggs used. There are many nougat confectioners and, no matter how big or small the premises, visitors are always welcome to watch the preparation and choose a favorite flavor. Blocks of nougat are cut for you while you wait. One excellent outlet is that of Signora Anna Peddes in Tonara, at No. 6 Via Roma; she makes particularly delicious and fragrant nougat.

The Nougat Festival at Tonara

THE WESTERN COAST

EACH YEAR THOUSANDS OF FLAMINGOS *choose the marshes and wetlands of western Sardinia as their favored place for overwintering, creating clouds of pink against the vegetation of the maquis. The coastline is vulnerable to the cool mistral, and years of strong winds have sculpted massive dunes along the shore.*

The natural harbors and fertile land in this part of Sardinia have attracted foreign ships for centuries. The Phoenicians discovered the safe harbors of Sulki and Tharros as well as the great commercial potential of the obsidian from the slopes of Monte Arci. The Romans and Spaniards also left their mark at Bosa; the latter transforming Alghero into a Catalonian town.

The area around Oristano is one of the most important wetland areas in Europe. As well as freshwater pools and marshy lakes, there are saltwater lagoons, sandbanks, and sand dunes. A combination of the waters of the Tirso River and the mistral is responsible for this particular ecosystem. Over the course of centuries massive dunes have formed at the river mouth, whipped up by the violent winds from the west, effectively blocking the flow of water out to sea. At the turn of the century, this marshland was infested with malaria-transmitting mosquitoes but, thanks to land reclamation in the 1930s and the Rockefeller-funded antimalaria campaign, the soil can now be cultivated without risk. Today this is one of the most fertile areas in Sardinia, producing spring vegetables as well as olives and citrus fruits for sale to mainland Italy. Vineyards cover the land around Oristano and near the beaches in the Sinis region, yielding quantities of white Vernaccia wine. The coastline is lovely – small beaches and seaside resorts nestle against sand dunes shaded by thick pine forests. Some beaches are made of grains of translucent quartz, which suits wild lilies. Some stretches of cliff, wild and rocky, can be reached only by boat or after a lengthy trek.

The historic town of Bosa seen from the Temo river

◁ A lateen-sail dinghy off the coast near Stintino

Exploring the Western Coast

THE WESTERN COAST OF SARDINIA offers a wide variety of activities – whether you prefer to explore the towns and countryside, or relax on a beach at places like Is Arenas, Is Arutas, or Bosa Marina. There are extensive nature preserves teeming with wildlife and fortified cities with Romanesque cathedrals. One of Sardinia's best-known wines, Vernaccia, is made in this region, from the vineyards north of Oristano. At Tharros you can explore the ruins of a Phoenician coastal town, founded in the 8th century BC. The relatively short distances between sights and the flattish terrain, especially in the Sinis and Campidano di Oristano regions, make this area ideal for bicycle tours. Hikers may prefer the trails, and horseback riders can choose from the bridle paths that converge at the riding school in Ala Birdi. At the headland of Capo Caccia you can explore caves and grottoes, some of which extend for miles under the cliff.

Limestone rocks at Capo Caccia and the island of Foradada

SEE ALSO

Archaeological excavations at Tharros

AL

MAR DI SARDEGNA

BOSA

SAN SALVATORE

THARROS

GOLFO DI ORISTANO

ORISTANO

CABRAS

SANTA GIUSTA

ARBOREA

ALES

Sanluri

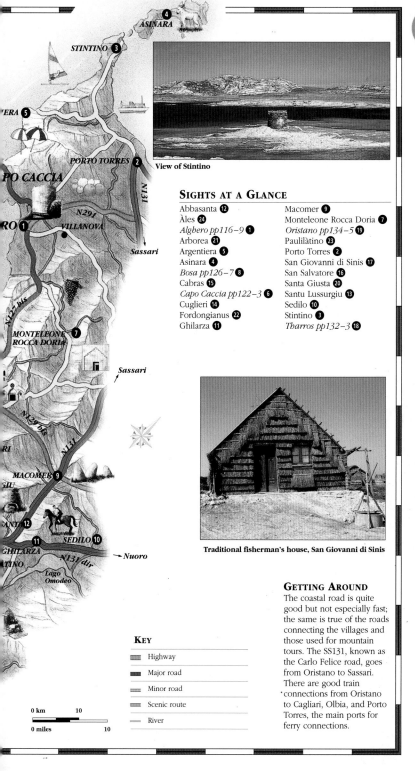

ASINARA

STINTINO

ERA

PORTO TORRES

PO CACCIA

RO

VILLANOVA

N291

N131

Sassari

MONTELEONE
ROCCA DORIA

Sassari

RI

MACOMER

GIU

ANTA

GHILARZA

TINO

SEDILO

Lago
Omodeo

Nuoro

N131 dir

View of Stintino

SIGHTS AT A GLANCE

Traditional fisherman's house, San Giovanni di Sinis

GETTING AROUND

The coastal road is quite good but not especially fast; the same is true of the roads connecting the villages and those used for mountain tours. The SS131, known as the Carlo Felice road, goes from Oristano to Sassari. There are good train connections from Oristano to Cagliari, Olbia, and Porto Torres, the main ports for ferry connections.

KEY

▬▬ Highway

▬▬ Major road

▬▬ Minor road

▬▬ Scenic route

— River

0 km   10

0 miles   10

Street-by-Street: Alghero ❶

42

**Old street
number**

IN THE EARLY 12TH CENTURY, the aristocratic
Doria family from Genoa decided to
establish two strongholds in Sardinia, which
became Castelgenovese (now Castelsardo)
and Alghero. Because of the abundant
quantities of algae off the coast, the latter
city was named Alquerium – *s'Alighera*
in Sardinian dialect and *l'Alquer* in Catalan.

After a very short period of Pisan rule, Alghero was
conquered by the Aragonese in 1353 and has always
been the most Spanish city on the island. The old
center lies within the ancient fortified quarter, and the
local economy is based on tourism and handicrafts –
particularly jewelry and other items made of coral.

★ San Francesco
*Parts of this jewel of Catalan
architecture date back to the first
half of the 14th century. The
lovely cloister becomes an open-
air concert venue in summer.*

Porta Terra tower

Sign in Catalan
*The street signs in Alghero
are still written in Catalan.*

**The Maddalena tower
and ramparts**

PIAZZA
CIVICA

MAGELLANO

VIA ROMA

VI

Lungomare
Each waterfront road (lungomare) *is
named after a great explorer from the
past. The buildings are painted in
sunny Mediterranean colors.*

LUNGOMARE

LUNGOMARE

Torre di
Sant'Erasmo

Torre della
Polveriera

★ Duomo Doors
*Built in the mid-
1500s, the carved
doorway and the
bell tower are the
oldest parts of
Alghero's cathedral.*

KEY

- - - - - Suggested route

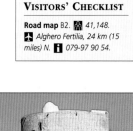

Torre di San Giovanni

San Michele
This Baroque church contains two stucco altars dating from the second half of the 17th century.

VISITORS' CHECKLIST

Road map B2. 41,148.
Alghero Fertilia, 24 km (15 miles) N. 079-97 90 54.

Torre dell'Esperò Real
This is one of the towers in the walls surrounding Alghero. It overlooks Piazza Sulis, the heart of city life.

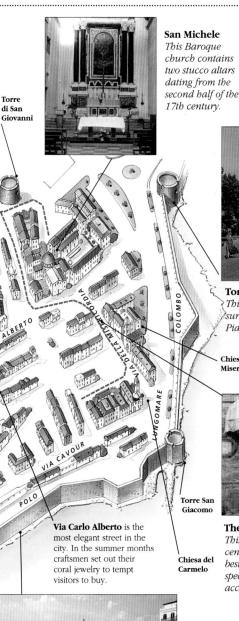

VIA C. ALBERTO
VIA DELLA MISERICORDIA
COLOMBO
VIA CAVOUR
LUNGOMARE
POLO

Chiesa della Misericordia

Torre San Giacomo

Via Carlo Alberto is the most elegant street in the city. In the summer months craftsmen set out their coral jewelry to tempt visitors to buy.

Chiesa del Carmelo

The Al Tuguri Restaurant
This small restaurant in the historic center of Alghero offers some of the best food in Sardinia. Al Tuguri specializes in fresh fish cooked according to old Catalan recipes.

0 meters	50
0 yards	50

★ Ramparts
Positioned between the old city and the sea, the ramparts are now popular places for strolling, especially on warm evenings.

STAR SIGHTS

★ San Francesco

★ Duomo Doors

★ Ramparts

Exploring Alghero

DESPITE THE CONSIDERABLE DAMAGE wrought by Allied bombardments in World War II, the heart of the old city is, for the most part, intact and can easily be explored on foot. The main roads from Bosa (to the south) and Sassari (to the northwest) lead to the city walls, and the best way to explore is to leave your car outside and walk around the narrow, high-sided streets of the old city. Strongly influenced by Spanish culture, Alghero remains the most Spanish city in Sardinia. The Alghero dialect is closely related to that of Catalonia, so much so that since 1970, street signs have been printed in Italian and Catalan, and you are likely to hear as much Catalan spoken on the streets as Italian.

🚇 Porta a Terra
Piazza Porta a Terra.
This 14th-century city gate now has a rather stranded air, as most of the associated fortifications were demolished to make room for present-day Via Sassari. The gate was once known as Torre degli Ebrei (dels Hebreus in Catalan), or Tower of the Jews, because of the contribution made by the Jewish community to Catalan king Pietro III's conquest of the city. The tower was originally one of two gates. A drawbridge linked Porta a Terra and the large Gothic arch, which is now a war memorial. The ground floor, covered by a stone vault, is now used as a small exhibition center.

🚇 Torre dell'Esperò Real
Piazza Sulis.
Facing Piazza Sulis, the heart of city life, is the impressive Torre dell'Esperò Real

A window at Palazzo d'Albis

(Tower of the Royal Spur), which was built in its present form in the first half of the 16th century to replace an older military structure. This 23-m (75-ft) high tower has an interesting interior with a number of superimposed chambers connected by means of a spiral staircase.

🚇 Lungomare and Forte de la Magdalena
Around sunset locals and tourists alike enjoy the pleasant stroll along the seafront. Starting from the south, Lungomare Dante is followed by Lungomare Cristoforo Colombo and Lungomare Marco Polo, which has a series of ramparts with towers (the Torre di San Giacomo, the Mirador rampart, the Torre de la Polvorera, the Torre de Castilla), leading to the port. Not far from the steps which run from the water to the old Porta a Mare city gate, is Forte de la Magdalena,

the city's most important Spanish fortification. On its walls a plaque commemorates Giuseppe Garibaldi's landing here on August14, 1855.

🚇 Palazzo d'Albis
Piazza Civica (Plaça de la Dressana).
This 16th-century palace with twin lancet windows is also known as Palazzo de Ferrera. It is a rare example of Catalan civic architecture and is famous for having hosted Charles V in October 1541.

The old town, Alghero

Charles V stopped here at Alghero with his fleet on the way to Algiers and was very flattering in his reactions to the city. According to tradition, the emperor spoke to the populace from the balcony of Palazzo d'Albis, and had the following to say about the city: "Bonita, por mi fé, y bien assentada." ("Beautiful, by my faith, and quite solid") and told the inhabitants "Estade todos caballeros" ("You are all gentlemen"). The monarch's sojourn ended with a massive requisition of cattle, which he needed for the Spanish troops. The animals were then slaughtered after an impromptu bullfight, held by the palazzo in Piazza Civica.

🛐 Cattedrale di Santa Maria
Piazza Duomo. **[** 070-97 92 22.
◐ 6:30am–noon, 5–8pm.
The doorway of Alghero's Cathedral opens out onto the small Piazzetta Duomo. The cathedral, dedicated to Santa Maria, was first built in the 14th century. In the mid-1500s the building was restructured in the Catalan-

The massive Torre dell'Esperò Real

View of the harbor and broad waterfront in Alghero

inspired late Gothic style. The unusual octagonal bell tower dates from the same period.

In the interior there is a striking difference between the layout of the central part, which is late Renaissance, and that of the 16th-century Gothic presbytery. Items of Catalan jewelry are on display in the sacristy.

Displays of coral jewelry

🏛 Via Principe Umberto

This narrow street, which begins at the Cathedral, was one of the main arteries in the old walled city. Of interest are the Casa Doria (16th century), Palazzo della Curia, and in Piazza Vittorio Emanuele II, the 19th-century Savoyard Teatro Civico.

⛪ San Francesco and Cloister

Via Carlo Alberto. 📞 070-98 03 30.
🕐 6.30am–noon, 5–8pm.
San Francesco may very well be the most important Catalan monument in the whole of Sàrdinia. Built at the end of the 1300s and then partially rebuilt when some of the structure collapsed, the

church clearly displays different stylistic influences. The bell tower is Gothic, with a hexagonal body set on a square base. The cupola, dressed with multicolored tiles, has become the symbol of Alghero.

Coral earrings

The two-aisle, white sandstone interior still has Baroque altars made of carved wood and, under the star-spangled Gothic vault of the presbytery, there is an 18th-century altar. The sculptures include a *Dead Christ* and *Christ at the Column*.

The cloister, accessible from the sacristy, is well worth a visit. It is an eclectic sandstone construction, built in different periods. The lower part dates from the 14th century, while the upper part was added in the 1700s. The 22 columns are in two sections, with round or polygonal bases and sculpted capitals. During the summer music season, the Estate Musicale Internazionale di Alghero, concerts, and other cultural events are held in these lovely surroundings. In other seasons of the year events and art exhibitions are held in the old refectory.

The Beaches

The Alghero port has never been an important trading place, partly because of its position and the low-lying coast. There is no heavy industry here, and consequently the sea is not polluted. A series of resorts can be found just outside the old town. The best-known

beach is the Bombarde, a strip of pure white sand bordered by crystal-clear sea, 8 km (5 miles) northwest of the city. Another good beach nearby is the Lazzaretto, which owes its name to the hospital for the poor located there during the period of the black plague. When the weather is clear, the impressive vertical profile of Capo Caccia stands out on the horizon.

ENVIRONS: To the north is the coastal town of **Fertilia**, a small yacht harbor built during the Fascist era as the center of the land reclamation plan. Just north is the mouth of the Calich lagoon, where eels, gilthead bream, and mullet are raised. Nearby you can still see the 13 arches of the Roman bridge at the ancient city of Carbia. At one time the bridge connected Carbia to Portus Nympharum, now Porto Conte bay. A few minutes away stands the site of **Palmavera Nuraghe**.

Entranceway to the prehistoric site of Palmavera Nuraghe

Porto Torres ❷

Road map B2. 🚶 *21,326.*
🚉 *079-51 50 00.*

THE CHIEF PORT in northern Sardinia lies in the Golfo dell'Asinara. Porto Torres was known to the Romans as Turris Libisonis and was once a prosperous colony. Trade with the city of Kàralis (today's Cagliari) was carried out along the main road on the island. Relations with Rome were very close, as can be seen from the ancient mosaics at the Foro delle Corporazioni in Ostia Antica.

After a lengthy period of decline that began in the Middle Ages, Porto Torres began to recover in the 19th century, when it became the port for Sassari, and again in the 20th century with the development of local industries.

The basilica of **San Gavino** is one of the most important Romanesque churches in Sardinia, built in the Pisan style in 1111. Noteworthy elements are the portal in the northern facade, with its 15th-century bas-relief, and the other Gothic doorway, which shows Catalan influences.

Gold bracelet from the Porto Torres excavations

Inside there is a crypt, with access to an area of late Roman-Early Christian ruins, as well as the 18th-century statues of the martyrs Gavino, Proto, and Gianuario, plus a medieval inscription celebrating emperor Constantine.

The **Terme Centrali** archaeological area presents a reasonably faithful picture of an ancient Roman quarter, and the **Antiquarium Turritano** contains finds from the excavations here. Not far away, the 135-m (440-ft), seven-arched **Ponte Romano** (Roman bridge), crosses the Mannu River.

ENVIRONS: A short distance from here lies one of the most interesting sites in ancient Sardinia, the pre-

San Gavino, in Port Torres

nuraghic **Santuario di Monte d'Accoddi**. From Porto Torres, head toward Sassari along main road SS131; a short distance after the Platamona junction (at kilometer marker 222.3) a dirt road leads to the archaeological site. The sanctuary dates from the Copper Age (2450–1850 BC) and provides the only example of a megalithic altar in the entire western Mediterranean. The shape is that of a truncated pyramid with a trapezoid base, supported by walls of stone blocks. On the southern side, a ramp leads to the top, about 10 m (33 ft) high, while the base of the altar is about 30 m by 38 m (98 ft by 124 ft).

Around the altar you can see foundations for houses, some sacrificial stone slabs and fallen menhirs. A group of *domus de janas* (rock-cut tombs) was once part of this complex. The materials found at this site, including ceramics, are on display at the Museo Nazionale in Sassari *(see p163)*.

🏛 **Antiquarium Turritano**
📞 *079-51 44 33.* ⏰ *9am–1:30pm Tue–Sat, 9am–1pm Sun.* 🖼
⛪ **Santuario di Monte d'Accoddi**
⏰ *at all times.*

Stintino ❸

Road map B2. 🚶 *1,192.*
🚉 *Pro Loco (079-52 30 53).*

THE ROAD to Capo Falcone, the northwestern tip of Sardinia, passes by the large wind turbines at the Alta Nurra ecological energy plant. Beyond this is the pleasant fishing village of Stintino (named from the Sardinian word *s'isthintinu*, or narrow passageway, the traditional name for the inlet where the village lies). Now a vacation spot, Stintino was once important for its tuna fishing grounds, off the island of Asinara. In the summer, at the old harbor, there is an exhibition devoted to the subject of Sardinian tuna fishing traditions. The two ports, Portu Mannu and Portu Minori, have facilities for aquatic sports of all kinds.

North of Stintino, the road skirts the coastline as far as **Capo Falcone**. The place is still "defended" by a tower on its highest point and by the two Spanish fortifications at Pelosa and Isola Piana, in the inlet of Fornelli, opposite the island of Asinara.

Portu Mannu, one of the two harbors in Stintino

The barren cliffs on the island of Asinara

Asinara ❹

Road map B1.

THIS RUGGED ISLAND is closed to visitors because of the Fornelli maximum security prison there, and it is still administered by the Italian Ministry of Justice. Asinara is less than 18 km (11 miles) long and 6 km (4 miles) wide and ends at the headland of Scomunica. The island's ecosystem is unique in the entire western Mediterranean and, because of its rare or endangered animal species, the island has been incorporated into the recently established Gennargentu National Park *(see pp82–3)*.

In fact, the pristine coastline and lack of traffic on its 50 sq km (19 sq miles) make Asinara an ideal refuge for raptors, various species of sea birds, moufflons, and wild boar. There is also a rare species of small endemic albino donkey, after which the island must have been named (*asino* means donkey). The rocky, volcanic terrain still supports a small holm oak forest, and the typical low-level maquis brush shields many rare plants.

Asinara can only be visited by naturalists and zoologists who have been authorized to carry out research by the island's prison administration.

Albino donkey from Asinara

Argentiera ❺

Road map B2.

MANY PLACES IN Sardinia still carry reminders of the island's former mining industries. At Argentiera, not far from the modern town of Palmadula, the ancient Romans, and the Pisans in the Middle Ages, dedicated themselves to mining the precious metal that gave its name to the area (*argento* means silver).

In the 19th century, mining complexes with wooden and masonry buildings were constructed along the coast, and the mined silver could then be transported by sea to other destinations, where it could be processed and eventually sold.

In recent years restoration and restructuring projects, many of which are yet to be completed, have changed the face of the town, but it still remains one of the most fascinating examples of industrial archaeology in Sardinia.

In the summer, the tranquil bay at Argentiera, with its crystal-clear water, is a great favorite with visitors.

The old mine buildings at Argentiera

Capo Caccia ❻

Towering above the sea, the Capo Caccia promontory, with a lighthouse perched on the outermost point, offers wonderful views of Alghero. Wild pigeons, swifts, peregrine falcons, and herring gulls nest in the crevices and gullies of the precipitous cliffs. On the western side of the headland – opposite the barren profile of the island of Foradada – 656 steep steps (known as the Escala del Cabirol, or Roe-deer's Staircase) take you down the cliff to the fascinating caves of the Grotta di Nettuno (Neptune's Grotto). The cave can also be reached in about three hours by boat from Alghero.

Griffon vulture
Only a few of these rare creatures survive in Sardinia.

Herring gulls
These birds nest in cliff crevices and ravines.

Gabbiano reale

Torre del Tram

Torre Pegna

Cala d'infern

Peregrine falcons
These raptors prefer calm, open spaces with rocky cliffs – Capo Caccia is a favored ground.

Capo Caccia
In the past this promontory was frequented by travelers and prominent naturalists such as Alberto La Marmora. The name Capo Caccia derives from the caccia, or wild pigeon hunting, which was once popular here.

VISITORS' CHECKLIST

Grotta di Nettuno
Alghero (079-97 90 54).
Apr–Sep: 9am–7pm daily;
Oct: 10am–5pm daily; Nov–Dec &
Jan–Mar: 9am–2pm daily.

Grotta Verde
The name of this large cave, Green Grotto, derives from the color of the moss and other plants that cover the stalagmites and stalactites. On the shores of a small lake at the far end of the gallery, ancient graffiti has been discovered.

Escala del Cabirol
From the ridge of land separating the headland from the lighthouse point, the Escala del Cabirol steps wind down to the entrance of the Grotta di Nettuno.

Punta del Quadro

Punta del bollo

Lago La Marmora

Isola Foradada

Grotta di Nettuno
Neptune's Grotto, one of the most picturesque caves in Sardinia, was first explored in the 1700s. The grotto extends for 2,500 m (8,200 ft), but the guided tour covers only 200 m (650 ft).

Romanesque Santo Stefano, at Monteleone Rocca Doria

Monteleone Rocca Doria ❼

Road map B3. 🏠 136.

Sᴵᴛᴜᴀᴛᴇᴅ ᴏɴ ᴛʜᴇ ᴛᴏᴘ of the Su Monte cliff (420 m, 1,380 ft), the little village of Monteleone Rocca Doria has a sweeping view of Lake Temo and the Nurra plain. It is tranquil today, although inhabitants look back proudly on a noble, warlike past. In the 13th century the Doria family from Genoa built a fortress here that was totally destroyed in 1436 after a ferocious three-year siege by troops from Aragon, Sassari, Bosa and Alghero.

Many inhabitants departed to found the town of Villanova Monteleone, but a few people remained behind. Monteleone was not included in development plans, and at one point, locals tried to improve their lot by putting the village up for sale. In the center of Monteleone is the 13th-century Romanesque parish church, **Santo Stefano**.

Bosa ❽

See pp126–7.

Macomer ❾

Road map C3. 🏠 11,480.
ℹ️ *Town Hall (0785-79 08 00).*
📅 *Jan 17: Sant'Antonio Abate.*

Bᴜᴵʟᴛ ᴏɴ ᴀ ᴘʟᴀᴛꜰᴏʀᴍ of volcanic rock, Macomer is one of the most important commercial centers in the interior of Sardinia. Macomer developed around key communication routes – the Carlo Felice road (the N131 that runs through most of the island) and the railroad – and owes its prosperity to agriculture, livestock raising, dairy products, and light industry, while retaining traces of its past. The parish church of **San Pantaleo** is an example of 17th-century Spanish Gothic. On the evening of January 17 the traditional *Sa Tuva* celebration is held in honor of Sant'Antonio Abate. The event takes place in the large square in front of Santa Croce, and a huge bonfire lights up the entire quarter.

San Pantaleo, in Macomer

ENVIRONS: Not far from the town center, near the Carlo Felice road, a short walk will take you to the impressive **Santa Barbara Nuraghe**. Its sheer size means that it dominates a series of smaller towers and ramparts.

Sedilo ❿

Road map C3. 🏠 2,609.
ℹ️ *0785-590 28.* 📅 *Jul 5-8: S'Ardia at Santu Antine sanctuary.*

Tʜᴇ ʀᴏᴄᴋʏ ᴛᴇʀʀᴀᴵɴ in the Abbasanta plateau gave the people of Sedilo the raw material to build their houses. There are still a few originals remaining, representing a style that has virtually disappeared. The main sight of interest is the church of **San Giovanni Battista** in the center of town. However, Sedilo's most important claim to fame is the **Sanctuary of Santu Antine**, otherwise known as San Costantino, or Constantine, after the early champion of Christianity who is much revered in Sardinia. The church, with the typical *cumbessias* houses for pilgrims, stands on a cliff overlooking Lake Omodeo. In the area there are numerous nuraghic sculptures on display, including the so-called *Perda Fitta*, a monolith that, according to legend, is actually the body of a woman who was turned into stone because she was disrespectful toward the patron saint.

The open space opposite the sanctuary is the setting for the annual *S'Ardia*. This horse race ends the July festivities commemorating Constantine the Great's victory over Maxentius in the battle of the Milvian Bridge in AD 312. The inside walls of Santu Antine are covered with great numbers of ex votos.

The S'Ardia horse race run around the Santu Antine sanctuary, Sedilo

The Losa nuraghe near Abbasanta

Ghilarza ⓫

Road map C3. 🏚 *4,616.*
ℹ *Town Hall (0785-540 38).*

An UNFINISHED Aragonese tower stands in the center of Ghilarza, but the place is known principally as the town where the famous Italian political thinker and writer Antonio Gramsci spent his childhood years. A small door on Corso Umberto leads to the **Casa di Gramsci**, now occupied by a research and study center. There is also an exhibition of historical material relating to the Communist leader, who died in prison during the Fascist era. On the second floor is the small bedroom that was Gramsci's from 1898 to 1908.

ENVIRONS: A short distance from Ghilarza, on the road to Nuoro, you will find the beautiful church of **San Pietro di Zuri**, which was relocated, along with the village of the same name, after the artificial lake Omodeo was created in 1923.

The original church dates from 1291. The building was commissioned by Mariano d'Arborea, and designed by architect Anselmo da Como. The architecture is prevalently Romanesque, with some interesting details which anticipate the transition toward the Gothic style.

🏛 **Casa di Gramsci**
Corso Umberto 57. 📞 *0785-541 64.*
🕐 *10am–noon, 4–7pm.*

Abbasanta ⓬

Road map C3. 🏚 *2,700.*
ℹ *Town Hall (0785-540 58).*

This VILLAGE, the center of which still has some old traditional houses made of dark local basalt stone, revolves around the parish church of Santa Cristina, with its impressive Renaissance-inspired architecture. Situated in the middle of a highly developed agricultural region, Abbasanta owes its importance to its strategic position near main artery routes, both ancient and modern.

In the vicinity are two of the most important archaeological sites in the whole of Sardinia: the **Losa Nuraghe** and the **Santa Cristina** nuraghic complex near Paulilàtino *(see p137)*. In order to reach the Losa Nuraghe, take the Carlo Felice road toward Cagliari until you reach kilometer marker 123 (indicated on a road sign). Here, a right turn leads to the entrance to the archaeological site, which is fenced off. Together with the monuments at Barùmini *(see pp64–5)* and Torralba *(see pp22–3)*, this nuraghic complex is one of the most important remaining sites from the immediate pre-Punic period.

In the middle of this vast structure is a keep thousands of years old, dating from the second millennium BC, while the ramparts were built some centuries later. The outer defensive walls were the last to be built, and date from the 7th century BC.

Inside the nuraghe you can visit three roofed chambers with a great many niches, which were probably used for storage. A spiral staircase leads to the upper floor, which has a terrace above.

All around the main structure are the foundations of a series of later buildings, dating from the Bronze Age to the Middle Ages.

A small **Antiquarium** stands about 100 m (328 ft) from the nuraghi themselves. It houses an interesting exhibition of plans and illustrations of many of the nuraghic monuments in this part of Sardinia.

Losa Nuraghe
SS Carlo Felice 123.5 km. 📞 *0785-548 23.* 🕐 *9am–1pm, 4–7pm daily.*

ANTONIO GRAMSCI

Antonio Gramsci was born at Ales at Ales in 1891 of humble family. After completing his studies at Turin, he entered politics full time. He was one of the co-founders of the radical weekly *L'Ordine Nuovo* and in 1921 helped to found the Italian Communist Party, later becoming its Secretary-General. He was elected to parliament but was arrested by the Fascists in 1926 and given a 20-year prison

The young Gramsci

sentence. He did not see freedom again but died in prison in 1937. The complete edition of his writings, *Quaderni del Carcere* (Prison Notebooks) was not published until 1976. *Lettere dal Carcere* (Letters from Prison) are a moving statement of his sufferings as a prisoner.

Bosa ➑

DOMINATED BY the Castello dei Malaspina, the pastel-colored houses of Bosa lie on the right bank of the Temo River, the only navigable river in Sardinia. The town was originally founded by the Phoenicians on the opposite bank of the river. In the Middle Ages, under threat from constant pirate raids, the **Locally made jewelry** townspeople sought the protection of the Malaspina family on the slopes of the hill of Serravalle. Bosa was granted the status of royal city under Spanish rule and always maintained a close relationship with the Iberian peninsula. Today the town is still fascinating, with the buildings of the Sas Conzas quarter mirrored in the calm waters of the river. In the Sa Costa medieval quarter, a labyrinth of cobblestone alleys and steps, you can still see women sitting outside their homes making lace. Environmentalists say the nearby seaside is the cleanest in Italy.

Interior of the Cathedral in Bosa, with Baroque ornamentation

⛪ Cathedral

Piazza Duomo. **[** 0785-37 32 86.
⊙ 7am–7pm daily.
Dedicated to the Virgin Mary, this cathedral was rebuilt in the 19th century in the majestic late Baroque Piedmontese style. In the interior is a statue of the *Madonna and Child*, of the Catalan school, sculpted in the 16th century. On either side of the main altar are two marble lions killing dragons. The side altars are made of multicolored marble.

⛪ Corso Vittorio Emanuele II

The main street in Bosa, paved with stone, runs parallel to the river. It is lined with aristocratic buildings and goldsmiths' workshops where filigree and coral jewelry are made.

🏛 Pinacoteca Civica

Casa Deriu, Corso
Vittorio Emanuele II 59.
⊙ 10am–1pm, 6–9pm
Mon–Sat; 10am–1pm
Sun.
Casa Deriu is a typical 19th-century Bosa building that has been transformed into an exhibition center. The first floor features traditional locally made products such as cakes, wine,

Detail of the architrave of San Pietro

and bread as well as a display of old black-and-white photographs. On the second floor is a fine reconstruction of the elegant Deriu apartment, with its olive wood parquet, frescoed vaulted ceiling, majolica tiles from Ravenna, and locally made lace curtains.

The top floor houses the Pinacoteca Civica (municipal art gallery), featuring the collection of Melkiorre Melis, a local artist and one of the leading promoters of 20th-century applied arts in Sardinia.

The works on display span a 70-year period of graphic art, oil painting, ceramics, and posters. Also shown here are the Arab-influenced works of Melis, executed while he headed the Muslim School of Arts and Crafts in Tripoli.

⛪ Castello Malaspina

Via Ultima Costa 14. **[** 0785-37 30
30. **⊙** 10am–1pm, 3–6pm daily
(May–Sep: 4–7:30pm).
Built in 1112 by the Malaspina dello Spino Secco family, this castle is still impressive, even though only its towers and outer walls have survived. It was enlarged in the 1300s and covers a large area. Very little remains of the castle itself: only parts of the wall on the northeast corner, at the foot of the main tower. The tower was built of light ocher trachyte in the early 1300s and is now being restored.

View of Bosa from the Temo River, with fishing boats

Aerial view of Bosa Marina with its Aragonese tower

Inside the walls the only building left standing is the church of **Nostra Signora di Regnos Altos**, built in the 14th century. Restoration carried out in 1974–5 brought to light a cycle of Catalan school frescoes, one of the few left in Sardinia. From the ramparts there are splendid views of the church of San Pietro, the lower Temo River valley, and the red roofs of the Sa Costa quarter. You can walk down to the center of town by following the steps skirting the walls that once defended Bosa to the east.

Sas Conzas
The buildings on the left bank of the Temo River were once used as tanneries. Abandoned years ago after a crisis in the leather goods market, the buildings are still waiting to be restored. In the meanwhile a small restaurant is housed

here. The Sas Conzas quarter can best be admired from the palm-lined street on the other side of the river, Lungotemo De Gasperi, where the fishermen of Bosa moor their boats.

San Pietro
ask custodian at cathedral for key.
About 1 km (half a mile) east of the left bank of the Temo stands the church of San Pietro, built in red trachyte stone, one of the most interesting of Sardinia's Romanesque churches. It was built in different periods, beginning in the second half of the 11th century, while the bell tower, apse, and side walls were added the following century. The facade combines some elements of Romanesque with touches of

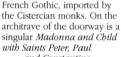

Bosa coat of arms

French Gothic, imported by the Cistercian monks. On the architrave of the doorway is a singular *Madonna and Child with Saints Peter, Paul and Constantine*. Unfortunately, it is difficult to arrange a visit to the interior.

ENVIRONS: Bosa Marina, just over 2 km (1 mile) from the center of town, has a lovely secluded beach with dark sand. Isola Rossa is linked to the mainland by a long jetty. The Aragonese tower is open in July and August and hosts temporary exhibitions.
The coastline between Bosa and Alghero is spectacular. Part of the Trenino Verde route *(see pp92–3)* goes from Bosa Marina to Macomer, skirting the Pedras Nieddas (black stones) beach before going up the Rio Abba Mala valley to Modolo, Tresnuraghes, and Sindia.

The Castello Malaspina in Bosa

The paired horse race held during Carnevale at Santu Lussurgiu

Santu Lussurgiu ⑬

Road map B3. 🏛 *2,829.* 🚉
ℹ️ *Via Santa Maria 40.*
📅 *Carnevale: horse race in town center; Jun 2-3: Horse Fair; Aug 21: San Lussorio.*

Santu Lussurgiu lies at 500 m (1,640 ft) above sea level on the eastern slope of Mount Montiferru, laid out like an amphitheater on the edge of a volcanic crater and surrounded by olive groves.

The historic center is fascinating, with its steep, narrow streets and tiny squares surrounded by beautiful tall stone houses painted in bright colors. Some have decorated architraves and wrought-iron balconies. In Via Roma, an elegant 11-room 18th-century building houses the **Museo della Tecnologia Contadina**, (Museum of Rural Culture), founded by the local Centro di Cultura Popolare. The "Su Mastru Salis" collection is the work of Maestro Salis, the museum curator, who in over 20 years has collected more than 2,000 objects related to the culture and traditions of Santu Lussurgiu.

A guided visit to this interesting museum is like making a trip backward in time. Room after room contains fascinating displays of everyday items used by the farmers, shepherds, and coal merchants who worked at the foot of Mount Montiferru. Among the most interesting exhibits are in the sections given over to spinning and weaving, cooking, and crafts. The room devoted to wine-making is also interesting. Equipment includes a fulling-mill, the implement used to soften and felt fabric. Over 40 of them were once in use in the Santu Lussurgiu area.

In the upper part of town is the 15th-century church of **Santa Maria degli Angeli**, which has a fine 18th-century carved wooden altar.

There are still craftsmen in Santu Lussurgiu who specialize in making knives and fittings for horseback riding (bridles, bits, saddles, and leather riding boots).

At Carnevale the street in front of the museum is turned into a track for a breakneck horse race between pairs of riders dressed as knights.

The Museum of Rural Culture

FLAMINGOS IN THE SALE PORCUS PRESERVE

The Sale Porcus marsh is one of the most important preserves on the Sinis peninsula, its many white sand dunes covered with maquis vegetation. In winter and spring over 10,000 flamingos and thousands of cranes, wild geese, cormorants, and mallards make their home here, making the area look like an East African lake. In summer, drought reduces the water

level, transforming the lake into a white area with a thick, hard salty crust that you can walk across. The Flamingo Center is run by the Lega Italiana per la Protezione di Uccelli (LIPU), the Italian Society for the Protection of Birds. An exhibition illustrates the life cycle of the birds through dioramas and panels. The museum is the starting point for all trails through the Sale Porcus marsh.

🦅 **Oasi LIPU Sale Porcus**
🕐 *daily.* 📞 *0783-522 00.* ✉️

Flamingos in the Sale Porcus preserve

One of the seven springs at San Leonardo de Siete Fuentes

ENVIRONS: A few kilometers from Santu Lussurgiu there is a forest of pine, holm oak, and oak near the village of **San Leonardo de Siete Fuentes,** which is famous for its seven springs of radio-active, diuretic water that flow out of seven fountains at a constant temperature of 11°C (52°F). The streams pass through a wood popular for family outings. In the center of town is the small church of San Leonardo, which once belonged to the Knights of Malta. It was constructed with dark trachyte stone in the 12th century and acquired its present Romanesque-Gothic appearance the following century. The single-nave interior bears the insignias of the Knights of Malta. Opposite the church stands a small public library.

In early June, San Leonardo plays host to an important saddle-horse fair.

🏛 Museo della Tecnologia Contadina
Via T Meloni 1. 📞 0783-55 06 17.
⭕ by appt only. 📷 📹

Cuglieri ⑭

Road map B3. 🏘 3,342.
ℹ️ Viale Regina Margherita (0785-391 55). 📅 Good Friday: procession and 'Iscravamentu; Aug 5: Madonna della Neve.

THE AGRICULTURAL town of Cuglieri lies 500 m (1,640 ft) above sea level on the western slopes of Mount Montiferru, with its panoramic view of the sea. It is dominated by the striking church of **Santa Maria della Neve**, which has an 18th-century facade and twin bell towers. The walk up to the church is lovely, winding through alleyways and stepped streets lined with tall stone houses.

The square in front of Santa Maria offers a fine view of the town and the coast between Santa Caterina di Pittinuri and Porto Alabe.

Santa Maria della Neve, in Cuglieri

ENVIRONS: The coast is 15 km (9 miles) away on main road **292. Santa Caterina di Pittinuri** is a seaside town set around a white-stone inlet enclosed by a limestone cliff, where the Spanish Torre del Pozzo tower stands. This stretch of coast is scenic, with rocky headlands and white sand and pebble beaches. The most famous sight is **S'Archittu,** a large natural bridge created by coastal erosion. A dirt road off main road 292, between Santa Caterina di Pittinuri and S'Archittu, goes to the ruins of the Punic-Roman city of **Cornus,** the setting for the last battle between the Romans and Sardinian-Carthaginians led by Amsicora (215 BC).

In the 9th century the city was abandoned because of repeated Saracen raids, and the inhabitants founded a new city, Curulis Nova, present-day Cuglieri, on the nearby mountain-side. The dirt road peters out just before the Early Christian town of Columbaris, and the acropolis of Cornus is visible on the hill to the southwest. Although the archaeological site may seem abandoned, it still has some sarcophagi and the remains of a three-nave basilica. It seems likely that all of these date back to the 6th century.

The cliff with the famous S'Archittu di Santa Caterina natural bridge at Pittinuri, near Cuglieri

Aerial view of the Cabras marsh area

Cabras ⑮

Road map B4. 🕍 *9,030.* 🚌 🛈 *Via Palestro 2 (0783-29 03 72).*

THE TOWN of Cabras lies a short distance from Oristano and is characterized by its old, one-story houses. It stands on the edge of the largest freshwater lake and marsh in Sardinia (5,000 acres) and is connected to the water via a series of canals.

The presence of both fresh and salt water attracts coots, marsh harriers, peregrine falcons, and purple gallinules. The water itself is rich in mullet and eels.

In the past, local fishermen used long, pointed boats, called *is fassonis*, which were made of dried rushes and other marsh plants, using a technique similar to that known to the Phoenicians. Another Phoenician survival is the marinading technique called *sa merca*, in which fresh fish is wrapped in plant leaves from the lake and left to soak in salt water.

ENVIRONS: At the northern end of the Golfo di Oristano is the **Laguna di Mistras**. Separated from the sea by two sandbars, in wetlands of international scientific importance, this lagoon makes an ideal habitat for flamingos, cormorants, gray herons, and ospreys. The nearby Mar 'e Pontis marshland is also rich in ornithological interest. At the Peschiera Pontis, once a fish farm, you can still see the old sluices and gratings.

San Salvatore ⑯

Road map B4. 🛈 *Cabras.* 🎪 *end of Aug–first Sun in Sep: Corsa degli Scalzi di San Salvatore.*

TYPICAL WHITE houses for pilgrims, or *cumbessias*, surround the country church of San Salvatore. They are occupied for nine days each year in late August and early September for the novena of the saint's feast day.

In the 1960s the church's central square was used as a location for "spaghetti" westerns. San Salvatore was built in the 17th century on the site of a nuraghic sanctuary for the worship of sacred waters. In the 6th century the site was transformed into an underground church. In the left-hand nave stairs lead to the hypogeum, which has six chambers: two rectangular ones flanking a corridor leading to a circular atrium with a well, around which three more chambers lie. The hypogeum was partly hewn out of the rock; the vaulted ceilings are made of sandstone and brick. On the walls are graffiti of animals (elephants, panthers, and peacocks) and heroes and gods (Hercules fighting the

The annual Corsa degli Scalzi (barefoot race) at San Salvatore

Marsh samphire, a typical plant growing in the Cabras marshes

Nemean lion, Mars, and Venus with a small winged cupid). There are even Arabic writings about Allah and Mohammed and numerous depictions of ships, which experts believe are ex votos.

The Latin letters RVF, interlaced as in a monogram and repeated several times, seem to derive from the Phoenician language and are said to stand for "cure, save, give health."

On the first Saturday in September, the feast day of San Salvatore is celebrated. The event is marked with a barefoot *(scalzi)* race in memory of local youths, who, in the Middle Ages, left the village to escape from the Saracens but returned to save the statue of the saint.

Just east of the sanctuary are the ruins of the Domu 'e Cubas Roman baths.

San Giovanni di Sinis ⑰

Road map B4. 37. Cabras.

AT THE EDGE OF THE Sinis peninsula there is a swimming resort that was once famous for its fishermen's huts made of wood and reeds *(see p115)*.

Today only a few have survived; the largest group lies east of the highway, not far from the famous archaeological site of Tharros *(see pp132–3)*.

As you enter the small village of San Giovanni di Sinis you will see the early church of **San Giovanni**. This and San Saturnino in Cagliari are the oldest churches in Sardinia. It was built in the 5th century, but much of the present-day church was the result of 9th- and 10th-century rebuilding. The three-nave interior is barrel vaulted.

ENVIRONS: Near San Giovanni is the WWF **Torre 'e Seu** preserve, where some of the last dwarf palms in the area survive. A dirt road at the northern end of San Giovanni di Sinis leads to the preserve. At the gate there is a path to the sea and the Torre 'e Seu Spanish tower.

THE VERNACCIA WINE OF SARDINIA

Vernaccia grapes

The countryside north of Oristano is one of the most fertile areas in Sardinia, carpeted with grapevines, orange groves, and olive trees. The cultivation of tangerines dates from the 14th century, thanks to the Camaldolite monks from the large monastery at Bonarcado. However viticulture is a great deal older: wine jugs, glasses, and amphoras have been found at Tharros *(see pp132–3)*. The Vernaccia made in Oristano is perhaps Sardinia's most famous white wine and is produced in the towns of San Vero Milis, Cabras, Zeddiani, Narbolia, Riola and Baratili. The wine is full-bodied and strong, with high alcohol content, and is aged for at least three years in large oak barrels. You can tour the wine-producing zone, and pause for a wine-tasting at the Cantina Sociale della Vernaccia, where the entrance is framed by an impressive 18th-century gate.

The 18th-century gate, Cantina Sociale

Wine barrels in the Cantina Sociale della Vernaccia

Rows of Vernaccia vines

Tharros 🔞

1st-century AD oil lamp

Tᴏ HE CITY OF THARROS was founded by the Phoenicians in about 730 BC, on a spit of land called Capo San Marco, which offered safe anchorage for cargo-laden ships from all around the Mediterranean. By the 6th and 5th centuries BC, Tharros had become a flourishing port and this prosperity continued under the Romans, from 238 BC on. With sea on two sides, this is one of the most intriguing ancient sites in the Mediterranean. Only a third of the area has been unearthed so far. The southern section contains the Punic and Roman city, with baths, houses, and sanctuaries, while to the north lies the Tophet, the nuraghic village of Murru Mannu, and the Roman walls.

7th–6th century BC necklace
Made of gold and carnelian, this necklace was found in the southern necropolis.

The necropolis, of Roman origin, was used until the 3rd century AD.

San Giovanni Spanish tower

Capo San Marco
The tip of the Sinis peninsula, Capo San Marco, was settled in the Middle Neolithic era. In the Bronze Age the area was fortified with nuraghi.

Section of the Punic Walls
Squared blocks of basalt and sandstone were used alternately in the 4th-century BC walls, which were 4 m (13 ft) thick.

STAR SIGHTS

★ **Corinthian Columns**

★ **Cistern**

Ancient Baking Oven
The bakery dates from Roman times. It is still possible to recognize the millstone, which was turned by mules and slaves, and the basins made of basalt, used to mix flour and knead dough.

Drainage System
A drain ran along the middle of the paved road. The system was linked to the rows of houses on either side of the street.

VISITORS' CHECKLIST

Road map B4. *San Giovanni di Sinis.* **i** *Cooperativa Penisola Sinis (0783-37 00 19).* ☐ *9am–9pm summer, 8am–1pm, 3–6pm winter.* 🌀 📷

Arena   **Tophet**   **Sanctuary of Demeter**

The Castellum Acquae
was a square construction used as a cistern. The vault was supported by eight brick pillars. It dominates the Compitum, the small piazza in the center of Tharros.

Head of Goddess
Found in the Punic necropolis, this 5th-century BC head is now in Cagliari museum (see p58).

★ Corinthian Columns
These columns have become the symbol of Tharros but are not, in fact, the originals. They were reconstructed by one of the many archaeologists who have worked on this site.

Baths

Baths

★ Cistern
Made of large blocks of sandstone, this well supplied water for the sacred rites celebrated in the temple adorned with Doric half columns.

Oristano ⑲

Interior of Cathedral dome

P LACED AT THE NORTHERN BORDER of the Campidano region, between the mouth of the Tirso River and the Santa Giusta marshlands, Oristano is the most important town in western Sardinia. It was founded in 1070, after the powerful and prosperous city of Tharros was abandoned, the inhabitants defeated by constant pirate raids. The period between 1100 and 1400 saw the rise of the city under enlightened rulers such as Mariano IV and his daughter Eleonora, who controlled most of Sardinia. Oristano became the provincial capital only in 1974. The town stands in the middle of a fertile plain with a network of pools, well-stocked with fish. The historic center, once protected by the city walls, is small and mostly a pedestrian-only zone.

The Cathedral of Oristano with its octagonal campanile

🚪 Cattedrale
Piazza Mannu. **⌖** 0783-786 84.
🕐 8:30am–noon, 5–8pm daily.
Dedicated to the Blessed Virgin Mary, the cathedral was built in 1228 by Lombard architects and masons for Mariano di Torres. It was totally rebuilt in the 17th century in the Baroque style and now displays a mixture of influences. The remaining original elements are the octagonal bell tower with its onion dome and brightly colored majolica tiles, the bronze doors, and the Cappella del Rimedio, which has a fine marble balustrade decorated with Pisan bas-relief sculpture depicting Daniel in the lions' den. The Renaissance choir behind the main altar is another important work. The rich and varied Tesoro del Duomo, the cathedral treasury, is housed in the chapterhouse, and silverwork, vestments, and illuminated manuscripts can be seen on request.
On Piazza del Duomo are the Palazzo Arcivescovile (archbishop's palace) and the Seminario Tridentino.

🗼 Torre di Mariano II
Piazza Roma.
Also called Torre di San Cristoforo or Porta Manna, this sandstone tower at the northern end of the former city walls was built in 1291 by the ruler of the Arborea principality, Mariano II. This and the Portixedda tower, just opposite, are the sole surviving remains of the old city walls. At the top of the tower is a large bell made in 1430. The Torre di Mariano is open on its inner facades and looks over Piazza Roma, the heart of city life, with its fashionable shops and outdoor cafés.

🗼 Corso Umberto
This pedestrian street, also known as Via Dritta, is the most elegant in Oristano with impressive buildings such as Palazzo Siviera, once the residence of the Marquise

---

THE KNIGHTS OF THE STAR

The Sa Sartiglia procession and tournament is centuries old and is held on the last Sunday of Carnival and on Shrove Tuesday. It was probably introduced in 1350 by Mariano II to celebrate his wedding. On February 2 the procession leader, *su Componidori*, is chosen. On the day of the event he is dressed by a group of girls. A white shirt is sewn on him, his face is wrapped in fasciae and covered with a woman's mask, and a bride's veil and black hat are placed on his head. He then leads a procession of knights, trumpeters, and drummers through the city to the tournament grounds by the Arcivescovado and the cathedral. At a given signal the tournament begins. The leader has to run his sword into the hole in the middle of a star hanging from a string, and pick it up. If he succeeds, this signals a prosperous year.

The Sa Sartiglia tournament at Oristano

d'Acrisia, which has a dome on top, and Palazzo Falchi, built in the 1920s. Oristano's best shops are here, and it is the most popular street for the traditional evening stroll.

🎭 Piazza Eleonora D'Arborea

This long, irregular, tree-lined square is named after the ruler who established the famous Carta de Logu body of laws in 1392. A 19th-century statue of Eleonora stands in the middle of the square. This piazza

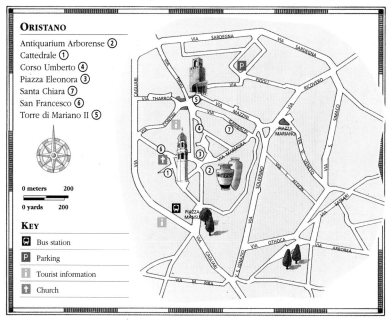

Eleonora d'Arborea

also boasts such noble buildings as Palazzo Corrias and the Palazzo Comunale, or town hall, once the Scolopi monastery. The octagonal church of San Vincenzo was part of the monastery.

🏛 San Francesco

Piazza Mannu. 🕻 0783-782 75.
◯ 7–11:30am, 5–8pm daily.
This Neo-Classical church was built over the remains of a Gothic church that was completely destroyed in the early 19th century. The facade has six columns with Ionic capitals. In the interior is one

of the most interesting statues in Sardinia: a crucifix executed by an unknown late 14th-century Catalan artist. Another important work, by Pietro Cavaro, depicts *The Stigmata of San Francesco*.

🏛 Santa Chiara

Via Garibaldi. 🕻 0783-780 93. ◯ 5–6pm daily.
The Gothic church of Santa Chiara was built in the 14th century. The façade displays sandstone ashlars, a severe rose window, and small bell gable. The interior has wooden Gothic corbels with carved animal figures.

🏛 Antiquarium Arborense

Palazzo Parpaglia, Via Parpaglia 37.
🕻 0783-744 33. ◯ summer: 9:30am–1pm Tue–Fri, 4:30–8:30pm Tue–Sun; winter: 9:30am–1pm, 4:30–7pm Tue–Sun. 🎫
Housed in the Neo-Classical Palazzo Parpaglia, this museum features archaeological finds from Tharros, an art gallery, and a section devoted to medieval Oristano. The gallery has interesting altarpieces in Catalan style:

the San Martino *retablo* (15th century) attributed to the workshop of the Catalan artist Ramon de Mur; the *Retablo di Cristo* (1533), by followers of Pietro Cavaro, of which only nine panels remain; and the *Retablo della Madonna dei Consiglieri* (1565) by the Cagliari artist Antioco Mainas, representing the councillors of Oristano kneeling before the Virgin Mary.

The archaeological collection contains over 2,000 Neolithic obsidian scrapers, bone barrettes, small amphoras from Greece and Etruria, and Roman glass objects and oil lamps. These all belong to the Collezione Archeologica Efisio Pischedda.

Among the most important objects are a terra-cotta mask used to ward off evil spirits, scarabs made out of green jasper, and carved gemstones from the Roman period.

ORISTANO

Antiquarium Arborense ②
Cattedrale ①
Corso Umberto ④
Piazza Eleonora ③
Santa Chiara ⑦
San Francesco ⑥
Torre di Mariano II ⑤

0 meters 200
0 yards 200

KEY

🚌 Bus station

P Parking

ℹ Tourist information

✝ Church

Fishermen using *fassonis*, traditional sedge boats, on the Santa Giusta lake

Santa Giusta 20

Road map B4. 🏛 *4,116.*
ℹ *Via Amsicora 17 (0783-35 96 14).*
🎉 *May: 14 Sagra di Santa Giusta.*

THIS AGRICULTURAL TOWN, built on the banks of the Santa Giusta lake and marsh, was built over the ruins of the Roman city of Ottona. The cathedral of **Santa Giusta**, a jewel of Pisan Romanesque architecture blended with Arab and Lombard elements, is seen on the hill as you enter the town. The cathedral was built in the first half of the 12th century and has a narrow facade, with a triple-lancet window. The

columns in the interior are in various styles and originally came from the nearby Roman cities of Neapolis, Tharros, and Othoca. From the sacristy there is a lovely view of the lake, one of the best fishing areas in Sardinia, where you can still see the long *is fassonis* sedge boats of Phoenician derivation. On the feast day of Santa Giusta in May, a lively regatta is held here. The local gastronomic specialty is *bottarga* (salted mullet roe).

Soapstone scarab found in Santa Giusta digs

🏛 **Santa Giusta**
Via Manzoni. 📞 *0783-35 92 05.*
🕘 *9am–1pm, 2–4:20pm daily.*

Arborea 21

Road map B4. 🏛 *3,828.* ℹ *Via Roma (0783-80 13 07).* 🎉 *Good Friday: living representation of the Passion of Christ.*

ARBOREA was founded in 1930 during the Fascist period and was initially

named Mussolinia. The town was built on a regular grid plan typical of modern cities. All the civic buildings (school, parish church, hotel and town hall) are found in Piazza Maria Ausiliatrice, from which the main streets radiate.

The avenues are lined with trees and the two-story Neo-Gothic houses are surrounded by gardens. In the **Palazzo del Comune** (town hall) there is a small collection of archaeological finds from excavations in the area, including the Roman necropolis of S'Ungroni, north of Arborea, discovered during work on land reclamation.

About 9 km (6 miles) to the southwest is the fishing village of Marceddi, on the edge of the marsh of the same name, dominated by the 16th-century Torrevecchia.

🏛 **Palazzo del Comune**
Piazza Maria Ausiliatrice. 📞 *0783-803 31.* 🕘 *10am–1pm Mon–Fri.*

Fordongianus 22

Road map C4. 🏛 *1,168.* ℹ *Via Traiano 7 (0783-601 23).* 🎉 *Apr 21 & Aug 20: Festa di San Lussorio.*

ANCIENT FORUM TRAIANI was once the most important Roman city in the interior. Located in the Tirso River valley, it was fortified against the local Barbagia people. Today the center consists of houses in red and gray stone.

Cathedral of Santa Giusta, a masterpiece of Romanesque architecture

One of the best preserved is Casa Madeddu, a typical old "Aragonese house" of the early 1600s with Catalan-style doorways and windows. On the same street is the 16th-century parish church of San Pietro Apostolo, in red trachyte, which has been almost entirely rebuilt. The **Roman Baths**, currently being restored, lie on the banks of the river. The rectangular pool still contains warm water from the hot springs, and the local women use it to do their washing. The portico and the rooms with mosaic pavements are closed to the public at the present time.

A short distance south of Fordon-gianus stands the little rural church of San Lussorio, built by Victorine monks about AD 1100, over an early Christian crypt.

Earrings found at the Forum Traiani

Panoramic view of Àles at the foot of Monte Arci

Paulilàtino ㉓

Road map C4. ![pop] 2,961. ![info] Via Pia 4 (0785-556 23). ![fest] second Sun in May: Sagra di Santa Cristina.

THIS RURAL VILLAGE at the edge of the Abbasanta basalt plateau is surrounded by olive groves and cork oak woods. The houses are built of dark stone and have Aragonese doorways and small wrought-iron balconies. The same stone was used to build the church of San Teodoro in the 17th century. This Aragonese Gothic church has a stained-glass rose window and a bell tower with an onion dome. **Palazzo Atzori** houses a museum of folk culture with domestic tools and objects on display.

🏛 **Palazzo Atzori**
Via Nazionale 127. ![tel] 0785-554 38. ![open] 9am–1pm, 5–8pm Tue–Sun.

ENVIRONS: About 4 km (3 miles) from town, a turn off state road 131 takes you to the nuraghic village of **Santa Cristina**. A stone wall encloses the archaeological area, where there is a well temple dedicated to the local

mother-goddess dating from the 1st millennium BC. The well is in a good state of preservation. Broad stairs lead down to a vaulted chamber. Nearby is an enclosure that was probably used for general assemblies. The sacred nature of this site has been maintained over the centuries with the construction of a church dedicated to Santa Cristina. Worshipers continue to flock to the church, which is surrounded by a village of *muristenes*, houses intended for those who come here for novena on the saint's feast day.

To the right of the church, among the olive trees, another archaeological zone includes a well-preserved nuraghe and two rectangular nuraghic-age stone dwellings. The best preserved of these is 14 m (46 ft) long and 2 m (6 ft) high.

🏛 **Santa Cristina**
Km 114,300, SS131 Cagliari–Sassari. ![info] Cooperativa Archeotur (0336-81 17 56). ![disabled]

Steps leading to the temple of Santa Cristina at Paulilàtino

Àles ㉔

Road map C4. ![pop] 1,633. ![fest] first Sun in Aug: Santa Madonna della Neve.

ÀLES, THE MAIN VILLAGE in the Marmilla area, lies on the eastern slope of Monte Arci. In the upper part stands the cathedral of San Pietro, built in 1686 by Genoan architect Domenico Spotorno, who used the ruins of the 12th-century church on this site as material for his construction.

Twin bell towers with ceramic domes rise above the elegant facade, while in the Baroque interior, the sacristy has lovely carved furniture and a rare 14th-century crucifix. The Archivio Capitolare contains elegant gold jewelry.

In the same square stand the Palazzo Vescovile and the seminary and oratory of the Madonna del Rosario.

Àles is also the birthplace of Antonio Gramsci (1891–1937) *(see p125).* The house is marked with a plaque.

ENVIRONS: Àles is a good starting point for a hike to the top of Trebina Longa and Trebina Lada, the highest peaks on **Monte Arci** and remnants of an ancient crater. Along the way you are likely to spot pieces of obsidian, the hard black volcanic glass that was cut into thin slices and used to make arrowheads, spears, and scrapers. The obsidian of Monte Arci was in great demand, and not only supplied the whole of Sardinia but was also sold throughout the Mediterranean in the 4th–3rd millennia BC.

THE NORTH AND THE COSTA SMERALDA

ORTHEASTERN SARDINIA's *beauty is familiar from the classic images of a rugged coastline, beautiful inlets, sparkling turquoise sea, and beaches of brilliant white sand. To the north, the islands crowded in the Straits of Bonifacio, a stone's throw from Corsica, have great appeal for those in search of unspoiled calm.*

The most famous development in the northeast is the famous Costa Smeralda, founded by a consortium of financiers, including the Aga Khan, in 1962. In the space of 35 years, few areas in Sardinia have undergone such profound changes as the northeastern coastline. Villas and residential hotels have sprung up almost everywhere, and small harbors have been equipped as marinas. The surroundings are undeniably beautiful, with spectacular scenery at headlands such as Capo d'Orso and Capo Testa. The perfume of the Mediterranean maquis still manages to reach the beaches of pure white sand, and there are still unspoiled areas that have resisted the encroachment of vacation homes. Tourism brings its own problems however, and there is increasing recognition of the need for stricter controls on building, if the growing influx of visitors is not to damage the island's unique environment.

In the interior, the Gallura region displays quite a different character, with extensive forests of cork oak trees and rough, rocky terrain. Granite outcrops create enchanting landscapes like the Valle della Luna near Aggius *(see p152)*. This part of Sardinia is characterized by its wholesome cooking, the continuing practice of traditional crafts, and frequent reminders of its long history. As well as prehistoric nuraghe, an exceptional series of Romanesque churches survives in the Logudoro area *(see pp156–7)*, culminating in the black-and-white striped stone church of Santissima Trinità di Saccargia *(see pp158–9)*.

The island of Caprera, ideal for swimming and sunbathing

◁   Two coves on the island of Mortorio, separated by a thin strip of land

Exploring the North and the Costa Smeralda

THE PORT AND AIRPORT in Olbia handle most of the visitors headed not only for the Costa Smeralda resort villages but the rest of Sardinia as well. The appeal of the northern part of Sardinia is the beautiful long coastline, with its magnificent beaches and wind-eroded cliffs. From Olbia the road winds northward to Santa Teresa di Gallura, then turns westwards, beyond the Castelsardo headland, until it reaches Porto Torres. In the interior, Tempio Pausania, capital of the Gallura region, makes an excellent starting point for local tours.

The bearlike cliff at Capo d'Orso

SIGHTS AT A GLANCE

ISOLA ROSSA ㉔

CASTELSARDO ㉓

GOLFO DELL'ASINARA

Porto Torres

SASSARI ㉒

TOUR OF THE LOGUDORO ⑳

SANTISSIMA TRINITÀ DI SACCARGIA ㉑

PLOAGHE

MÓRES

OZIERI ⑲

Macomer

A stretch of coast at Capo Testa

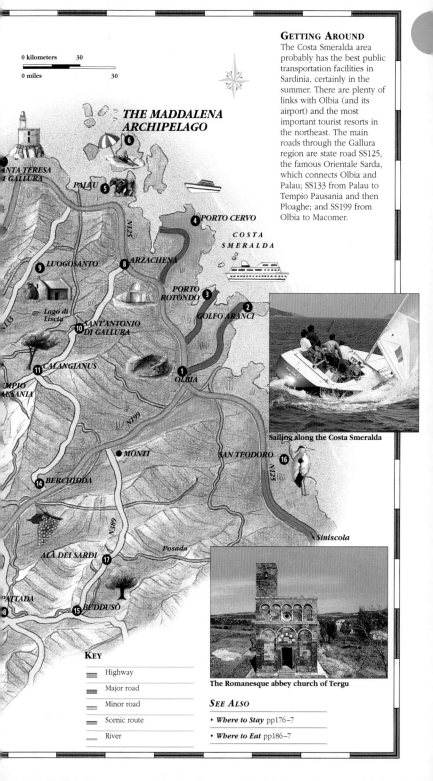

0 kilometers 30

0 miles 30

**THE MADDALENA
ARCHIPELAGO** 6

ANTA TERESA
I GALLURA

PALAU 5

PORTO CERVO 4

COSTA
SMERALDA

LUOGOSANTO 9

ARZACHENA 8

PORTO
ROTONDO 3

GOLFO ARANCI 2

N125

Lago di
Liscia

SANT'ANTONIO
DI GALLURA 10

OLBIA 1

CALANGIANUS 11

N133

MPIO
USANIA

N199

MONTI

SAN TEODORO 16

N125

Siniscola

BERCHIDDA 14

N389

Posada

ALÀ DEI SARDI 17

PATTADA

BUDDUSÒ 15

GETTING AROUND
The Costa Smeralda area
probably has the best public
transportation facilities in
Sardinia, certainly in the
summer. There are plenty of
links with Olbia (and its
airport) and the most
important tourist resorts in
the northeast. The main
roads through the Gallura
region are state road SS125,
the famous Orientale Sarda,
which connects Olbia and
Palau; SS133 from Palau to
Tempio Pausania and then
Ploaghe; and SS199 from
Olbia to Macomer.

Sailing along the Costa Smeralda

The Romanesque abbey church of Tergu

KEY

	Highway
	Major road
	Minor road
	Scenic route
	River

SEE ALSO

• **Where to Stay** pp176–7

• **Where to Eat** pp186–7

The ruins at Cabu Abbas

Olbia ❶

Road map D1 & 2. 👤 *42,707.* 🚤
ℹ️ *Azienda Autonoma Soggiorno
(0789-214 53).*

THE TOWN OF OLBIA is only
200 km (125 miles) from
the port of Civitavecchia on
the mainland of Italy and has
always been the main arrival
point on the island, rather
than the capital Cagliari. The
building of the airport just
outside Olbia, to serve the
Costa Smeralda, has con-
firmed this role.

Olbia is a modern city and
usually considered as a stop-
off on the way to the coast.
Of interest in the town are a
Roman cistern in Piazza
Margherita, proof of ancient
Roman occupation, and the
Romanesque **San Simplicio**.
This church was built from
the 11th century onward and
enlarged in the 13th century.

ENVIRONS: There are two
interesting prehistoric sites
near Olbia: the **Cabu Abbas**
nuraghic complex (4 km, 2
miles to the northeast) and
the **Sa Testa** holy well.

To reach Cabu Abbas from
the old port of Olbia, go
along Corso Umberto and
then Via d'Annunzio. Once
past the railroad you will see
the country church of Santa
Maria Cabu Abbas. From here
a dirt path winds up toward
the top of the mountain,
another 15 minutes on foot.
The site offers a magnificent
view of the island of Tavolara.
There is a central well with
a tower where remains of
sacrifices – burned bones and
pieces of pottery – were
found in 1937. This large
megalithic zone extends for
about 200 m (656 ft).

To reach the Sa Testa holy
well, take road SP82 to Golfo
Aranci as far as the Pozzo
Sacro hotel. This site consists
of a wide paved courtyard,
from which 17 covered steps
lead down to a well chamber.

Golfo Aranci ❷

Road map D1. 👤 *2,048.*
ℹ️ *Town Hall (0789-216 72).*

THE NAME "ARANCI" means
oranges, but you will not
see orange groves here. Golfo
Aranci owes its name to a
mistaken interpretation of
the local place-name *di li
ranci,* meaning "some crabs."

Formerly a part of Olbia,
the village of Golfo Aranci
became an independent
town in 1979. Since 1882
increasing numbers of ferries
from the mainland have used
Golfo Aranci as a stopping
place. It is also the official
port of call for the Ferrovie
dello Stato (Italian State
Railroad) ferries.

The Porto Rotondo Yacht Club

Porto Rotondo ❸

Road map D1.
ℹ️ *Azienda Autonoma di Soggiorno
di Arzachena (0789-826 24).*

PORTO ROTONDO is not so
much a town as a large,
well-planned tourist village
that grew from nothing
during the Costa Smeralda
boom. The buildings, placed
around the inevitable yacht
marina, were designed to fit
in as much as possible with
the natural surroundings. The
result is certainly pleasant,
and Porto Rotondo has been
a great success as a tourist
resort, despite its perhaps
slightly artificial air.

Mussel beds at sunset in the Bay of Olbia

Aerial view of Porto Rotondo

The Porto Rotondo dock and Piazzetta San Marco are lined with famous designer shops, and throughout the summer the cafés and restaurants are crowded with visitors, lunching, dining, meeting friends, listening to music, and just watching the world go by. Out of season Porto Rotondo is quiet and even deserted.

The church of San Lorenzo, designed by Andrea Cascella, holds wooden statues by Mario Ceroli depicting Biblical figures.

Just outside Porto Rotondo is the lovely headland called Punta della Volpe, separating the Golfo di Marinella from the Golfo di Cugnana.

Architecture on the Costa Smeralda

MORE THAN 30 YEARS have passed since a stretch of coastline in northeastern Sardinia was transformed into the most exclusive tourist resort in the Mediterranean, the Costa Smeralda, or Emerald Coast. In 1962 the beaches were the preserve of grazing cattle, then taken to overwinter on the islands of Mortorio, Soffi, and Li Milani. The Consorzio Costa Smeralda was formed to transform the area. The group initially consisted only of the landowners but expanded to include property owners. Building regulations were established and an architectural committee was founded to supervise any new building in the area. The prominent architects Luigi Vietti, Jacques Couelle, Giancarlo and Michele Busiri Vici, Antonio Simon, Raimond Martin, and Leopoldo Mastrella were appointed to design the resorts. The area has since changed beyond recognition. Luxury hotels, sumptuous villas, and huge vacation villages have gone up, together with sports facilities: the famous Yacht Club and one of the most attractive golf courses in the Mediterranean, as well as small villages such as Porto Cervo.

The Neo-Mediterranean style is a combination of the various elements frequently seen in Mediterranean architecture.

In planning Porto Rotondo, the architects decided that only native plants should be used, so trees such as pine, poplar, and eucalyptus are banned because they would not blend in with the local strawberry trees, myrtle, mastic trees, oleanders, and mimosa.

The materials used must be traditional – local stone, pebbles, curved tiles, and brick.

An aerial view of Porto Cervo

Porto Cervo **4**

Road map D1. ℹ️ *Azienda Autonoma Soggiorno di Arzachena (0789-826 24).*

THE HEART OF the Costa Smeralda and a paradise for VIPs, Porto Cervo is centered around two yacht harbors with some of the most spectacular private craft in the world. In summer there is a series of top sports events, including regattas and golf tournaments. The traditional evening stroll along the dock is almost obligatory, with fashionable designer shops on one side and luxury yachts on the other. The church of Stella Maris has a canvas attributed to the painter El Greco.

ENVIRONS: There are plenty of good beaches around Porto Cervo, such as Liscia Ruja to the south, framed by the sheltered Cala di Volpe.

Palau **5**

Road map D1. 🏔️ *3,238.*
ℹ️ *Azienda Autonoma Soggiorno (0789-70 95 70).*

THE LOGICAL departure point for a trip to the Maddalena archipelago, Palau also owes its success to the appeal of the narrow-gauge Sassari-Tempio-Palau railroad. Life here is rather frenetic in the summer and revolves around the ferry boat wharf and the yacht harbor. From Palau you can travel to some of the most fascinating and famous places on the coast, such as

the jagged Capo d'Orso (Bear Cape) promontory, which ends in a large, bear-shaped rock, sculpted by the wind.

To get to Punta Sardegna, take the road that goes up to Monte Altura, and then go down to the beach of Cala Trana, on the tip of this headland. There is an extraordinary view of the coast and the islands, which is particularly lovely in the early morning

and at sunset, despite the fact that 20th-century construction work is slowly but surely spoiling the unique beauty of this part of Sardinia.

The Maddalena Archipelago **6**

See pp146–9.

Santa Teresa di Gallura **7**

Road map C1. 🏔️ *4,127.*
ℹ️ *Azienda Autonoma Soggiorno (0789-75 41 27).*

THE AREA around Santa Teresa was inhabited in Roman times and was also important to the Pisans, who used the local granite for building. The present-day town was built from scratch during the Savoyard period. It has a regular grid plan with streets intersecting at right

Sunset at Palau, departure point for the Maddalena Archipelago

---

THE AGA KHAN AND THE COSTA SMERALDA

The Consorzio Costa Smeralda group of foreign investors was founded in 1962 with Prince Karim Aga Khan IV at its head. The Harvard-educated prince, rich and charismatic, was then in his mid-twenties. He is reputed to have spent more than 1 billion dollars in creating an opulent jet-set playground, complete with yachting marinas, luxury hotels, villas, and elegant restaurants along the Gallura coastline, all designed to harmonize with the rugged Sardinian landscape. The project has proved very successful: Porto Cervo and the nearby villages quickly became popular vacation spots, especially for the wealthy and famous of the international jet set, who can be seen on the docks of Porto Cervo in the summer.

Aga Khan IV

Overlooking Santa Teresa di Gallura

angles, in the middle of which is a small square and the church of San Vittorio. The local economy is based on fishing (including coral fishing) and tourism.

On the rocky headland stands the Torre Longosardo, a tower built in the 16th century during the Aragonese period; it gives a magnificent view of Porto Longone bay and, in the distance, the white cliffs circling the city of Bonifacio in Corsica, which is only 12 km (7.5 miles) away.

To the left the coast falls away to the beach of Rena Bianca, which ends not far from the Isola Monica, a tiny island that has remains of an abandoned quarry.

The Capo Testa lighthouse

ENVIRONS: About 5 km (3 miles) away is **Capo Testa**, a rocky promontory connected to the mainland by a thin sandbar. The headland can be reached via a very nice route around the bays of Colba and Santa Reparata. A walk through the ancient and modern quarries – which supplied the Romans with the granite for the columns in the Pantheon – accompanied by the sweet fragrance of the maquis, will take you to the Capo Testa lighthouse.

Arzachena ➑

Road map D1. 🏠 9,963.
ℹ️ *Azienda Autonoma Soggiorno (0789-826 24).*

AROUND THIRTY YEARS AGO, Arzachena was a peaceful shepherds' village in the interior. Today it is the center of one of the most famous tourist resorts in the world, the Costa Smeralda and has undergone considerable change. Towering above the houses is a curious rock formed by wind erosion, called the Fungo (mushroom), and there are many traces of prehistoric settlements in the vicinity. Among the most interesting sites for a tour are the **Albucciu Nuraghe**, the **Tomba di Giganti Coddu Vecchiu,** and the **Li Muri Necropolis**.

♙ Albucciu Nuraghe
▢ *At all times.*
From Arzachena, take the road to Olbia and after about 600 m (650 yds), at the end of town, follow the turn-off and then take the trail on the right. Once at the nuraghe, go up the ladder to the upper level to visit the side section.

The protruding stone brackets that once supported the original wooden structure are still intact.

♙ Tomba di Giganti Coddu Vecchiu
▢ *At all times.*
To get to the Giants' Tomb, take state road SS427 toward Calangianus and, after about 3 km (2 miles), take the turn to the right marked "Luogosanto." After about 1,800 m (1 mile) you join the Capichera road, and another 500 m (550 yds) farther on there is a path leading to the tomb, which lies to the right. In the middle of the funerary monument there is a stele about 4 m (13 ft) high, surrounded by a semicircular wall of stone slabs set into the earth.

♙ Li Muri Necropolis
▢ *At all times.*
Once outside Arzachena, follow signs for Calangianus (SS427) and then the right-hand turn for Luogosanto. Continue for about 4.5 km (3 miles) and take another right turn onto a dirt road, which goes to the necropolis of Li Muri.

This site includes a number of ancient tombs: burial chambers surrounded by as many as five concentric circles of stones. These funerary circles constitute the most important monumental complex left from the era archaeologists now refer to as the Arzachena Culture.

The mistral whipping up the surf off Capo Testa

The Maddalena Archipelago 6

Subalpine warblers

SEVEN ISLANDS (Maddalena, Caprera, and Santo Stefano to the southeast, Spargi, Budelli, Razzoli, and Santa Maria to the northwest) make up the Arcipelago della Maddalena. Beyond lie the Straits of Bonifacio, which became a marine preserve of international status at the beginning of 1997. Rugged, jagged coasts, rocks hewn by wind and water erosion, and tenacious maquis vegetation characterize this group of islands, known during the Roman period as *Cuniculariae*, or "rabbit islands." In the 18th century Maddalena was used as a military base – it is a convenient landing place and lay in a strategically important position. A tour of the island would be incomplete without a visit to Caprera, to see the places where the Italian hero Giuseppe Garibaldi lived and is buried.

LOCATOR MAP

RAZZOLI

SANTA MARIA

BUDELLI

SPARGI

LA MADDALENA

Spargi
Uninhabited, like Budelli, Razzoli, and Santa Maria, this island has marvelously clear water and secluded beaches, making it an ideal site for swimmers, snorkelers, and scuba divers.

A scenic route of just over 20 km (12 miles) runs around the island, providing magnificent views of the archipelago, Corsica, and the four Corsican islands of Lavezzi.

Bird Life
The many rock formations in this archipelago are frequently visited by sea birds such as cormorants, to the delight of bird-watchers.

★ **La Maddalena**
This is the most important town in the archipelago. Town life centers around Piazza Umberto I and Piazza Garibaldi. There is a wide choice of boat trips to the nearby islands from the harbor.

Regattas
*The west wind, an almost constant presence
in the Maddalena archipelago, makes this a
popular place for yachting competitions.*

VISITORS' CHECKLIST

Road map D1. 🚢 *from Palau,
departures every 20 mins in the
summer (once an hour after
midnight) and winter.*
ℹ️ *Azienda Autonoma di
Soggiorno La Maddalena
(0789-73 63 21).*
Caprera *can be reached
from Maddalena via a 600-m
(2,000-ft) bridge on the Passo
della Moneta.*

Guardia Vecchia is the
highest mountain on the
island. The Savoy rulers chose
it as the site for the fort of
San Vittorio, which is now
occupied by a lighthouse.

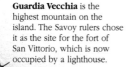

Monte Teialone
is the highest
point on Caprera.

**The Bridge on Passo della
Moneta**
*Constructed in 1891, this
bridge links the islands of
Maddalena and Caprera.*

SANTO
STEFANO

CAPRERA

Caprera
*The island of Caprera
extends over nearly
3,950 acres.*

★ **Tomb of Garibaldi**
*The "hero of two worlds" was
buried here on June 2, 1882.*

STAR SIGHTS

★ **La Maddalena**

★ **Tomb of Garibaldi**

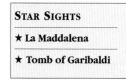

Exploring the Maddalena Archipelago

T HE SMALL Maddalena Archipelago is a favorite with sailing fanatics, fans of subacqua fishing and with people who appreciate tranquillity and unspoiled surroundings. Except for the two largest islands, the archipelago is uninhabited and, together with the many other small islands, make perfect summer destinations for boat trips, sunbathing, and swimming in solitude.

The Sardinia Regional Naval headquarters at La Maddalena

La Maddalena
Road map D1. 🏘 11,235.
🛈 Azienda Autonoma Soggiorno,
Via XX Settembre 24 (0789-73 63
21). 🚢 from Palau. 🎉 Jul 20-22:
Santa Maria Maddalena.

The town that is now the capital of the island was founded in 1770 and replaced a small village built on the shores of the Cala Gavetta bay. After the unsuccessful invasion on the part of the French in 1793, British admiral Horatio Nelson stopped at La Maddalena in 1804 and in 1887 the entire Maddalena Archipelago was turned into a naval base by the Savoy rulers. On Via Amendola, which runs along the waterfront, a series of 19th-century buildings bears witness to the rapid development of the town in this period. In Piazza Garibaldi, the Municipio (town hall) has on display a French bomb dating from France's attempt to conquer Sardinia in 1793.

In the evening, particularly in summer, the traditional evening stroll centers around Via Garibaldi. Not far away is the church of Santa Maria Maddalena, which has two candelabra and a silver cross given by Admiral Nelson to

the island's inhabitants. La Maddalena is still the head-quarters of the Sardinia Regional Navy.

🏞 The Scenic Route
The road around the island is about 20 km (12 miles) long and goes through the Cala Spalmatore, Stagno Torto, and Baia Trìnita bays.

On your way from La Maddalena, you will see the church of the Trinità, then the turn-off for Monte Guardia Vecchia, on the summit of which is the Savoyard fort of San Vittorio, and lastly the island of Giardinelli, which is connected to La Maddalena

by a narrow strip of land. Farther north are Porto Massimo, the inlets of Abbatoggia and Cala d'Inferno, and the other large fortification on the island, Forte dei Colmi. On the first part of this tour is the **Museo Archeologico Navale "Nino Lamboglia,"** the maritime museum with finds from the "ship of Spargi," an ancient Roman cargo vessel discovered in the 1950s.

🏛 Museo Archeologico Navale "Nino Lamboglia"
Località Mongiardino. ⏰ 8am–1:30pm
Tue–Sun. 🎫 0789-79 06 60. 🖼

Caprera
Road map D1. 🛈 Azienda
Autonoma Soggiorno della
Maddalena (0789-73 63 21).
This small island has 34 km (21 miles) of coastline and is connected to the island of Maddalena by the 600-m (1,968-m) Passo della Moneta bridge. Energetic hikers will enjoy the climb up the steps to the top of Monte Teialone (212 m, 695 ft).

The island of Caprera became the property of Giuseppe Garibaldi in 1856. His estate is now part of the **Compendio Garibaldino** museum area. A visit here includes a fascinating tour of the entire residential complex, the stables, moorings, and the Casa Bianca (white house) where Garibaldi lived. The stable still has a period steam-engine used for threshing, and the Casa Bianca contains mementoes of Garibaldi's adventurous life: weapons, flags, portraits, the hero's

GARIBALDI AND CAPRERA

The legendary Italian hero and revolutionary Giuseppe Garibaldi escaped to the island of Caprera in 1849, after the fall of the Roman Republic. He returned in 1855 after the death of his wife, Anita, and decided to buy most of the island. The rest of the land was then given to him by some English friends. Garibaldi, who went on to play a key role in the unification of Italy, settled on Caprera permanently in 1857. He died there in 1882.

**Giuseppe Garibaldi wearing
the famous red shirt**

The famous pink sand beach at Budelli

clothes (including his famous red shirt), and a model of the Battle of Solferino.

Garibaldi's favorite room was the parlor, and he asked to be taken there before he died. The calendar and clocks in the room have not been changed since then; they show the exact time of his death: 6:20pm on June 2,1882.

Caprera also has a famous sailing school, the Centro Velico Caprera *(see p199)*.

Compendio Garibaldino

⬛ *9am–1pm, Tue–Fri, 9am–2pm, Sat & Sun.* ⬤ *public hols.* ▨

Santo Stefano

Road map D1.

🛈 *Azienda Autonoma Soggiorno La Maddalena (0789-73 63 21).*

This small island lies halfway between Palau and the island of Maddalena and can be reached via the boats that depart at regular intervals from La Maddalena harbor. Dominating the scene is the Santo Stefano (or San Giorgio) fortress, also known as Napoleon's fort, built at the end of the 18th century.

There is a tourist village on the beach of Pesce, on the western coast.

Spargi

Road map D1. 🚢 *from La Maddalena.* 🛈 *Azienda Autonoma Soggiorno La Maddalena (0789-73 63 21).*

Spargi is little more than 2 km (1 mile) in diameter, and the only inhabitants are a few shepherds. The terrain is fairly barren and the coast steep and inaccessible, but there is a lovely beach for swimming, even though it has no facilities. An ancient Roman ship was found opposite the Cala Corsara cove on the southern coast; its cargo is now in the Museo Archeologico Navale "Nino Lamboglia" at La Maddalena.

Budelli

Road map D1.

🛈 *Azienda Autonoma Soggiorno La Maddalena (0789-73 63 21).*

This beautiful uninhabited island is remarkable for its unique beach of rose-colored sand. Even though there are no facilities, Budelli is popular with visitors because of its beautifully unspoilt natural setting.

The clear, unpolluted water is also ideal for scuba diving, either to observe marine life or for underwater fishing.

SAILING IN NORTHERN SARDINIA

The Straits of Bonifacio are dotted with small islands and rocks with lighthouses, which create natural buoys, making the area ideal for yacht and dinghy racing. The wind is pretty constant, and in summer the west wind blows steadily at 40 km per hour (24 mph).

The Costa Smeralda Yacht Club at Porto Cervo, founded by the Aga Khan, is the main sailing facility in this area. This world-famous club organizes several important sailing races and other competitions. The most well-known are the Sardinia Cup, an international deep-sea championship held in even-numbered years, and the Settimana delle Bocche, a summer race for speedboats from all over Italy.

In the odd-numbered years the old harbor at Porto Cervo provides space for 50 or so vintage boats: from the *gozzo* with its characteristic lateen sail to 30-m (98-ft) schooners. This popular event, which has been held since 1982, is usually followed by the world yacht championship for boats in the Maxi class.

Other important races, such as the European and world championships of various yacht categories also take place here. The Costa Smeralda Yacht Club represented Italy in the 1983 America's Cup with the yacht *Azzurra*, and in 1987 the club organized regattas to select the Italian representative in the America's Cup in Perth, Australia.

Yachts racing in the Straits of Bonifacio

San Trano, a 12th-century hermitage near Luogosanto

Luogosanto ❾

Road map C1. 🏘 *1,873.* ℹ *Pro Loco (079-65 22 13).* 🎪 *first Sun in Aug: San Quirico's feast day.*

THE VILLAGE of Luogosanto is surrounded by maquis and is well known for the production of bitter honey, often served with *seadas (see p181)*. The village is typical of the Gallura region, backed by greenery and wind-eroded pinkish-gray rocks. Every seven years a colorful and solemn ceremony celebrates the opening of the Porta Santa (holy door) of the church of Nostra Signora di Luogosanto.

San Quirico's feast day ends with a dinner for all the villagers. The traditional dish *carr'e cogghju*, made with pork and cabbage, is served.

About 1 km (half a mile) to the east of Luogosanto is the **San Trano hermitage**, perched at 410 m (1,345 ft), dominating the landscape toward the north of the town. This small church was built in the 12th century in memory of the hermit saints San Nicola and San Trano, who, according to the legend, lived in the small cave to the rear of the altar.

Nearby is the Filetta spring, whose waters are famous throughout the island. In recent years, squares, steps, and street lamps have been placed around the spring.

Sant'Antonio di Gallura ❿

Road map D1. 🏘 *1,653.* 🚍 ℹ *Town Hall (079-66 90 13).* 🎪 *first Sun in Sep: Sant'Antonio's feast day.*

THIS VILLAGE HAS always been an important farming and sheep-raising center. In the heart of town, situated on a rocky spur, is a small, recently founded archaeological park, known for its intricate landscape of wind-sculpted rocks. This same site was inhabited in prehistoric times. During the first week of September, the feast days of Sant'Antonio, San Michele and Sant'Isidoro are celebrated with a procession. Decorated oxen and tractors follow the statues of the saints through the streets.

ENVIRONS: 2 km (1 mile) away is the artificial lake of Liscia, capable of holding 150,000,000 cubic m (5 billion cubic ft) of water.

Calangianus ⓫

Road map C2. 🏘 *4,706.* 🚍 ℹ *Pro Loco (079-66 11 48).* 🎪 *third Sun in Sep: Sant'Isidoro's feast day.*

IN THE FORESTS around the town of Calangianus you can see evidence of cork harvesting everywhere: the barked cork oaks have the characteristic reddish color that will remain until the bark grows again, while the cork sheets themselves are heaped up in large piles to dry.

Calangianus is the cork production center of the Gallura region, and there are numbers of workshops and factories for processing the material. There is also an important trade school whose program focuses on the cultivation of cork oaks and

The artificial lake of Liscia near Calangianus

making the maximum use of cork bark. In September every year Calangianus hosts an exhibition and trade fair of cork oaks and their many by-products, both on an industrial and domestic scale.

In the center of the old town, in a small, isolated square, is the small parish church of Santa Giusta, which was built in the 17th century.

Cork items produced in the Gallura region

ENVIRONS: Near the village of **Luras** (northwest of Calangianus), a series of prehistoric dolmens is open to visitors. To reach the site, go through the village in the direction of Luogosanto and then turn right just before the end of town. At the point where the paved road ends, take the dirt road on the right, which takes you to the **Ladas Dolmen**, the most impressive of them all. It has a rectangular plan, is roofed with two granite slabs, and is 6 m (19 ft) long and 2.20 m (7 ft) wide.

Tempio Pausania ⑫

Road map C2. 🏛 *13,961*. 🚉
ℹ *Pro Loco (079-63 12 73).*

THE CAPITAL OF Gallura, Tempio Pausania consists of a large number of modern buildings, which tend to obscure the charming old town. Investigate further and discover two- and three-story buildings with dark granite stone walls and characteristic balconies. A short walk from the central Piazza Gallura, site of the town hall and other public buildings, is the **Cathedral** – founded in the 15th century but rebuilt in the 1800s. Also nearby are the Oratorio del Rosario and the small **Santa Croce** church, all well worth seeing.

Detail of Santa Croce

Not far from town are the **Rinaggiu springs**, whose mineral water is famous for its beneficial qualities. As well as the traditional festivals, an international folklore festival is held here in July.

ENVIRONS: A short distance away, on state road SS133, is the turn-off for the **Maiori Nuraghe**, one of the best preserved megalithic structures in the area.

By heading south from the town on state road 392 for 17 km (10 miles) you will pass close to the summit of **Monte Limbara** (1,359 m, 4,459 ft), which can be reached in a few minutes on foot from the paved road.

Along the way you will see the Curadoreddu road house (about 6 km, 4 miles, from Tempio Pausania); here, a left turn will take you to an abandoned fish farm, from which you can admire an impressive view of mountain rock pools and waterfalls. Water flows from one great mass of rocks to the other, creating cascades and hollows. The spectacle is at its most striking during the winter months.

The bed of the mountain stream near Curadoreddu

CORK AND THE HANDICRAFTS OF GALLURA

Cork is obtained from the stripped bark of cork oak trees *(Quercus suber)* and has always been a fundamental part of the Gallura regional economy. The material is used for everyday purposes as well as local handicrafts. Among kitchen utensils in use are cork spoons and ladles (such as the *s'uppu*, a small ladle used to collect water), buckets and different containers for water and wine, and large serving dishes – called *agiones* in dialect – for roasts and other dishes. Today the Tempio Pausania region produces 90 percent of the bottle stoppers used in Italy, although the cork is also used as a building and insulating material. Cork is very versatile, thanks to its lightness, impermeability to air and water, its insulating properties, and long life.

Strips of cork bark ready for processing

Cork cannot be stripped before the tree is at least 25–30 years old. The first layer stripped is porous and elastic and of little commercial use. Only nine to ten years after this first barking process is the true – and profitable – new layer of cork obtained. The trees are then stripped every nine to ten years and the layers thoroughly seasoned before use.

A barked cork oak tree

The Valle della Luna (Valley of the Moon) near Aggius

Aggius ⑬

Road map C1. 🚶 1,776. 📍 Pro Loco (079-62 04 88). 🎉 first Sun in Oct: feast days of Santa Vittoria and Madonna del Rosario.

NATURAL FEATURES have shaped this village and its surroundings. A granite outcrop dominates the landscape of Aggius, both in the high ground of the Parco Capitza, which towers over the town, and in the amazing labyrinth of rock formations in the nearby Valle della Luna.

Once the dominion of the Doria family from Genoa, and then ruled by the Aragonese, Aggius owes its present prosperity to the quarrying and processing of granite. Local crafts are also important to the economy – especially rug making, every stage of which is carried out using traditional techniques.

The center of Aggius is a pleasant place to walk thanks to the loving care with which the old stone houses have been preserved; they are among the most attractive in the Gallura region. On the first Sunday in October traditional festivities are held, including the *di li 'agghiani*, for unmarried men, at which the Gallura *suppa cuata* (bread and cheese soup) is served.

The road to Isola Rossa quickly brings you to the **Valle della Luna**, with its weird rock formations, the result of glaciation.

On a left-hand curve a dirt road veers right. Follow this almost up to the bridge, then continue along the small road on the right, which leads to the **Izzana Nuraghe** in the middle of the valley.

Rock formations above Aggius

Berchidda ⑭

Road map C2. 🚶 3,333. 🚉 📍 Town Hall (079-70 46 90).

BUILT ON THE SOUTHERN slopes of Monte Limbara, in a hilly landscape that stretches as far as Monte Azzarina, Berchidda is a large village whose economy is based on sheep raising, dairy products, cork processing, and viticulture. The leading local wine is Vermentino (one of the best known of Sardinian white wines), and the local pecorino cheese is also of excellent quality.

About 4 km (2 miles) from the center of Berchidda, a steep climb will take you to the ruins of the **Castello di Montacuto**, which was the fortress of Adelasia di Torres and her husband Ubaldo Visconti before becoming the domain of the Doria and Malaspina families from the mainland. Monte Limbara, the geographical heart of the Gallura region, towers in the background.

Cheese and white Vermentino wine, locally made produce from Berchidda

Buddusò ⑮

Road map C2 & D2. 🚶 6,399. 📍 Town Hall (0789-21 453).

THE TOWN OF Buddusò is fairly prosperous, thanks to sheep farming, granite quarrying, and the processing and sale of cork.

The stone-paved streets in the old part of town wind around buildings made of dark stone. In the Roman era the main road from Kàralis

(Cagliari) to Olbia crossed the town, then known as Caput Thirsi. The church of **Santa Anastasia** and the paintings in the sacristy are worth a visit. A tour through the **Monti di Alà** is another worthwhile excursion.

ENVIRONS: Nearby are the **Iselle Nuraghe** (toward Pattada) and **Loelle Nuraghe**, on the road to Mamone.

A *cuile*, or shepherd's hut

San Teodoro 16

Road map D2. 2,889.
Azienda Autonoma Soggiorno di Olbia (0789-21 453).

To the south of the Capo Coda Cavallo headland, just opposite the rocky island of Tavolara, the village of San Teodoro has grown rapidly in recent years due to increasing numbers of tourists.

The village also makes an excellent starting point for excursions to the Cinta beach, a long strip of sandy terrain that separates the **Stagno di San Teodoro** from the sea. Fairly close to the Orientale

THE ISLAND OF TAVOLARA

This island is a mountain of limestone rising from the sea to a height of 500 m (1,640 ft). The eastern side is an inaccessible military zone, but the low sandy area called Spalmatore di Terra has beaches, a small harbour, a couple of restaurants and a few houses. Together with the neighbouring islands of Molara and Molarotto, home to over 150 mouflons, Tavolara is due to become a marine reserve. The granite cliffs are pierced by caves and crevices. Sea lilies grow in the Spalmatore di Terra area and the rock is covered with juniper, helichrysum, rosemary and lentiscus. According to tradition, Carlo Alberto, the king of Piedmont and Sardinia, landed on the island to find the legendary "goats with golden teeth" (a phenomenon caused by a grass they eat), and was so fascinated by the island that he officially dubbed its only inhabitant, Paolo Bertolini, "king of Tavolara". In the summer there is a regular boat service to the island from Olbia *(see p142)*.

The unmistakable profile of the island of Tavolara

Sarda road, this large 494-acre lake and marsh is one of the few remaining coastal marshes that once lay south of the Bay of Olbia. Mallards and coots are easily sighted on the water. When the birds glimpse a bird of prey or some other danger, they gather in large groups and make loud noises to defend themselves. Gray and red heron as well as Kentish plovers can be seen searching for food, and another common sight is the hovering kestrel, one of Italy's smallest raptors.

Granite outcrops are used as a resting place by ducks.

Kestrel

The clear, still water is rich in food for birds.

Gray heron

The shores are ideal for mud-dwelling creatures.

Lapwing

The Stagno di San Teodoro

The village of Alà dei Sardi

Alà dei Sardi ⑰

Road map D2. 🏛 *1,981.*
🅸 *Buddusò Town Hall
(079-71 40 03).* 🎉 *Oct 4: countryside feast day of San Francesco.*

ROCKS AND MAQUIS and
forests of enormous cork
oaks with the characteristic
marks of recent peeling make
up the landscape of Alà dei
Sardi and its plateau, the last
tract of the rocky interior
overlooking the Bay of Olbia.
    The main street of the
village is lined with the
small granite stone houses
characteristic of this region.

ENVIRONS: Not far from Alà
dei Sardi, off the road which
leads to Buddusò, is the **Ruju
nuraghe**, with the remains of
a prehistoric village almost
buried in the scrub.

Following signs to the town
of Monti, the route crosses a
large plateau studded with
astonishingly varied rock
formations. At a fork, the
road deviates for the
sanctuary of San Pietro
l'Eremita and passes
through some stunning
scenery, with gaps
allowing occasional
views of the sea and
the unmistakable
profile of the island of
Tavolara *(see p153)* in
the distance. The
Romanesque church of
San Pietro l'Eremita
has been restored
relatively recently.
Every year in August
at Ferragosto
(Assumption Day), the
church is crowded
with pilgrims from the
surrounding villages.

Pattada ⑱

Road map C2. 🏛 *3,724.*
🅸 *Buddusò Town Hall (079-71 40
03).* 🎉 *Aug 29: Santa Sabina.*

SITUATED IN THE middle of a
territory rich in prehistoric
nuraghi and other vestiges of
the past, Pattada is world-
famous for the production of
steel knives, which began
here because of a rich vein of
iron ore that has been
worked for centuries. The
village blacksmiths still carry
on the tradition of making
steel blades, and handles
from animal horn. Dozens of

The Sa Fraigada forest near Pattada

THE KNIVES OF PATTADA

The best-known style of shepherd's knife
made in Pattada is the *resolza* (the word
derives from the Latin *rasoria*, or razor). The
resolza is a jackknife with a steel blade that
may be as much as 14 cm (5 inches) long.
The blacksmiths of Pattada only use
traditional materials. Steel is hammered into shape in a
forge and on an anvil; the handle is made from wood or
from moufflon, sheep, or deer horn. The production of
Pattada knives dates from the mid-19th century, and the

Sheath

The handles are
made of wood
or horn.

The blade is
made of hand-
wrought steel.

best knives are
still handmade
by skilled
craftsmen.
Among the masters at work today some, like
Salvatore Giagu and Maria Rosaria Deroma,
draw inspiration from the oldest types of
Pattada knives, such as the fixed-blade *corrina*,
which dates back to the 18th century. It is not
easy to find real Pattada knives for sale, and you
should avoid imitations. Production is a slow
and complicated affair, but it is possible to
order a custom-made Pattada knife, although
this procedure will take about a year.

An assortment of Pattada knives

The artificial lake created by the Rio Mannu at Pattada

imitations of these famous Sardinian knives can now be found on the Italian mainland.

ENVIRONS: In the vicinity of Pattada is the **Fiorentini** – an area of greenery resulting from reforestation – and the ruins of the medieval castle of Olomene.

Ozieri ⑲

Road map C2. 🏘 11,782. 🚏
ℹ️ Pro Loco (079-77 00 77) or Comunità Montana del Monte Acuto (079-78 61 13). 🎉 second Sun in May: Sant'Antioco di Bisarcio.

O ZIERI LIES in a natural hollow, and its position is one of the most attractive sights in northeast Sardinia. Both the traditions and archi-tecture here are interesting, and the town has a fascinating history that goes back millennia and has added to the knowledge of the remote pre-nuraghic cultures that developed in Ozieri.

The fabric and layout of the town are quite varied and blend in well with the slopes of the hills. Among the tall houses the occasional covered roof terrace filled with flowers can be glimpsed.

The major sights in the old town are **Piazza Carlo Alberto** and **Piazza Fonte Grixoni**, centered around an ancient fountain. On the edge of the historic quarter is the Neo-Classical **cathedral**, which contains a splendid 16th-century Sardinian polyptych by the painter

known as the Maestro di Ozieri. The painting depicts the famous miracle of the Sanctuary of the Madonna of Loreto and reveals Spanish influences as well as traces of Flemish mannerism. The 17th-century San Francesco monastery houses the **Museo Archeologico**, with finds from the archaeological digs in the area. Most of this material belongs to the era of the Ozieri civilization, the predominant culture here from 3500 to

Earthenware found in the Grotta di San Michele

2700 BC. It is also known as San Michele, from the name of the cave where the most important material was found.

The territory surrounding Ozieri is also rich in historic and archaeological sites and ruins, such as the *domus de janas* at Butule, the San Pantaleo necropolis, and the dolmen at Montiju Coronas.

The **Grotta di San Michele** is a cave that lies behind the Ozieri hospital, near the track and field stadium (in fact, during the construction of the stadium, part of the cave was destroyed). Large quantities of decorated ceramics were found here as well as human bones, a mother-goddess statuette, and pieces of obsidian from Monte Arci.

All these finds support the theory that there was some continuity from the earlier Bonu Ighinu culture to the time of the Ozieri.

🏛 **Museo Archeologico di Ozieri**
Piazza Canonico Spano.
📞 079-78 76 38. ⏰ 9am–1pm, 4–7pm Tue–Sat; 9:30am–12.30pm Sun.
Grotta di San Michele, Ozieri Hospital.
🎟 combined ticket for both sites.

Terraces of houses climbing the slopes of the town of Ozieri

Tour of the Logudoro ⑳

Detail, Sant'Antioco di Bisarcio

AFTER THE FALL of the Roman Empire, Sardinia did not return to a central role in the Mediterranean until after the year 1000, when Pisan and Genoese merchants, soldiers, and preachers came into contact with the different regional cultures of the island. The Romanesque churches in the north of Sardinia are the result of these encounters. It is difficult to assess how much of each single monument was created by local artists and artisans and how much by those from Pisa and Genoa. Whatever the facts, east of Sassari there are many Romanesque churches that are unequaled in the rest of mainland Italy.

Nostra Signora di Tergu ⑦
This church was built over the remains of a monastery founded by monks from Montecassino in Tuscany.

Santissima Trinità di Saccargia ①
The Santissima Trinità, built in striped layers of black and white stone, is the most significant example of Romanesque architecture in northern Sardinia. The apse is decorated with frescoes of Christ and the saints. The church was restored in the early 1900s (*see pp158–9*).

San Michele di Salvènero (Ploaghe) ②
In the 12th century the monks of Vallombrosa built this church near the village of Salvènero, which has since disappeared. The church now stands abandoned in the middle of a series of crossroads. Restored in the 13th century and again in 1912, this splendid monument needs to attract greater care and respect to safeguard its future.

Santa Maria del Regno (Ardara) ③
Santa Maria was consecrated in 1107, and is different from the Pisan Romanesque churches. The facade faces south, perhaps to soften the severity of the dark stone and squat bell tower.

Castelsardo

N200

N134

N132

Nuraghe di Cannarzu

N672

Ploaghe

N131

N597

San Pietro di Simbranos (or delle Immagini) ⑥

The traditional name of this church derives from the bas-relief on the facade depicting an abbot and two monks (the *immagini* or "images"). San Pietro, in the Bulzi area, was first built in 1113 and rebuilt in its present form a century later. This isolated and tranquil monument has a particular fascination because of its desertlike setting among canyons and rocks.

┌─────────────────────────────────────┐

VISITORS' CHECKLIST

Road map C2.
**Santissima Trinità di Saccargia
and Sant'Antioco di Bisarcio**
☐ *normal opening hours;* **San
Michele di Salvènero** ⬤
Nostra Signora di Castro
☐ *variable, the cumbessias
precinct can be visited;* **Santa
Maria del Regno di Ardara,**
inquire at priest's house; **Nostra
Signora di Tergu** ⬤ *can usually
only be seen from outside;*
San Pietro di Simbranos ☐
*normal opening hours, or ask
Bulzi parish priest.*

└─────────────────────────────────────┘

Nostra Signora di Castro (Oschiri) ⑤

Dominating Lake Coghìnas, this church blends Lombard and local architectural elements. It was built in the second half of the 12th century and is surrounded by the *cumbessias* enclosure of pilgrims' houses, built at a later date.

(Map showing Lago di Castel Doria, Pérfugas, Coghìnas, Monte Sassu, Lago di Coghìnas, Oschiri, Ozieri, Ardara, with roads N132, N597)

0 kilometers 5
0 miles 5

Sant'Antioco di Bisarcio (Ozieri) ④

Sant'Antioco is a combination of Pisan Romanesque and French influences. Sant'Antioco was built from the second half of the 11th century to the late 12th century and was initially the cathedral of the Bisarcio diocese. It differs from the other churches on this tour in its architectural complexity, shown in the unusual two-story porch, small windows, and the decorative detail on the facade.

KEY

▬	Tour
▬	Highway
=	Other roads
—	River

Santissima Trinità di Saccargia ㉑

Portico frieze

BOTH SIMPLE and impressive, Sardinia's most famous Romanesque church stands in the middle of a windswept valley. Its name probably derives from *sa acca argia*, "the dappled cow." According to legend, this animal used to kneel in prayer on the site, which is why there are carvings of the cow on four sides of one of the capitals in the portico. Another account relates how, around the year 1112, the ruler of the region, Constantine, donated the small church to the Camaldolesi monks, who then decided to enlarge it with the help of Tuscan architects, craftsmen, and laborers. Initially they added the apse and the bell tower with its alternating layers of black trachyte and white limestone. At a later stage they built the porch, the only one on a Sardinian church. The austere interior, with a tall, narrow nave lit by small openings or slots in the side walls, is very atmospheric.

Animal frieze
The severity of the exterior of the church is lightened with sculptures of animals.

★ The Facade
Two rows of blind arches adorn the facade, each level decorated with rose windows and multi-colored diamonds. The central arch has an opening in the form of a cross.

The campanile
is 41 m (134 ft) tall and each side is 8 m (26 ft) wide.

★ The Carved Cows
It may be that the church was named after the carved cows on this capital, even though the portico was built after the main church.

Double-lancet Windows
These date from the late 12th century.

The black and white stripes reveal Pisan influence.

Monastery Ruins
Only a few black and white stone archways are left of the first and most important Camaldolese monastery in Sardinia.

Fresco of Christ
Christ is depicted holding a book in the act of benediction.

★ The Apse Frescoes
Romanesque frescoes are rare in Sardinia – these are attributed to Pisan artists.

The aisleless nave was built after the apse, which dates from 1116.

The Portico Capitals
The portico is supported by columns with carved capitals. They carry the classic Romanesque motifs of plants and animals.

STAR FEATURES

★ The Apse Frescoes

★ The Facade

★ The Carved Cows

Sassari ❷

Coat of arms of Sassari

Sardinia's second most important city commercially, politically and culturally, Sassari lies on a tableland that slopes down to the sea among olive groves and fertile and well-cultivated valleys. The city has a long history of invasions, conquests, and raids but also holds a tradition of stubborn rebellion and uprisings. Pisans, Genoese, and Aragonese have all attempted to subdue the city, but the indómitable spirit of the Sassari citizens has always succeeded in asserting independence. The city's hero is a rebel named Carlo Maria Angioj, who headed a revolt in 1796 against the Savoyard government, which had sought to impose a feudal system. Two presidents of the Italian Republic, Antonio Segni and Francesco Cossiga, were born in Sassari as was the prominent Communist Party leader Enrico Berlinguer.

The *Li Candareri* festival in Sassari

Exploring Sassari

The old town, with its winding alleyways branching off from the main streets, was once surrounded by walls that ran along present-day Corso Vico, Corso Trinità, Via Brigata Sassari, and Corso Margherita. Only a few parts of the city walls (such as the section at the beginning of Corso Trinità) have survived the effects of time, but the old center has preserved its original layout, even though it is now somewhat dilapidated.

A morning should be enough for a walk around the old town. The main sights are the Duomo (cathedral), the Fontana del Rosello fountain, the churches of Sant'Antonio, Santa Maria di Betlem and San Pietro in Silki, and the Sanna museum.

⛪ Duomo

Piazza Duomo. 🕻 *079-23 20 67.*
⏰ *8am–noon, 3.30–8pm daily.*
Sassari cathedral is dedicated to San Nicola (St. Nicholas). Its impressive Baroque facade is in rather striking contrast to its size and to the small, simple and elegant 18th-century Piazza Duomo with

its characteristic semicircular shape. The end result of successive enlargements and changes carried out over the centuries, the Duomo was originally built on the site of a Romanesque church. The base of the facade and bell tower are still intact.

At the end of the 15th century the original structure underwent radical transformation that not only changed its shape but created today's unusual proportions. The side walls were propped up by buttresses decorated with gargoyles of mythical and monstrous animals, while the interior was rebuilt in the Gothic style.

In the late 18th century the upper portion of the facade was radically changed with the addition of some grandiose decoration: volutes, flowers, cherubs, and fantastic figures. In the middle, the statue of San Nicola is surmounted by the figures of the three martyr saints, Gavino, Proto, and Gianuario, set in three niches. At a later stage, an octagonal section decorated with multicolored majolica tiles was superimposed on the original Lombard-style lower part of the campanile. The interior, which has been totally restored, has retained its simple Gothic lines despite the presence of lavishly decorated Baroque altars. The choir, the work of 18th-century Sardinian artists, is particularly striking.

The Museo del Duomo, reached through the Cappella Aragonese (Aragonese chapel) on the right, houses the processional standard, a panel painting by an

Detail of the facade of Sassari Cathedral

The Fontana del Rosello, dating from the Renaissance

VISITORS' CHECKLIST

Road map B2. 121,889.
Ente Provinciale Turismo, Viale Caprera 36 (079-29 95 44 or 29 95 46).
last Sun of month: Antiques Show in Piazza Santa Caterina; Easter Week: Maggio Sassarese; penultimate Sun in May: Cavalcata Sarda; Aug: 14 Festa de li Candareri.

anonymous 15th-century artist. There is also a silver statue of San Gavino, embossed using a Mexican technique that was in fashion in the late 17th century.

▓ Fontana del Rosello
Via Col di Lana.
On the right-hand side of the church of Santissima Trinità, in Piazza Mercato, a small stone stairway known as the Col di Lana will take you to the Fontana del Rosello, the fountain at the lower end of

the Valverde gorge. Very little remains of the steep valley and woods that were once the natural backdrop for this little jewel of late Renaissance art. However, this lack has not diminished the locals' love for their fountain.

This was once the haunt of the enlightened bourgeoisie and the place where the local water-carriers drew water from the eight lions' mouths at the base of the fountain. It has become one of the city's

favorite symbols. The fountain was created in the early 1600s by Genoese artists, who still had a preference for the classical styles of the Renaissance.

The base consists of two white and green marble boxes. The lions' mouths are surrounded by statues symbolizing the four seasons (the originals were destroyed in the 1795–6 uprisings).

In the middle, a bearded divinity, known as Giogli, is surrounded by small towers symbolizing the city. On the top of the fountain are two arches that protect the figure of San Gavino.

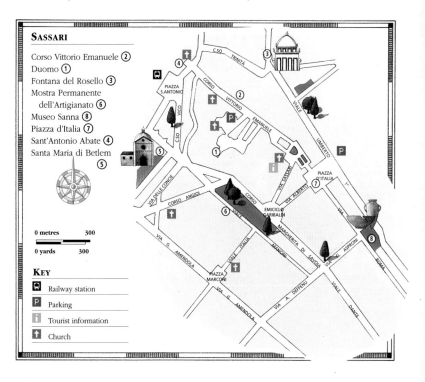

SASSARI

Corso Vittorio Emanuele ②
Duomo ①
Fontana del Rosello ③
Mostra Permanente dell'Artigianato ⑥
Museo Sanna ⑧
Piazza d'Italia ⑦
Sant'Antonio Abate ④
Santa Maria di Betlem ⑤

0 metres 300
0 yards 300

KEY

🚊 Railway station
🅿 Parking
ℹ Tourist information
✝ Church

🔒 Sant'Antonio Abate

Piazza Sant'Antonio. 📞 *079-26 00 24.* ⏰ *8–10am, 4:30–6pm daily.*

Dating from the early 1700s, the stately Baroque facade of this church, with its simple elegance and harmonious proportions, dominates the tree-lined square at the end of Corso Trinità.

The upper part of the portal still bears the emblem of the brotherhood responsible for building the church. The Latin cross interior has one of the most elegant high altars in Sassari, which bears a carved and gilded wooden altar-piece. The panels were executed in the late 18th century by the Genoese painter Bartolomeo Augusto.

The church stands in Piazza Sant'Antonio, once the site of the old northern gate of the same name, and formerly the hub of the city's commercial and political life. The only vestiges of the past are a part of the medieval city walls, and a battlemented tower to the left of the church.

🔒 Santa Maria di Betlem

Piazza Santa Maria. ⏰ *7:30am–noon, 5–7pm daily.*

The church of Santa Maria di Betlem is situated in the square of the same name, at the northwestern entrance to the city. Built by Benedictine monks in 1106, it was later donated to the Franciscans. Unfortunately, the elegant original structure was the subject of frequent rebuilding in the 18th and 19th centuries, and the church has lost its early qualities of light-ness and purity of form. The only intact part of the earlier church

The Romanesque church of San Pietro in Silki, Sassari

is the 13th-century facade, decorated with small columns and capitals and pierced by a lovely 15th-century rose window. The Gothic interior, once austere, has been spoiled by the heavy-handed Baroque decoration and altars; yet the original side chapels are intact, each dedicated to a craftsmen's guild as a reminder of the social role the church played in the community. To this day, on August 14, the date of the *De li Candareri* festivities, the votive candles donated by the various guilds are carried here in procession from the Chiesa del Rosario.

Detail of an Art Nouveau style house

The cloister is partly walled in but can still be visited. It contains the 14th-century granite stone Brigliadore fountain, once the source of most of Sassari's water supply.

🔒 San Pietro in Silki

Via delle Croci. 📞 *079-21 60 67.* ⏰ *6:30am–noon, 3:30–6pm daily.*

The Romanesque church of San Pietro in Silki faces a lovely tree-lined square and

was most probably named after the medieval quarter built here in the 1100s. Its simple 17th-century facade has a large atrium leading to the Gothic nave with four side chapels. The first of these was dedicated to the Madonna delle Grazie in the second half of the 15th century. It is named for a statue of the Virgin Mary, found inside a column from the square in front of the church. The statue is one of the best examples of Catalan Gothic sculpture in Sardinia.

On the other side of the square, opposite San Pietro, is the Frati Minori monastery, which houses one of the island's richest libraries. The collections consist of over 14,000 volumes, removed from Franciscan monasteries after their closure.

🏛 Corso Vittorio Emanuele

The city's main street crosses the heart of the old town and connects Piazza Sant'Antonio and Piazza Cavallino. The Corso is lined with 19th-century houses and 16th-century Aragonese buildings, and you can often catch a glimpse of courtyards and interiors that testify to their former splendor. This is Sassari's main shopping street, with stores of all kinds, from clothing to hardware.

🏛 Mostra Permanente dell'Artigianato

Viale Mancini. 📞 *079-23 01 01.* ⏰ *9am–1pm, 4:30–7:30pm Mon–Sat.*

Facing the Emiciclo Garibaldi public gardens, a shop in a modern building houses the Permanent Exhibition of

The church of Santa Maria di Betlem in Sassari

Sardinian Handicrafts, a collection of the best work from the island's various crafts cooperatives. The large rooms overlook an inner garden, which allows light into the display cases housing the most precious objects. These include filigree necklaces and earrings, coral jewelry designed according to old drawings, and pottery and ceramics created using traditional techniques.

Hanging on the walls are traditional Sardinian rugs, which resemble abstract paintings with their geometric patterns. There is also fine bobbin lacework and – still interesting though not so valuable – baskets of dwarf palm wood, terra-cotta pots and other everyday objects whose design and techniques have been handed down over centuries of tradition.

⛫ Museo Archeologico Nazionale "GA Sanna"

Via Roma. ☎ 0781-835 90.
🕐 9am–1pm, 3:30–7pm daily. 🖼
🚻 ♿

The Sassari archaeological museum was donated to the Italian state by the Sanna family, who built the premises in 1931 to house finds collected by Giovanni Antonio Sanna, an important figure in the island's history and director of the local mine.

Two entire floors are given over to various periods of Sardinian civilizations, from the Neolithic to the Middle Ages. Arrowheads, nuraghic bronze statuettes, amphoras, furnishings, weapons, tools,

Entrance to the Museo Nazionale "GA Sanna" in Sassari

ceramics, and jewels are on display in chronological order. On the ground floor, panels illustrate the evolution of Sardinia, and every room has time charts on display.

There are also architectural reconstructions of prehistoric buildings such as dwellings, *domus de janas* (rock-cut tombs), and giants' tombs. In the last hall, among floor plans, sarcophagi, and statues there is a reconstructed mosaic floor from a patrician Roman villa in nearby Turris Libisonis (present-day Porto Torres). The mosaic shows lobsters, sea horses, and seals chasing one another in an eternal circle. The next room contains a small art gallery with works by Sardinian artists from the 14th to the 20th centuries.

There is also a traditional crafts section of four rooms with jewels, costumes, musical instruments, and craftsmen's tools, almost all of which are still used in central-northern Sardinia.

♙ Piazza d'Italia

This large square is laid out at the edge of the 19th-century quarter of Sassari. It is a well-proportioned public space, surrounded by elegant Neo-Classical buildings and with tall palm trees and well-kept flower beds, guarded by a statue of Vittorio Emanuele II.

One of the finest buildings is the Palazzo della Provincia (provincial government building), built in pure Neo-Classical style. The council chamber on the first floor is open to the public. On the walls are 19th-century paintings depicting important events in the city's political history, such as *The Proclamation of the Sassari Statutes* and *Carlo Maria Angioj Entering Sassari*. You can also see the adjacent royal apartments, built in 1884 for the occasion of the King of Sardinia's visit. In summer the courtyard is used for concerts and plays.

The lovely 19th-century Bargone and Crispi arcades on the northwestern side of Piazza d'Italia shelter the city's oldest bars and *pasticcerie* (pastry shops) and lead to Piazza Castello.

♟ Santa Caterina

Via Santa Caterina. ☎ 0781-23 16 92. 🕐 pm for mass.
This church was built at the end of the 16th century for the Jesuits and combines Sardinian Gothic style with Renaissance elements.

In the interior there are paintings by the artist Giovanni Bilevelt.

Sassari's Piazza d'Italia, framed by the Neo-Classical Palazzo della Provincia

The harbor at Castelsardo

Castelsardo ㉓

Road map C2. 🏚 *5,017.* 🛈 *Pro Loco (079-47 15 00).* 🎭 *Easter Monday: Lunissanti procession.*

PERCHED ON a volcanic headland, Castelsardo has known a number of name changes in its history. The town was founded in 1102 by the aristocratic Doria family from Genoa and was originally known as Castelgenovese, a name it kept until 1448, when it became Castellaragonese, after the town's new conquerors. The present name of Castelsardo dates from 1776.

The town is dominated by the castle (**Castello**), which now houses a museum with exhibits of traditional basketweaving. Overlooking the sea is the cathedral of Sant'Antonio Abate.

Local basketwork

The alleyways of the center of town are lined with small shops selling all kinds of local crafts. Fish-lovers will do well here, as the local cuisine is based on freshly caught fish and lobsters.

On Easter Monday, the traditional **Lunissanti** procession is held in Castelsardo. The streets are lit by flaming torches, and traditional hooded figures form a slow procession, to the sound of three songs, *Lu Stabat, Lu Jesu,* and *Lu Miserere.* These songs are centuries ol, and probably date from before Catalan rule. They have been handed down by word of mouth ever since. The solemn procession, one of the most famous of Sardinia's Easter festivals, ends at the church of **Santa Maria**.

🏯 **Castello and Museo dell'Intreccio**
Via Marconi. ⭘ *9am–1pm, 2–5pm (Apr–Oct: 9am–midnight) daily.* 🎟
This fortress was built in the 13th and 14th centuries. The place is now occupied by the **Museo dell'Intreccio** (museum of wickerwork). Local baskets are made from traditional materials such as palm, cane, and asphodel. From the castle terraces there are lovely views of the Golfo dell'Asinara, and on clear days you can even see the hills on Corsica.

Sant'Antonio Abate in Castelsardo

🏛 **Cattedrale di Sant'Antonio Abate**
Via Seminario. ⭘ *8am–6pm daily.*
Constructed in the 17th century on the site of an existing Romanesque church, the cathedral has a bell tower roofed with majolica tiles. From the tower there is a splendid view of the water below. The cathedral contains fine 16th-century carved wooden furnishings.

The town of Castelsardo and the castle above

The Roccia dell'Elefante (Elephant Rock) near Castelsardo

The village is not an island (*isola*) but was given its name ("red island") after the small, reddish-colored rock island out in the bay. Fishing boats are drawn up on the beach below the village after each day's catch is brought in.

The coastline either side of Isola Rossa is worth visiting, especially toward the east, where Monte Tinnari overlooks the sea. To the west, the coast gently slopes to meet the mouth of the Rio Coghina, a short distance from Castelsardo.

Santa Maria
Via Vittorio Emanuele. ☐ *ask priest for keys.*
In the heart of the old town, the upper part of Castelsardo, stands the church of Santa Maria. The building does not have a facade, and entry is gained through the side door. In the interior is a 14th-century crucifix known as the *Cristo Nero* (Black Christ). The church is the focus of the Lunissanti Easter procession, which starts and ends here.

La Roccia dell'Elefante
To one side of the road near Multeddu, not far from Castelsardo, stands the impressive Roccia dell'Elefante (Elephant Rock). This massive block of dark trachyte rock has been gradually sculpted by the wind into the shape of an elephant with its trunk raised. In ancient times the rock was used as a burial place. At the base you can still see small carved openings for several *domus de janas* (rock-cut tombs).

Isola Rossa ㉔

Road map C1.

THE HILLS of Gallura slope down toward the sea, forming a landscape characterized by rose-colored crags, sculpted into strange shapes by wind erosion. The small fishing village of Isola Rossa lies on a headland, at the foot of an impressive 16th-century sentinel tower.

The fishing fleet at Isola Rossa

ENVIRONS: A short distance from Isola Rossa is the small agricultural town of **Trinità d'Agultu**, which developed in the late 19th century around the church of the same name. As is so often the case in Sardinia, the simple country church became a sanctuary and pilgrimage site. As a result, it is also an important trade and commercial center during the associated religious festivities and pilgrimages.

THE FISHING INDUSTRY

The Sardinians are historically a nation of shepherds. Despite this, fishing is still an important activity, even though for centuries it has been carried out almost exclusively by non-Sardinian immigrants: people from the island of Ponza at Castelsardo, and Neapolitans, who founded the village of Isola Rossa in the early 20th century. Today an important source of income in these two places is the cultivation of mussels and shellfish. Tuna fishing, once widespread off the northwest coast, no longer survives in Sardinia, the small trawlers unable to compete with deep-sea fishing, now practiced on an industrial scale.

Craftsman at work making a lobster pot

TRAVELERS' NEEDS

WHERE TO STAY

THE LEGENDARY ALLURE of the beaches in Sardinia has resulted in a boom in tourist facilities, especially along the coast, and visitors can now choose from a wide range of hotels and resort villages. The exclusive and world-famous hotels built in the Costa Smeralda in the early 1960s cater to the wealthy, but it is not difficult to find less expensive accommodations. You can find luxury hotels and resorts in the south, while the western coast offers reliable family-run lodgings. On the eastern coast, comfortable and well-equipped tourist villages are easily found, many offering efficiencies as an option. There are some excellent hotels in the interior, especially in the Gennargentu and Barbagia areas, where you can also take advantage of organized tours and hikes. For more information, listings, and descriptions of hotels, farm vacations, and resort villages, turn to page 171 and pages 174–7.

Logo of ESIT, the Sardinian Tourist Board

The Hotel Torre Moresca at Cala Ginepro, Orosei *(see p175)*

GRADES OF HOTEL

HOTELS IN SARDINIA are graded on a star-rating system, from one star, which stands for minimum comfort and service, to five stars for luxury accommodations. The four-star category offers first-class service without the very high prices of five-star hotels. Three-star lodgings, especially family-run establishments, sometimes offer better value for your money, but this is generally the exception rather than the rule.

Most Sardinian hotels also have a restaurant which is usually open to nonresidents as well. The majority of hotels, whatever their category, provide a range of facilities. Along the coast, for example, hotels are likely to offer beach equipment such as umbrellas and deckchairs.

RESORT VILLAGES

THE RESORT VILLAGES OF Sardinia, mostly situated on or near the coast, offer a variety of types of accommodations. The choice varies from vast establishments with hundreds of rooms and good facilities and service to smaller sites, which may be elegant and expensive. The larger resort villages offer more than one type of lodging within a single site. At Forte Village, for example, there are six different hotels, each in a different style, ranging from the 38-room Le Dune to the 152-room Castello. At some places you can choose between serviced apartments *(residence)* or a normal three- or four-star hotel, with a range of charges. Some of these villages offer all-inclusive packages that even include drinks at the bar. Sardinian resorts often require guests to take half or full board, as do many hotels.

Logo of the Hotel Sporting at Porto Rotondo

In some resorts guests may choose to rent an efficiency apartment or bungalow and then decide whether to have the other services and facilities included in the package. These services usually include the use of sports facilities and entertainment, such as a disco or night club, baby-sitters for those traveling with small children, beach facilities, the swimming pool, and use of the various bars and restaurants. Many villages offer an excellent range of equipment for water sports.

Renting an apartment in a tourist resort is a worthwhile alternative to renting a villa, especially if you plan to be on vacation for less than a month. It allows you to be independent while at the same time giving you access to a range of services and facilities should you find you need them.

For a listing of these resorts see page 171.

A café in the small square at Porto Cervo

The Hotel Victoria at Tortolì, near Arbatax *(see p175)*

PRICES

ITALIAN LAW REQUIRES every hotel to place the National Tourist Board price list, with the maximum prices for the current year, on the door of each room. The prices quoted should never be exceeded. Room prices shown on this list, or quoted by the hotel staff when you reserve, normally include taxes and service. However, it is advisable to check whether breakfast is included, to avoid any misunderstandings.

Hotels on the coast usually require guests to take half or full board. In off season you could try asking for a bed and breakfast rate, but this is unlikely to happen in tourist season. Winter rates are quite different from summer rates: in the summer prices may be as much as double. Hotel prices reach their peak in the two middle weeks of August. This is also true of the tourist villages (except that rates here are calculated on a weekly basis).

The location of your hotel will also affect the price. Hotels, villages and even pensions on the coast are always more expensive than lodgings in the interior.

You may be able to negotiate special rates for groups or for longer stays.

EXTRAS

GENERALLY SPEAKING, you will pay separately for drinks consumed with your meal, anything taken from the mini-bar in your room, room service, and telephone calls. A word of warning: phone calls in particular can be subject to very high surcharges.

In some cases air-conditioning may be charged as an extra. Glimpses of Sardinia's lovely coast may also be regarded as chargeable, and you may pay extra for rooms with a view. It is always a good idea to check on extras like this when reserving or choosing your room.

OFF SEASON

IF YOU PLAN TO GO to Sardinia in any season other than summer, it is a good idea to check beforehand on the availability of accommodations. Most hotels are run on a seasonal basis and tend to open around Easter and close in the autumn. The end of the season may very well depend on such unpredictable circumstances as a sudden turn of bad weather.

BOOKING AND PAYING

IF YOU DECIDE to travel during the summer, especially in the Italian vacation months of July and August, and if you want to stay on the coast, you must book well in advance, since the island is overflowing with visitors in this period. If you are booking your hotel separately from your travel arrangements, you may be asked to send some money as a deposit. This can be done by credit card or international money order. When you arrive at your hotel or village, the person at the reception desk will ask for your passport; this is to register travelers with the police, a legal requirement. You will be given a receipt on checking out, another legal formality.

CAMPING

TOGETHER WITH *agriturismo*, or farm vacations, camping is the most inexpensive way of staying on the island. Sardinia has a number of good campsites, some of which are located in quiet areas with lovely views. Most of them are situated along the coast, often in eucalyptus or pine woods. There are far fewer sites in the interior.

Campsites, like hotels, get extremely crowded in the summer. If you are traveling around and have not booked in advance, you need to start looking for a place to stay as early as noon.

Some campsites also have a small number of bungalows with a bathroom and kitchen area, but the prices can be very expensive.

Most Sardinian campsites are open from Easter to October. Some may be open for the Christmas period, offering bungalows or heated campers.

Camping outside official sites is strictly forbidden, and camping on the beach is particularly frowned on. You need permission to camp on private property (from the owner), and in state forests.

The Hotel Hieracon, on the island of San Pietro *(see p174)*

The L'Agnata vacation farm at Tempio Pausania

FARM VACATIONS

A FARM VACATION *(agriturismo)* is an excellent way of coming into direct contact with Sardinian customs and traditions. Unlike other regions in Italy, Umbria and Tuscany in particular, Sardinia can offer a genuinely rustic atmosphere. Very few rooms have private bathrooms, though many farm managers are now taking steps to remedy this situation. Farmhouses in Sardinian tend not to be placed in isolated countryside: true to tradition, at least half the farms are in villages. Local farmers and shepherds often live in villages and travel some distance to work the fields or take their sheep to pasture.

The highest concentration of farms offering vacations is found in the provinces of Sassari and Oristano, while there are very few in the Cagliari region. The only drawback – depending on your point of view – might be a certain lack of privacy: everybody eats at the same table, guests and host family alike. You will probably find yourself becoming almost a part of the family before you leave. Meals consist of produce grown on the farm – cheese, meat, vegetables and honey – all cooked according to local tradition. It is an excellent way of getting to know the specialties of the region. In general, farms offer accommodations by the week on a half- or full-board basis. Many of them also organize hikes, horseback riding, and mountain bike and canoe excursions.

VILLA RENTAL

R ENTING A HOUSE for two weeks or a month is the most economical solution for a family or a group of friends who want to spend their entire vacation by the sea. This option is especially recommended for families with small children and babies. Note, however, that the charge for cleaning tends to be the same for a week as for a longer stay.

If you are looking for a house to rent you should contact the local Pro Loco and Azienda di Soggiorno information offices (given in the information for each town in this guide). Tourist offices sometimes offer a specialized service supplying lists of private homes available in the vicinity and their prices. Travel agents and tour companies can also arrange this type of accommodation.

Prices for rental are usually quoted on a weekly basis, and a deposit is normally requested. When you rent a house or apartment it is advisable to ascertain the exact size of the house and number of bedrooms. In some houses the living room also functions as a bedroom. Before signing any contract, also check whether gas, water, electricity, and telephone expenses are part of the rent or are considered "extras." Make a note of the readings on the meters on arrival if these items are extra.

A typical vacation house for rent in the Sulcis region of Sardinia

---

USING THE LISTINGS

The hotels on pages 174–7 are listed according to area and price.

▤ air-conditioning
🛁 all rooms with bath and/or shower
🍸 minibar in room
📺 television in all rooms
🛗 elevator
🌳 garden or terrace
🧒 facilities for children
🅿 hotel parking available
♿ wheelchair access
🍴 restaurant in hotel
🏊 swimming pool
💳 credit cards accepted
AE American Express
MC MasterCard
DC Diners Club
V VISA

Price categories show the maximum per night for a double room with breakfast or, where shown, for half or full board per day and per person.
Ⓛ under L100,000
ⓁⓁ L100,000–200,000
ⓁⓁⓁ L200,000–300,000
ⓁⓁⓁⓁ L300,000–400,000
ⓁⓁⓁⓁⓁ over L400,000.

DIRECTORY

TOURIST OFFICES

ESIT (Ente Sardo Industrie Turistiche)
Via Mameli 97, Cagliari.
070-602 31.
freephone 167 131 53.

RESORT VILLAGES

Club Méditerranée
Caprera,
Isola La Maddalena.
Road map D1.
0789-72 70 78.
FAX 0789-72 74 14.

Club Méditerranée Santa Teresa
Località La Marmorata,
Santa Teresa di Gallura.
Road map C1.
0789-75 15 20.
FAX 0789-75 15 25.

Club Vacanze Cala Moresca
Località Bellavista,
Arbatax.
Road map D4.
0782-66 73 66.
FAX 0782-28 85 00.

Ventaclub Capo Boi
Località Piscadeddus,
Villasimius.
Road map D6.
070-79 80 15.
FAX 070-79 81 16.

Ventaclub Monte Turri
Località Bellavista,
Arbatax.
Road map D4.
0782-66 75 50.
FAX 0782-66 78 92.

Villaggio Valtur
Santo Stefano,
Isola La Maddalena.
Road map D1.
0789-70 85 74.
FAX 0789-70 85 73.

CAMPING

Arcobaleno
Località Porto Pozzo,
Santa Teresa di Gallura.
Road map C1.
0789-75 20 40.

Baia Blu La Tortuga
Località Vignola Mare,
Aglientu (Sassari).
Road map C1.
079-60 20 60.

Baia Chia
Località Chia, Domus De
Maria (Cagliari).
Road map C6.
070-92 30 185.

Cala Fiorita
Località Agrustos,
Budoni (Nuoro).
Road map D2.
0784-84 62 90.

Cala Gonone
Cala Gonone,
Dorgali (Nuoro).
Road map D3.
0784-931 65.

Camping Garden Cala Sinzias
Castiadas,
Cala Sinzias (Cagliari).
Road map D6.
0781-85 21 12.

Europa
Località Torre del Pozzo,
Cuglieri (Oristano).
Road map B3.
0783-380 58.

Is Arenas
Is Arenas (Oristano).
Road map B5.
0783-522 84.

Isola dei Gabbiani
Località Porto Pollo,
Palau.
Road map D1.
0789-70 40 19.
FAX 0789-70 40 77.

La Caletta
Carloforte,
Località La Caletta.
Road map B6.
0781-85 21 12.

L'Isuledda
Località Cannigione,
Arzachena.
Road map D1.
0789-881 01.
FAX 0789-881 01.

Nurapolis
Narbolia (Oristano).
Road map B4.
0783-522 83.

Porto Pirastu
Località Capo Ferrato,
Muravera (Cagliari).
Road map D5.
070-99 14 37.

Senniscedda
Pau (Oristano).
Road map C4.
0783-93 92 81.

Sos Flores
Tortolì, Arbatax (Nuoro).
Road map D4.
0782-66 74 85.

Spiaggia del Riso
Località Campolungo,
Villasimius.
Road map D6.
070-79 10 52.
FAX 010-79 71 50.

Telis
Località Porto Frailis,
Tortolì (Nuoro).
Road map D4.
0782-66 71 40.

FARM VACATION ASSOCIATIONS

Agriturist
Via Bottego 7,
Cagliari.
Road map C6.
070-66 83 30.

Coop. Agrituristica Gallurese
Tenuta Valentino,
Località Calangianus.
Road map C2.
0789-508 81.

Cooperativa Allevatrici Sarde
Via Duomo 17,
Oristano.
Road map B4.
0783-739 54 or
41 80 66.

Terranostra
Via Roma 231, Cagliari.
Road map C6.
070-66 83 67.
FAX 070-66 58 41.

Turismo Verde
Via Libeccio 31, Cagliari.
Road map C6.
070-37 37 33 or
37 39 66.
FAX 070-37 20 28.

FARM VACATIONS

L'Agnata
di Fabrizio De Andrè,
Valle di Baldu,
Tempio Pausania (Sassari).
Road map C2.
079-67 13 84.

Azienda di Gino Camboni
Località L'Annunziata,
Castiadas (Cagliari).
Road map D6.
070-99 49 152.

Azienda di Giovanna Maria Addis
Riu-Riu, Tergu (Sassari).
Road map C2.
079-47 61 24.

Azienda di Lucia Sotgiu
Via Amsicora 9,
Nurachi (Oristano).
Road map B4.
0783-41 02 96.

Cunzadu Mannu
Via Marconi 23,
Burgos (Nuoro).
Road map C3.
070-66 83 67.

La Rosa dei Venti
Località San Pietro,
Castiadas (Cagliari).
Road map D6.
070-66 83 67.

Fenu
Località Sa Tuerra,
Teulada (Cagliari).
Road map C6.
070-92 83 013.

Le Querce
Località Valli di Vatta,
Porto Cervo
(Sassari).
Road map D1.
0789-992 48.

Sa Perda Marcada
Sa Perda Marcada,
Arbus (Cagliari).
Road map B5.
070-66 83 67.

Zeminariu
Zeminariu,
Atzara (Nuoro).
Road map C4.
070-66 83 67.

Sardinia's Best: Hotels

THE MAJORITY OF THE luxury hotels in Sardinia are found in the Gallura region and close to the beaches of the Costa Smeralda. However, there are increasing numbers of smaller hotels in other less famous and much less expensive areas of Sardinia. All the hotels on this map offer something special and are highly recommended for their particularly favorable position along the coast or in the mountains, for architecture that blends in with the landscape, and for excellent service. Reserve well in advance if you plan to visit in tourist season, and note that many hotels close for the winter.

Villa Las Tronas
This seaside villa at Alghero is now a comfortable hotel. All the rooms have views of the coast, and the only "noise" is that of the sea (see p175).

Le Dune
Tucked away among the Piscinas dunes, this hotel occupies two old mine buildings that have been restored with great attention to detail (see p174).

Forte Village
At this seaside vacation village the hotels are surrounded by Mediterranean maquis. Facilities for relaxation are excellent and include thalassotherapy pools (see p174).

Pitrizza
The most exclusive hotel on the Costa Smeralda is located at Liscia di Vacca. The service and facilities are impeccable (see p176).

0 km   20

0 miles   20

Hotel Cala di Volpe
The first hotel to be built on the Costa Smeralda was designed by Jacques Couelle in the 1960s (see p177).

Su Gologone
At the foot of Supramonte di Oliena, this hotel offers decor and cuisine in the best tradition of the Barbagia region as well as the chance to go horseback riding (see p175).

Tanka Village
Surrounded by woods, this resort near Villasimius has the feel of a tropical village. Tanka is perfect for water sports (see p175).

CAGLIARI AND THE SOUTH

ARBUS – INGURTOSU

Le Dune

Road map B5. Località Piscinas.
 070-97 71 30. **FAX** 070-97 72 30.
Rooms: 25. ▤ ⌨ 🍴 P ♿ 🍴
🏊 🍽 MC, V. ⬜ Jan–Dec. ⓛⓛ
half board.

A charming hotel in a recently restored mine building alongside the Piscinas dunes.

CAGLIARI

Calamosca

Road map C6. Viale Calamosca 50.
070-37 02 52. **FAX** 070-37 03 46.
Rooms: 47. ⌨ TV 🍴 P 🍴
🍽 MC, V. ⬜ Jan–Dec. ⓛⓛ

The only hotel in Cagliari right by the beach, 1.5 km (1 mile) from the center of town.

Hotel Mediterraneo

Road map C6. Lungomare Colombo
46. 070-30 12 71. **FAX** 070-30 12
74. **Rooms:** 140. ▤ ⌨ 🍴 TV 🔆
🍴 P ♿ 🍴 🍽 AE, DC, MC, V.
⬜ Jan–Dec. ⓛⓛ

A modern building, just a few minutes' drive from the center of Cagliari and the provincial roads leading to the coast.

Regina Margherita

Road map C6. Viale Regina
Margherita 44. 070-67 03 42.
FAX 070-66 83 25. **Rooms:** 100. ▤
⌨ 🍴 TV 🔆 🍴 P 🍽 AE, DC,
MC, V. ⬜ Jan–Dec. ⓛⓛⓛ

Below the Saint Remy ramparts and the Castello quarter, an ideal hotel for those who want to stay near the historic center of Cagliari.

DOMUS DE MARIA

Chia Laguna

Road map C6. Località Chia Laguna.
070-923 91. **FAX** 070-92 30 141.
Rooms: 315. ▤ ⌨ 🍴 TV
🍴 P 🍴 🍽 🍽 AE, DC, MC,
V. ⬜ Jan–Dec. ⓛⓛⓛ
half board.

A large hotel complex very similar to a resort village. The Chia Laguna is set in a scenic position overlooking the Chia bay, with one of the best beaches on the coast.

ISOLA DI SAN PIETRO

Hieracon

Road map B6. Località Carloforte,
Corso Cavour 63. 0781-85 40 28.
FAX 0781-85 48 93. **Rooms:** 21;
apartments: 7. ▤ ⌨ 🍴 TV 🔆
🍴 🍴 🍽 AE, V. ⬜ Jan–Dec.
ⓛⓛ

A villa with a good restaurant. The period rooms are nicer but noisier than those at the back.

ISOLA DI SANT'ANTIOCO

Maladroxia

Road map B6. Località Maladroxia.
 0781-81 70 12. **FAX** 0781-830 92.
Rooms: 21. ⌨ 🍴 P 🍴 🍽 AE,
MC, V. ⬜ Jun–Nov. ⓛⓛ

A big house on the seaside, with wooden furniture, large public rooms, and true family hospitality.

PORTOSCUSO

La Ghinghetta

Road map B6. Località Sa Caletta, Via
Cavour 28. 0781-50 81 43.
FAX 0781-50 81 44. **Rooms:** 8.
▤ 🍴 TV 🔆 🍴 🍴 🍴 🍽
🍽 AE, DC, MC, V. ⬜ May–Nov.
ⓛⓛ

This hotel on the beach has charming rooms furnished in different styles and a well-known restaurant with a Michelin star.

SANTA MARGHERITA DI PULA

Flamingo & Mare Pineta

Road map C6.  070-92 08 361.
FAX 070-92 08 359. **Rooms:** 134 &
60. ▤ ⌨ 🍴 TV 🍴 P ♿
🍴 🍽 AE. ⬜ May–Oct. ⓛⓛ
half board.

Two hotels with four- and three-star ranking, in Mediterranean style and overlooking a lovely sandy beach.

Is Morus

Road map C6. 070-92 11 71.
070-92 15 96. **Rooms:** 85. ▤ ⌨
🍴 TV 🍴 P 🍴 🍽
🍽 AE, DC, V. ⬜ May–Oct.
ⓛⓛⓛ half board.

A luxury hotel on the coast with access to the 18-hole golf course at the nearby Is Molas Hotel, run by the same management.

Forte Village

Road map C6.  070-921 71.
FAX 070-92 12 46. **Rooms:** 719.
▤ ⌨ 🍴 TV 🍴 🍴 P ♿
🍴 🍽 AE, DC, MC, V.
Mar–Oct. ⓛⓛⓛⓛ half board.

A Hollywood setting and first-class service distinguish the six hotels in this extensive resort. Facilities include a wide range of water sports and a health spa.

TEULADA

Baia delle Ginestre

Road map C6. Località Portu Malu.
 070-92 73 005. **FAX** 070-92 73
009. **Rooms:** 100; **villas:** 45.
▤ ⌨ 🍴 TV 🍴 P 🍴 🍽
🍽 AE, DC, MC, V.
⬜ Apr–Oct. ⓛⓛⓛ

A Mediterranean-style resort village, with small villas and rooms right on the gravel beach of the splendid Teulada coastline.

THE EASTERN COAST

BAUNEI

Santa Maria

Road map D4. Località Santa Maria
Navarrese. Via Plammas 30.
 0782-61 53 15. **FAX** 0782-61 53
16. **Rooms:** 37. ⌨ TV 🍴 P 🍴
🍽 AE, DC, MC, V.
⬜ Apr–Dec. ⓛⓛ

In the heart of town, only a five-minute walk from the sea, the Santa Maria hotel is also a good starting point for hikes in the Codula di Luna.

BARÌ SARDO

La Torre

Road map D4. Località Torre di Bar.
 0782-280 30. **FAX** 0782-295 77.
Rooms: 60. ▤ ⌨ 🍴 TV 🍴 P
🍴 🍽 AE, DC, MC, V.
⬜ Jan–Dec. ⓛⓛ

A modern, elegant hotel set in a superb location, opposite a 16th-century tower and with the sea directly in front.

DORGALI

Costa Dorada

Road map D3. Località Cala Gonone, Lungomare Palmasera 45. **C** *0784-933 33.* **FAX** *0784-934 45.* **Rooms:** *30.* 🎫 🛌 📺 📺 ♨ 🅿 🍽 📧 *AE, MC, V.* ⬜ *Apr–Nov.* ⓛⓛ *half board.*

A pleasant hotel, designed in a blend of Spanish and Sardinian styles, situated opposite the little beach of Cala Gonone.

MURAVERA

Free Beach Club

Road map D5. Località Costa Rei, Via Ichnusa 25. **C** *070-99 10 41.* **FAX** *070-99 10 54.* **Rooms:** *438.* 🎫 🛌 🅿 🍽 ♨ 📧 *AE, DC, MC, V.* ⬜ *Jun–Nov.* ⓛⓛ *full board.*

The Free Beach Club is right on the beach and offers accommodations in charming stone bungalows. There are assorted sports facilities and a baby-sitting service. The hotel asks an extra charge for air-conditioning.

OROSEI

Torre Moresca

Road map D3. Località Cala Ginepro. **C** *0784-912 30.* **FAX** *0784-912 70.* **Rooms:** *180.* 🎫 🛌 📺 📺 ♨ 🅿 🛗 🍽 ♨ 📧 *AE, V.* ⬜ *May–Oct.* ⓛⓛ *half board.*

Mediterranean-style architecture amid greenery, and only 100 m (330 ft) from the water. The Club Med-style service offers an assortment of activities and enter-tainment programs.

TORTOLÌ

Victoria

Road map D4. Via Mons. Virgilio 72. **C** *0782-62 34 57.* **FAX** *0782-62 41 16.* **Rooms:** *60.* 🎫 🛌 📺 📺 ♨ 🅿 🛗 🍽 ♨ 📧 *AE, DC, MC, V.* ⬜ *Jan–Dec.* ⓛⓛ

Recent renovation has upgraded this hotel considerably. It has spacious rooms, and an additional bonus is the large terrace where you can enjoy the marvelous views of the coast while having your breakfast.

VILLASIMIUS

Stella Maris

Road map D6. Località Campulongu. **C** *070-79 71 00.* **FAX** *070-79 73 67.* **Rooms:** *43.* 🎫 🛌 📺 📺 ♨ 🅿 🛗 🍽 📧 *AE, V.* ⬜ *May–Oct.* ⓛⓛⓛ *half board.*

This was once a vacation spot for the Jesuits, only 50 m (160 ft) from the beach. The building is now an elegant, modern hotel.

Tanka Village

Road map D6. **C** *070-79 51.* **FAX** *070-79 70 08.* **Apartments:** *968.* 🛌 ♨ 🅿 🍽 ♨ 📧 *AE, DC, MC, V.* ⬜ *May–Oct.* ⓛⓛⓛ

Situated in a fine location in the midst of greenery, this resort offers the best in facilities. There are different types of accommodations from independent lodging to the Domus with hotel-type service. Good sports facilities.

CENTRAL SARDINIA AND BARBAGIA

ARITZO

Sa Muvara

Road map C4. Via Funtana Rubia. **C** *0784-62 93 36.* **FAX** *0784-62 94 33.* **Rooms:** *65.* 🛌 📺 📺 ♨ 🅿 🛗 🍽 ♨ 📧 *AE, MC, V.* ⬜ *Apr–Nov.* ⓛⓛ

This is one of the most famous hotels in the Barbagia area, well placed for hikes up Mount Gennargentu and other sports activities such as canoeing and kayaking. There is also an excellent restaurant serving typical Sardinian food.

GAVOI

Gusana

Road map C3. Località Gusana. **C** *0784-530 00.* **FAX** *0784-521 78.* **Rooms:** *35.* 🛌 📺 📺 ♨ 🅿 🛗 🍽 📧 *AE, V.* ⬜ *Jan–Dec.* ⓛ

This small hotel is situated in a splendid position on Lake Gusana, surrounded by the Barbagia hills, with family hospitality and a good restaurant. Hikes and horseback riding.

NUORO

Fratelli Sacchi

Road map D3. Località Monte Ortobene. **C** *0784-312 00.* **FAX** *0784-340 30.* **Rooms:** *20.* 📺 🛌 🅿 🛗 🍽 📧 *AE, DC, MC, V.* ⬜ *Jan–Dec.* ⓛ

Only 7 km (4 miles) from Nuoro, the Fratelli Sacchi offers family hospitality. The well-known restaurant serves Barbagia cuisine.

OLIENA

Cooperativa Enis

Road map D3. Località Monte Maccione. **C** *0784-28 83 63.* **FAX** *0784-28 84 73.* **Rooms:** *17.* 🛌 🅿 🛗 🍽 ⬜ *Jan–Dec.* ⓛ

A three-star hotel, terraces with panoramic views and a good restaurant with Barbagia cuisine. Tours of the Gennargentu National Park are available.

Su Gologone

Road map D3. Località Su Gologone. **C** *0784-28 75 12.* **FAX** *0784-28 76 68.* **Rooms:** *65.* 🛌 📺 📺 ♨ 🅿 🍽 ♨ 📧 *AE, DC, MC, V.* ⬜ *Mar–Oct.* ⓛⓛ

A quiet location, characteristic architecture, fine cuisine, and warm hospitality. This is an ideal starting point for a tour of the Supramonte di Oliena.

THE WESTERN COAST

ALGHERO

Porto Conte

Road map B2. Località Porto Conte. **C** *079-94 20 35.* **FAX** *079-94 20 45.* **Rooms:** *148.* 🎫 🛌 📺 🅿 🍽 ♨ 📧 *AE, DC, MC, V.* ⬜ *Apr–Nov.* ⓛⓛ *full board.*

A pleasant, modern hotel over-looking the bay, ideal for a seaside vacation.

Villa Las Tronas

Road map B2. Lungomare Valencia 1. **C** *079-98 18 18.* **FAX** *079-98 10 44.* **Rooms:** *29.* 🎫 🛌 📺 📺 ♨ 🅿 🍽 📧 *AE, DC, MC, V.* ⬜ *Jan–Dec.* ⓛⓛⓛ

For key to symbols *see p170*

This beautifully restored late 19th-century Art Nouveau villa is in a unique position on a headland overlooking Capo Caccia.

ARBOREA

Ala Birdi

Road map B4. Strada a Mare 24. 📞 0783-80 10 83. **FAX** 0783-80 10 86. **Rooms:** 58; **villas:** 58. 🔳 🔂 📺 🔲 🔲 P 🔲 🔲 🔲 AE, DC, MC, V. ◯ Jan–Dec. Ⓛ Ⓛ

A hotel and 58 little villas in a lovely pine forest. The Ala Birdi is well known for its equestrian facilities. The hotel also organizes interesting guided tours.

BOSA

Turas

Road map B3. Località Turas. 📞 0785-35 92 30. **Rooms:** 38. 🔂 P 🔲 ◯ Jun–Nov. Ⓛ Ⓛ

This small hotel with typical 1970s architecture and decor is worth seeking out because of its splendid location at the end of the Bosa beach.

CUGLIERI – SANTA CATERINA

La Baja

Road map B3. Località Santa Caterina di Pittinuri 20. 📞 0785-381 05. **FAX** 0785-381 05. **Rooms:** 24. 🔂 🔲 P 🔲 🔲 AE. ◯ Jan–Dec. Ⓛ Ⓛ

Situated opposite the Torre Spagnola (Spanish tower), with rooms overlooking the bay. Horseback riding, hikes, and mountain biking are offered.

ORISTANO

Mistral 2

Road map B4. Via XX Settembre. 📞 0783-21 03 89. **FAX** 0783-21 10 00. **Rooms:** 132. 🔳 🔂 📺 📺 🔲 🔲 P 🔲 🔲 🔲 AE, DC, MC, V. ◯ Jan–Dec. Ⓛ Ⓛ

Only five minutes by car from the central square of Oristano, this well-appointed modern hotel has floors for nonsmokers, a swimming pool, and a restaurant on the premises.

STINTINO

Geranio Rosso

Road map B2. Via XXI Aprile 4. 📞 079-52 32 92. **Rooms:** 5. 🔂 📺 🔲 🔲 MC, V. ◯ Jan–Dec. Ⓛ Ⓛ

This tiny hotel with a restaurant attached is in the center of town, a mile or so from the white Pelosa beaches.

Rocca Ruja

Road map B2. Località Capo Falcone. 📞 079-52 92 00. **FAX** 079-52 97 78. **Rooms:** 99. 🔂 🔂 📺 📺 🔲 🔲 🔲 🔲 🔲 AE, MC, V. ◯ May–Oct. Ⓛ Ⓛ Ⓛ full board.

This modern complex includes a hotel and residence hotel, in a lovely setting facing the rocky island of Asinara.

TRESNURAGHES

Piccolo Hotel

Road map B3. Località Porto Alabe. 📞 0785-35 90 56. **FAX** 0785-35 90 80. **Rooms:** 20. 🔂 🔲 P 🔲 ◯ Jan–Dec. Ⓛ Ⓛ

The Piccolo is a family-run hotel in an enchanting location on the coast. Excellent fish is served.

THE NORTH AND THE COSTA SMERALDA

ARZACHENA

Residenza Capriccioli

Road map D1. Località Capriccioli. 📞 0789-960 16. **FAX** 0789-964 43. **Suites:** 34. 🔂 🔲 P ◯ May–Oct. Ⓛ Ⓛ

About 100 m (330 ft) from the beach of Capriccioli, one of the best in the Costa Smeralda, the Residenza offers good accommodations at reasonable prices for this area.

Le Ginestre

Road map D1. Località Porto Cervo. 📞 0789-920 30. **FAX** 0789-940 87. **Rooms:** 80. 🔳 🔂 📺 📺 🔲 P 🔲 🔲 🔲 AE, DC, MC, V. ◯ May–Oct. Ⓛ Ⓛ Ⓛ half board.

One of the most famous hotels in the Costa Smeralda. Set in a fantastic location on the Golfo

del Pevero, on pine-clad hills, Le Ginestre offers four-star hospitality and service.

Valdiola

Road map D1. Località Cala di Volpe. 📞 0789-962 15. **FAX** 0789-966 52. **Rooms:** 33. 🔳 🔂 🔲 P 🔲 🔲 🔲 AE, DC, MC, V. ◯ Jan–Dec. Ⓛ Ⓛ Ⓛ

The Valdiola is a well-appointed, pleasant hotel and offers a great bargain. You'll find an enchanting view, informal atmosphere, and good service.

Villaggio Le Magnolie

Road map D1. Località Liscia di Vacca. 📞 0789-56 94 99. **FAX** 0789-56 94 17. **Rooms:** 61. 🔂 📺 📺 🔲 🔲 P 🔲 🔲 🔲 AE, DC, MC, V. ◯ Apr–Oct. Ⓛ Ⓛ Ⓛ half board.

The Villaggio consists of three well-run residence hotels and a hotel situated between the scented maquis and the sea. Sports facilities and entertainment for everybody, children included.

La Bisaccia

Road map D1. Località Baia Sardinia. 📞 0789-990 02. **FAX** 0789-991 62. **Rooms:** 120. 🔳 🔂 📺 📺 🔲 🔲 P 🔲 🔲 🔲 AE, DC, MC, V. ◯ May–Oct. Ⓛ Ⓛ Ⓛ Ⓛ half board.

The Bisaccia is surrounded by maquis vegetation and faces the sea; it includes a four-star hotel and a three-star annex.

Pitrizza

Road map D1. Località Liscia di Vacca. 📞 0789-93 01 11. **FAX** 0789-916 29. **Rooms:** 50. 🔳 🔂 📺 📺 🔲 🔲 P 🔲 🔲 🔲 AE, DC, V. ◯ May–Oct. Ⓛ Ⓛ Ⓛ Ⓛ Ⓛ half board.

The most exclusive hotel in Sardinia deserves its worldwide fame. The style, service, and simple elegance are worthy of a five-star luxury hotel.

Villaggio Forte Cappellini

Road map D1. Località Baia Sardinia. 📞 0789-990 57. **FAX** 0789-990 57. **Rooms:** 59. 🔂 🔲 P 🔲 🔲 AE, V. ◯ May–Sep. Ⓛ Ⓛ Ⓛ Ⓛ full board.

This classic resort village is right on the water and features the usual range of sports activities and entertainment. Children under 15 are not allowed.

Cala di Volpe

Road map D1. Località Cala di Volpe. 📞 0789-97 61 11.
FAX 0789-97 61 67. **Rooms:** 123.
🍽️🛏️📺📶🅿️♿🏊 AE, DC, MC, V.
○ Apr–Oct. ⓁⓁⓁⓁⓁ
full board.

The spectacular architecture of one of the first and most exclusive hotels on the Costa Smeralda was the work of Jacques Couelle. Every luxury is provided.

Romazzino

Road map D1. Località Romazzino.
📞 0789-97 71 11. FAX 0789-962 58.
Rooms: 90. 🍽️🛏️📺
📶🅿️🏊 AE, DC, MC, V. ○ Apr–Oct.
ⓁⓁⓁⓁⓁ full board.

One of the loveliest buildings in the Costa Smeralda, built in the Neo-Mediterranean style, with fascinating views toward the islands of Soffi and Mortorio.

CASTELSARDO

Hotel Villaggio Pedraladda

Road map C2. Via Zirulia 50.
📞 079-47 03 83. FAX 079-47 04 99.
Rooms: 128. 🍽️🛏️🅿️🏊
AE, DC, V. ○ Apr–Oct.
ⓁⓁ full board.

Only 600 m (1 mile) from Castelsardo, the hotel and residence hotel both have terraces with sweeping views of the sea; tennis courts, and a disco. Scuba and skin-diving lessons provided.

LA MADDALENA

Cala Lunga

Road map D1. Località Porto Massimo. 📞 0789-73 40 42.
FAX 0789-73 40 33. **Rooms:** 65.
🍽️🛏️📺📶🏊 AE, DC, MC, V. ○ May–Oct.
ⓁⓁⓁ half board.

Cala Lunga is in a bay protected from the west and mistral winds, with private coves and a yacht harbor 6 km (4 miles) from the center of La Maddalena.

Giuseppe Garibaldi

Road map D1. Via Lamarmora.
📞 0789-73 13 14. FAX 0789-73 73 26. **Rooms:** 19. 🍽️🛏️📺📶
🅿️ AE, DC, MC, V.
○ Jan–Dec. ⓁⓁ

This small hotel in the old section of La Maddalena is named after the 19th-century hero. The closest beach is 10 minutes on foot, the farthest half an hour by car.

OLBIA

Sporting

Road map D1 & D2. Località Porto Rotondo. 📞 0789-340 05.
FAX 0789-343 83. **Rooms:** 27.
🍽️🛏️📺🅿️🏊
AE, DC, V. ○ May–Oct.
ⓁⓁⓁ half board.

This interesting hotel has always been a favorite with Porto Rotondo VIPs. It is elegant but informal. All the rooms have access to the beach.

PALAU

Capo d'Orso

Road map D1. Località Cala Capra. 📞 0789-70 20 00.
FAX 0789-70 20 09. **Rooms:** 60.
🍽️🛏️📺🅿️🏊
AE, DC, MC, V. ○ Apr–Oct.
ⓁⓁ half board.

A series of small terraced villas in the middle of luxuriant maquis undergrowth offers a splendid panoramic view.

SAN TEODORO

Due Lune

Road map D2. Località Puntaldia.
📞 0784-86 40 75.
FAX 0784-86 40 17. **Rooms:** 59.
🍽️🛏️📺🅿️♿🏊
AE, DC, MC, V. ○ May–Oct.
ⓁⓁⓁ half board.

A nine-hole golf course, and the island of Tavolara opposite. This charming complex consists of small villas of granite and stone.

SANTA TERESA DI GALLURA

Belvedere

Road map C1. Piazza della Libertà 2. 📞 0789-75 41 60.
FAX 0789-75 49 37. **Rooms:** 22.
🛏️📺 AE, MC, V, DC.
○ Mar–mid Dec. ⓁⓁ full board.

This small hotel is in a marvelous location near the Aragonese tower, with a panoramic view. Simply but elegantly appointed.

Grand Hotel Corallaro

Road map C1. Località Rena Bianca.
📞 0789-75 54 75.
FAX 0789-75 54 31. **Rooms:** 81.
🍽️🛏️📺📶🅿️♿
🏊 AE, DC, MC, V.
○ Apr–Oct. ⓁⓁ half board.

A four-star hotel that is ideal for those who want a vacation by the sea. It is right in front of you, with Corsica on the horizon.

Moresco

Road map C1. Via Imbriani 16.
📞 0789-75 41 88.
FAX 0789-75 50 85. **Rooms:** 44.
🛏️📺🅿️ MC, V.
○ Apr–Oct. ⓁⓁ half board.

The Moresco is a charming three-star hotel overlooking the Rena Bianca, the lovely white sandy beach of Santa Teresa, and very near the central square.

SASSARI

Grazia Deledda

Road map B2. Viale Dante 47.
📞 079-27 12 35. FAX 079-28 08 84.
Rooms: 127. 🍽️🛏️📺📶
🅿️ AE, DC, V. ○ Jan–Dec.
ⓁⓁ

In the heart of town, a short stroll from the Emiciclo Garibaldi gardens, is this modern, comfortable hotel named after Sardinia's Nobel-prize-winning novelist.

Leonardo da Vinci

Road map B2. Via Roma 79.
📞 079-28 07 44. FAX 079-28 07 44.
Rooms: 117. 🍽️🛏️📺🅿️♿
AE, DC, MC, V.
○ Jan–Dec. ⓁⓁ

A new, elegant bed and breakfast with spacious rooms near the central Piazza Italia, often described as Sassari's "living room." Discounts are offered for weekend stays.

TEMPIO PAUSANIA

Petit

Road map C2. Piazza Alcide De Gasperi 9/11. 📞 079-63 11 34.
FAX 079-63 17 60. **Rooms:** 40.
🍽️🛏️📺📶♿🅿️
AE, DC, MC, V. ○ Jan–Dec.
ⓁⓁ

Modern and quiet, with a great view of the main square. The restaurant offers the best in Gallura regional cuisine.

For key to symbols *see p170*

WHERE TO EAT

THE RELATIVELY RECENT arrival of tourism in Sardinia means that it is an excellent place for appreciating regional variations in cuisine. Fish and seafood fill restaurant menus along the coast, while meat and stuffed pasta are commonly found in the interior. In fact, restaurants that do not serve typical regional dishes are a rarity. The rhythm for mealtimes is Mediterranean, with lunch being served from

Lucia Pennisi and homemade, fresh pasta, Sant'Antioco

1–3pm and the evening meal from 9–10:30pm. In many cases restaurants stay open until 10:30–11pm, especially in summer. Almost all restaurants and trattorias close one day a week and are closed for a month for annual vacations, so check business hours if you have a particular destination. All the restaurants listed on pages 184–7 have been chosen as among the best in their category.

The Locanda Rosella at Giba, in the Cagliari region

TYPES OF RESTAURANTS

IN TERMS OF price, cuisine, and atmosphere, there is not much difference between a restaurant (ristorante) and a trattoria in Sardinia. Even a fairly expensive restaurant may still be decorated in a functional, country style, with simple furniture. The pizzerias are rarely luxurious but have the advantage of offering decent eating at lower prices. If you can, choose pizzerias with wood-burning ovens; the quality is better. In the summer, foodstands on the beaches sell sandwiches and fish and pasta dishes for those spending the day at the seaside. In general, the bars do not offer snacks and sandwiches for a quick meal.

PRICES AND PAYING

A THREE-COURSE meal will cost about L30–50,000. In top restaurants the bill may add up to L60–80,000 but

only rarely will it go above L100,000. In pizzerias you can have a two-course meal with a glass of beer or half-liter of wine for L20–30,000. The bill always includes a cover charge (coperto or pane e coperto), which varies from L2,000 to L5,000, and service. It is customary to leave 12–15 percent of your bill as a tip.

Restaurants are obliged by law to give customers a legal receipt (ricevuta fiscale) when they pay. This must have the name of the establishment and an official "fiscal number"; any other piece of paper is illegal, and you are liable to a fine if you leave the restaurant without one, so you have every right to demand a genuine bill. Many restaurants accept major credit cards (such as VISA, MasterCard, American Express, and Diners), but just in-case, be prepared to pay in cash, especially when you go to bars, cafés, or smaller, family-run establishments.

FIXED-PRICE MENUS

MANY RESTAURANTS offer menus at fixed prices (menù a prezzo fisso or menù turistico). Some prepare a menu of Sardinian specialties once a week, giving you a chance to try regional dishes such as porceddu (suckling pig), which you would otherwise have to order in advance. Upscale restaurants may offer a special menu called a menù degustazione or menù gastronomico, for a fixed price. This usually gives you the chance to taste five or six house specialties.

CLOSING DAYS

ALL RESTAURANTS close for one day each week, except during tourist season (July and August). The closing days for each establishment

Dal Corsaro, one of Cagliari's top restaurants (see p184)

recommended in this guide are clearly shown in the listings on pp184–7. Most places also close for about one month for annual vacations, usually in the winter, except for the restaurants in Cagliari, which are closed in August.

VEGETARIAN FOOD

SARDINIA is not ideal for strict vegetarians. People who eat fish but not meat will not have problems along the coast. In the interior the choice may be limited to pasta and soup dishes with fresh bread and cheeses. (However, don't forget that some soup dishes may be prepared with meat stock.)

A thirst-quenching snack of fresh fruit eaten on the beach

RESERVATIONS

RESTAURANTS are often crowded, particularly in the evening and during the summer. Consequently, it is advisable to reserve ahead even in the less expensive establishments, or at least arrive fairly early to avoid a long wait.

THE MENU

RESTAURANTS do not always provide a written menu. Where this happens, the waiter will give you a list of the day's dishes at your table and help you choose. You may wish to begin with an antipasto or appetizer, such as sliced sausage, cured hams, or vegetables in oil, artichoke

Aperitif time in an Alghero bar

hearts or perhaps olives. Coastal restaurants offer seafood appetizers (clams, mussels, cuttlefish, baby squid, sea anemones, and assorted mollusks). This is followed by the first course *(primo)*, which may consist of soup, pasta, ravioli, or occasionally, a rice dish. The second course *(secondo)* will be meat or fish and may include the famous *porceddu* (suckling pig). Some first courses, such as *pane frattau* *(carasau* bread in broth) or *fregula* pasta with clams, make substantial meals. The meal ends with cheese, fruit, or dessert such as ice cream, with coffee and perhaps a Sardinian liqueur.

WINE AND DRINKS

MOST RESTAURANTS, even those in the medium-price range, stock a good selection of regional wines and liqueurs *(see pp182–3).* Some may offer non-Sardinian wines. Almost all restaurants provide house wine.

CHILDREN

CHILDREN are welcome in restaurants, especially family run ones, where it is easier to prepare special dishes or half portions.

SMOKING

FEW RESTAURANTS in Sardinia have a no-smoking area; smoke-free restaurants are rare.

WHEELCHAIR ACCESS

ONLY A FEW restaurants in Sardinia are equipped to deal with the disabled (with ramps and toilet facilities). However, few restaurants have steps, and access is not normally a problem. It is a good idea to call the restaurant beforehand to guarantee an easily accessible table and assistance when you arrive.

USING THE LISTINGS

Key to the symbols in the listings on pages 184–7.

🍴	fixed-price menu
🍷	good wine list
♿	wheelchair access
🚭	no-smoking area
☂	outdoor tables
Ⓥ	vegetarian dishes
🧒	children's portions
▤	air-conditioning
⬤	closed

💳	credit cards accepted
AE	American Express
MC	MasterCard
DC	Diners Club
V	VISA

Average prices for a three-course meal for one, including half a bottle of wine, cover charge, taxes, and service.

Ⓛ under L40,000
ⓁⓁ L40,000–60,000
ⓁⓁⓁ L60,000–L80,000
ⓁⓁⓁⓁ L80,000–L100,000
ⓁⓁⓁⓁⓁ over L100,000.

What to Eat in Sardinia

DESPITE THE FACT THAT Sardinia is surrounded by water, the island's most famous dish is *porceddu*, suckling pig roasted over an open fire until it is *Sospiri pastries* tender and the skin crispy. It is often served on traditional cork trays strewn with myrtle leaves, on a layer of *carasau* bread. Meat roasted on the spit is still a classic dish for celebrations such as feast days or religious festivals. Lamb and mutton also feature strongly in the island's cuisine, and Sardinia's best-known cheese is pecorino, made from sheep's milk. Pasta is often handmade, and comes in a variety of forms, including the stuffed pasta called *culungiones* (ravioli). Fish and seafood are eaten along the coast, and Spanish influences are still evident in the cooking of the west, where lobster *alla catalana* can be found.

Malloreddus *are gnocchi (like dumplings), served with fresh tomato sauce and minced sausage, flavored with saffron.*

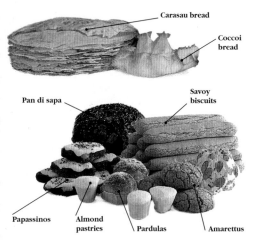

Carasau bread

Coccoi bread

Pan di sapa

Savoy biscuits

Papassinos   Almond pastries   Pardulas   Amarettus

Zuppa gallurese *is a soup made of dried durum wheat bread, stock, and grated pecorino cheese, baked in the oven.*

BREAD AND PASTRIES

There are countless different types of bread in Sardinia, from fat loaves to thin crispy circles. Perhaps the most famous is *carasau*, baked in a very thin, round layer. Pastries and cakes are usually made with flour, honey, and almonds, and vary from one village to the next.

Fregula *(or fregola) is a granular pasta, similar to couscous. It is served with clams, like pasta, or in broth as a soup.*

Succu *is fregula (like couscous) simmered in mutton stock and flavored with saffron and pecorino cheese.*

Culungiones *are large ravioli stuffed with potato purée, egg yolk, mint, onion, and a little cheese, served with tomatoes or meat sauce.*

Pane Frattau *is made with carasau bread rounds, softened in stock and flavored with pecorino cheese, tomato sauce, and eggs.*

Cordula *is a braid formed from lamb entrails, rolled onto a skewer, and roasted on a spit.*

Porceddu *is traditionally roasted for celebrations. A young suckling pig weighing about 4 kilos (9 lb) is spit-roasted over a fire and basted at intervals with melted lard.*

Stufato di capretto *is a rich casserole made with kid goat, wine, artichokes, and saffron. Sometimes eggs are added to make a kind of fricassée.*

Buccinis *(a type of mollusk) and* arselle *(clams), are often served as antipasti (appetizers).*

Burrida *is cooked fish, marinaded in garlic, parsley, hazelnuts, and vinegar for a day. There are many variations.*

Catalan lobster *is a typical specialty of Alghero. The lobster is served with a vinaigrette sauce made from lobster juices and egg, blended with a dash of olive oil and lemon.*

Seadas *(or* sebadas*) are fritters, stuffed with cheese and lemon peel, then fried. They are eaten with plenty of Sardinian honey.*

Pecorino

Ricotta

Fiore sardo

SARDINIAN CHEESES

Sardinian sheep or goat's cheese is either served newly made and fresh *(caprino, fiore sardo)* or mature (pecorino, *canestrato)*. Ricotta (sheep's milk) is always soft and creamy.

Pardulas *(also known as* casadinas*) are fresh cheese pastries, flavored with saffron, vanilla, and lemon or orange peel.*

What to Drink in Sardinia

GRAPEVINES FIRST CAME to Sardinia from the eastern Mediterranean, where the Phoenicians had long cultivated vineyards. The warm climate tends to yield very ripe grapes, which are then turned into strong, deeply colored wines, often used for blending. Today the general quality of Sardinian wines is rising rapidly, with better viticultural practices, more careful selection in the vineyard, and better hygiene in the winery. All types are made, from red *(rosso)*, white *(bianco)*, and rosé *(rosato)* to rich dessert wines. Many qualify for the status of *denominazione di origine controllata* (DOC), with guaranteed provenance and quality standards. Sardinian wines are almost always made from a single grape variety. Perhaps the best-known is Vernaccia di Oristano, the first to gain DOC in Sardinia.

Old winemaking equipment

Vernaccia

Slightly sparkling Sinis

Grape harvesting

RECOMMENDED WHITES

- **Cantina Sociale della Riforma Agraria, Alghero**
  Vermentino di Sardegna Aragosta
- **Cantina Sociale Gallura**
  Vermentino
- **Tenuta Sella & Mosca, Alghero**
  Terre Bianche

WHITE WINES

THE WHITE WINES of Sardinia go well with fish and seafood dishes, and some are sturdy enough to go with meat dishes such as pork. Nuragus is a widely planted white grape, producing rather neutral, soft, and fruity wines. Vermentino is also widely grown, and the wines have more complex flavors. Vermentino di Sardegna and Vermentino di Gallura, both made mostly around Sassari and Nuoro province, tend to be fairly strong. There is also a sparkling version. DOC Vermentino from Cala Viola and Usini is very good. The Campidano area produces the fruity, dry white Semidano.

RED WINES

THE MOST WELL-KNOWN red wine is Cannonau, which is usually full-bodied and strong, although some lighter versions are made. Most Cannonau is produced in the province of Nuoro in eastern Sardinia. It goes well with roast meat and game. Another wine to drink with game and mature cheese is Monica di Sardegna, a dry red with intense perfume that should be drunk while still young. Less common but equally good DOC reds are the light, dry Mandrolisai, Campidano di Terralba, and Carignano del Sulcis. Other reds, such as Tanca Farrà di Alghero and Terre Brune del Sulcis, are blends of native Sardinian and imported grape varieties.

Cannonau grapes

Nieddera rosé and Cannonau

RECOMMENDED REDS

- **Azienda Giuseppe Cabras, Nuoro**
  Cannonau
- **Tenuta Sella & Mosca, Alghero**
  Anghelu Ruju
- **Attilio Contini, Cabras**
  Nieddera

DESSERT WINES

Sardinia produces a number of sweet dessert wines, both white and red. Besides mature white Vernaccia and sweet red Cannonau, there is Moscato di Sardegna, made from Muscat grapes and bottled at three years old. It is sweet but has good acidity, and an alcoholic content of 15%. Tempio Pausania Muscat tends to be lightly fizzy, while the Cagliari version is strong and sweet. The red Girò di Cagliari and amber-colored Nasco are also strong and sweet. Two dessert wines made from semidried grapes come from the Alghero region: Torbato and Anghelu Ruju, both produced with Cannonau grapes. The Bosa and Cagliari Malvasia wines are similar to Vernaccia.

Cantina Sociale della Vernaccia at Oristano

Sparkling Vernaccia

Malvasia di Bosa

Vernaccia grapes

Malvasia grapes

Moscato grapes

Harvesting black grapes from Cannonau vines

RECOMMENDED DESSERT WINES

- **Centro Enologico Sardo, Villacidro**
  Malvasia
- **Centro Enologico Sardo, Villacidro**
  Moscato Dolce (Muscat)
- **Fratelli Serra, Zeddiani**
  Vernaccia
- **Meloni Vini, Selargius**
  Malvasia di Cagliari
  Cantina Sociale Dolianova
  Moscato di Cagliari

DIGESTIVI

The best-known spirit in Sardinia is *abbardiente* (named from the Spanish *aguardiente*), a grappa or eau-de-vie. Among the best are made from the strong-tasting Cannonau and the more delicate Malvasia. Grappa here is also called *fil'e ferru* (wire), from the wire used to mark hiding places for illegally produced grappa. Grappa flavored with wild fennel, juniper, and thistle is a relatively new style. The most famous liqueur, however, is Mirto, both red and white, made with wild myrtle leaves and berries. The Sardinians' favorite is Zedda Piras.

Cork-covered bottles with characteristic decorative motifs

CAGLIARI AND THE SOUTH

ASSEMINI

Su Zaffaranu

Road map C5. Via Coghinas 1.
(070-94 11 46. **V X ▤**
● Fri in winter, Christmas, Jan 1.
✉ AE, MC, V. **ⓁⓁ**

On state road SS130 connecting
Cagliari and Iglesias, 5 km (3
miles) from the airport and 10 km
(6 miles) from the center of
Cagliari, this fish restaurant
features mussels with spring
vegetables, crayfish tails with
arugula, pasta with artichokes and
salted mullet roe, gilthead bream
with Vernaccia or baked in salt,
seadas, and fresh cheeses.

BARUMINI

Su Nuraxi

Road map C4. Provincial road (SP).
(070-93 68 305. **¶●¶ V & V**
X ▤ ● Tue in winter. **✉** AE, DC,
MC, V. **ⓁⓁ**

Handy because of its proximity to
the nuraghi and the new mineral
museum. Typical homemade
dishes are available, such as
porceddu, *fregula* with sauce or
clams. Parking for RVs.

CAGLIARI

Antica Hostaria

Road map C6. Via Cavour, 60.
(070-66 58 70. **& V ▤**
● Sun, Aug, Christmas, Jan 1.
✉ AE, DC, MC, V. **ⓁⓁ**

This small, cozy place is on the
ground floor of an old building.
The specialties are seasonal:
risotto with radicchio, pappardelle
(wide noodles) with salmon and
shrimp, spaghetti with clams and
bottarga (dried mullet roe), salad
of porcini and ovoli mushrooms,
game, and fish.

Lillicu

Road map C6. Via Sardegna 78.
(070-65 29 70. **¶ V X ▤**
● Sun, Aug 10–Sep 1. **✉** MC, V.
ⓁⓁ

Lillicu, in the alley behind Via
Roma, is furnished with white
marble tables. The specialties are
fish dishes: dogfish (marinated in
garlic, nuts, vinegar and fish liver),
fish soup, and sea anemone.

Saint Remy

Road map C6. Via Torino 6.
(070-65 73 77. **¶●¶ V X**
▤ ● variable, Sat lunch and Sun.
✉ AE, DC, V. **ⓁⓁ**

Occupying a 17th-century
monastery, Saint Remy has a
special atmosphere. Food is
carefully prepared: ravioli with
ricotta, saffron and orange, *fregula*
with mussels, lamb with artichokes
or potatoes, squid with herbs
and potatoes, fish with Vernaccia.

Dal Corsaro

Road map C6. Viale Regina
Margherita 28. **(** 070-66 43 18.
¶●¶ V & V X ▤ ● Sun,
Aug, Christmas. **✉** AE, DC, MC, V.
ⓁⓁⓁ

Dal Corsaro is one of the best
restaurants in Sardinia. The menu
features squid salad with French
beans and balsamic vinegar, fish-
stuffed ravioli with fresh tomatoes,
clams, and shrmp, fillet of sea bass
with saffron and potatoes.

CALASETTA

Da Pasqualino

Road map B6. Via Roma 99.
(0781-884 73. **& X ▤**
● after 10pm, Tue in winter, Oct or
Feb. **✉** AE. **Ⓛ**

Fish is the specialty here: fish soup
with gurnard, scorpion fish, moray
eel, squid, shellfish as well as
mixed fish, grilled or pan-fried.

CARLOFORTE

Al Tonno di Corsa

Road map B6. Via G Marconi 47.
(0781-85 51 06. **▤ ▤**
● Dec 23–Jan 23. **✉** AE, MC, V.
ⓁⓁ

In the old part of town, on the hill
behind the seafront, Al Tonno
offers such typical local fare as
couscous, *musciame* (sun-dried
dolphin), and above all a varied
selection of tuna *(tonno)* dishes.

Da Nicola

Road map B6. Via Dante 46 (winter)
Corso Cavour 32 (summer). **(** 0781-
85 40 48. **¶ & ▤ X ▤ ●**
Mon in winter, Dec–Jan. **✉** AE, DC,
MC, V. **ⓁⓁ**

Da Nicola moves to the seafront in
summer. The cooking is a blend of
Arab and Ligurian: couscous with
vegetables, veal, and beef, lobster,
tuna, swordfish, and crayfish.

IGLESIAS

Villa di Chiesa

Road map B5. Piazza Municipio 9/10.
(0781-235 40. **& ▤ ▤ X ▤**
● Mon, except in Aug. **✉** V. **ⓁⓁ**

This fish restaurant in a medieval
square offers delectable dishes
such as spaghetti with salted
mullet roe and clams, or with
fresh tomatoes, as well as meat
and game specialties.

THE EASTERN COAST

ARBATAX

Del Porto

Road map D4. Via Bellavista 14. **(**
0782-66 72 26. **¶ X V ▤ ▤**
● Dec–Mar. **✉** DC, MC, V. **ⓁⓁ**

On the dock, 100 m (330 ft) from
the waterfront, Del Porto focuses
on fresh fish and features fish
risotto, *culungiones* and burrida
(marinated skate).

BAUNEI

Golgo

Road map D4. Località San Pietro.
(0337-81 18 28. **& ▤ X**
● Oct–Easter. **ⓁⓁ**

A typical stone construction in the
open country serving characteristic
Sardinian dishes: from *pane
frattau* with suckling pig to
macaroons with almond paste.

DORGALI

Colibrì

Road map D3. Via A Gramsci 15.
(0784-960 54. **& ▤ X**
● Oct–Easter. **Ⓛ**

This modern restaurant offers
typical Barbagia cuisine such as
pane frattau, *maccarones furriaos*
(baked macaroni), roast suckling
pig, mutton with herbs.

OROSEI

Su Barchile

Road map D3. Via Mannu 5. **(**
0784-988 79. **¶●¶ ▤ ▤ V X**
▤ ● Nov. **✉** AE, MC, V. **ⓁⓁ**

In the old town. In summer you can eat on the terrace garden: homemade bucatini pasta with shellfish, fish ravioli, and seafood risotto as well as meat dishes.

POSADA

Sa Rocca

Road map D2. Piazza Eleonora d'Arborea 30. **(** 0784-85 41 66. **&** **V** **†** **●** Mon in winter, Nov. **≋** AE. **①** **①**

This restaurant lies below the castle with a view of the sea (only .6 mi away). Classic Sardinian fare such as ravioli, gnocchi with clams, mixed grilled fish, grilled veal chops, and, if you call in advance, suckling pig and lobster.

TORTOLÌ

Da Lenin

Road map D4. Via San Gemiliano 19. **(** 0782-62 44 22. **♬** **&** **☷** **V** **†** **●** after 10pm, Sun, 20 Dec–20 Jan. **≋** AE, DC, MC, V. **①**

Excellent fish specialties as well as classic meat dishes. Ravioli with bottarga, black tagliatelle with salmon, grilled fish, and in the autumn, gilthead bream baked in foil with porcini mushrooms.

VILLASIMIUS

Carbonara

Road map D6. Via Umberto I 60. **(** 070-79 12 70. **♬** **&** **V** **†** **≣** **●** variable, Wed in winter. **≋** AE, DC, MC, V.

Risotto alla corsara with shellfish, spaghetti with clams and bottarga, and ravioli with Vernaccia are the house specialties at Carbonara.

CENTRAL SARDINIA AND BARBAGIA

ARITZO

Sa Muvara

Road map C4. Via Fontana Rubia 35. **(** 0784-62 93 36. **♬** **&** **☷** **V** **†** **●** 10pm, Dec–Easter. **≋** AE, DC, MC, V. **①** **①**

Good basic Barbagia food: risotto with chestnuts, pasticcio all'-aritzese (strudel with potatoes,

mushrooms, ham and fresh tomatoes), aromatic herb soups, sausages made on the premises, and roast meat dishes.

FONNI

Miramontes

Road map D3. Fonni–Dèsulo road. **(** 0784-573 11. **♬** **&** **V** **†** **●** Wed, Oct. **①**

One km (half a mile) from Fonni, on the road to Montespada, this country restaurant offers typical fare: ravioli, malloreddus, pane frattau, barbecued suckling pig and lamb, and their own sausages, made on the premises.

GAVOI

Gusana

Road map C3. Gusana. **(** 0784-521 78. **&** **†** **≣** **●** Mon. **≋** AE, DC, MC, V. **①**

A true selection of Barbagia cuisine, based on the staple of purpuzza (sausage meat): homemade gnocchi, and ravioli with meat sauce, plus eel and trout.

NUORO

Canne al Vento

Road map D3. Viale Repubblica 66. **(** 0784-20 17 62. **&** **†** **≣** **●** Sun, 10 days in Aug, Christmas. **≋** AE, DC, MC, V. **①** **①**

This restaurant in the center features Barbagia dishes: malloreddus, boar, mutton, horsemeat, suckling pig, and grilled, salted or wine-marinated fish.

Da Giovanni

Road map D3. Via IV Novembre 9. **(** 0784-305 62. **V** **†** **●** Sun. **≋** AE, V. **①**

Da Giovanni is in the heart of town and offers the typical Nuoro soup, filindeu (braided pasta simmered in mutton stock), fettuccine ribbon noodles with a sauce of wild boar meat, stewed wild boar, and baked fish.

OLIENA

Su Gologone

Road map D3. Località Su Gologone. **(** 0784-28 75 12. **♬** **&** **☷** **V** **‡** **●** Nov. **≋** AE, MC, V. **①** **①** **①**

Su Gologone is 12 km (7 miles) from Nuoro, surrounded by greenery, and is known for its typical meat dishes: roast suckling pig, lamb, and goat as well as pane frattau, ravioli, malloreddus and seadas with honey.

ORGOSOLO

Ai Monti del Gennargentu

Road map D3. Settiles. **(** 0784-40 23 74. **♬** **&** **V** **†** **≣** **●** Nov, Feb. **①** **①**

This restaurant in the countryside, 6 km (4 miles) from Orgosolo, has its own organic fruit orchard and kitchen garden. Among the many typical dishes are vegetable and ham soup and soup with homemade pasta, and tangy sheep's milk cheese.

THE WESTERN COAST

ALGHERO

Al Tuguri

Road map B2. Via Maiorca 113. **(** 079-97 67 72. **♬** **&** **V** **†** **≣** **●** Sun, Dec 20–Jan 20. **≋** MC, V.

This restaurant occupies three floors in a charming, rebuilt 15th-century building. The menu is seasonal: mussels and fava beans, fresh pasta with sea urchins, Majorca-style fish, onion soup with eggs.

Rafel

Road map B2. Via Lido 20. **(** 079-95 03 85. **♬** **&** **†** **●** Thu in winter, Nov. **≋** AE, DC, MC, V. **①** **①**

At Rafel's first courses are cooked while you wait: fresh sauces flavored with clams, sea urchin roe (in winter), and crab meat. Fish soup upon request. The fish on the menu varies according to the day's catch. House desserts include the special sorbets with fruit-of-the-season flavors, from lemon to strawberry and peach.

La Lepanto

Road map B2. Via Carlo Alberto 135. **(** 079-97 91 16. **♬** **&** **☷** **V** **†** **●** until late. **●** Mon in winter. **≋** AE, DC, MC, V. **①** **①** **①**

This restaurant is in the old town, with verandas overlooking the sea. The menu is mainly fish, often traditionally presented: lobster, spaghetti Alghero-style, pasta with eggplant and crayfish.

BOSA

Tatore

Road map B3. Via IV Novembre.
📞 *0785-37 31 04.* 🍴 🔓 🛗 **V**
🪑 🍽 🌙 *Wed.* Ⓛ

Tatore offers mostly fish dishes: spaghetti *allo scoglio* with shell-fish, risotto with seafood, fish soup, mixed grilled or fried fish.

CABRAS

Sa Funtà

Road map B4. Via Garibaldi 25.
📞 *0783-29 06 85.* 🔓 🛗 **V** 🪑
🍽 *Sun, Jan, Feb.* 🌙 *V.* ⓁⓁⒷ

A small, elegant establishment in Oristano tradition: soup with herbs (in winter), *bottarga* (dried mullet roe) as a first course, *burrida* (fish in spicy sauce), or fresh mullet.

CUGLIERI

Meridiana

Road map B3. Via Littorio 1.
📞 *0785-394 00.* 🍴 🔓 🛗 🪑
🍽 🌙 *Wed, mid-late Oct, two weeks in Jan.* 🌙 *V.* ⓁⓁⒷ

A range of fish specials: crayfish and mushroom salad, fried squid with zucchini, sea urchins on toasted bread, *bottarga* and figs, swordfish risotto, clam and mussel soup. Reserve early.

GHILARZA

Al Marchi

Road map C3. Via Concezione 4.
📞 *0785-522 80.* 🔓 🛗 **V** 🪑 🍽
🍽 *Mon, Aug, two weeks in Jan.*
🌙 *AE, DC, MC, V.* ⓁⒷ

In the heart of town. Traditional island appetizers, followed by raviolini with a light sauce of tomato and spinach, porcini mushrooms, mutton baked in foil, grilled meat in wine sauce.

ORISTANO

Da Gino

Road map B4. Via Tirso 13.
📞 *0783-714 28.* 🛗 🪑 🍽 🍽
Sun, from mid-Aug to early Sep. Ⓛ

In the heart of Oristano in a characteristic building, which has been completely restored, you can enjoy pasta with sea urchins or sea anemones, Gino's special lobster, and various game dishes.

Da Giovanni

Road map B4. Via Colombo 8.
📞 *0783-220 51.* 🍴 🔓 🛗 🌿
🪑 🍽 🌙 *Mon.* 🌙 *DC, MC, V.* ⓁⓁ

The owner exhorts people to enjoy "fish, fish, and more fish." It comes straight off the boat and arrives on the table as starters or first and second courses. Seafood sauce, spaghetti with sea urchins and *bottarga*, barbecued squid, bass with Vernaccia, stewed cuttlefish with peas, gilthead bream, dentex (fish), and lobster.

Il Faro

Road map B4. Via Bellini 25.
📞 *0783-700 02.* 🍴 🔓 🛗 🌿
🪑 🍽 🍽 *after 10pm, Sun eve.*
🌙 *AE, DC, V.* ⓁⓁⒷ

Il Faro is well known for its traditional cuisine and seasonal fish: mullet, sea bass, gilthead bream as well as ravioli with ricotta cheese and asparagus tips, and Sardinian desserts.

PORTO TORRES

Li Lioni

Road map B2. SS131, Località Li Lioni. 📞 *079-50 22 86.* 🔓 🛗 🌿
V 🪑 🍽 *after 10pm, Wed, Nov.*
🌙 *AE, DC, MC, V.* ⓁⒷ .

In the countryside, 3 km (2 miles) from Porto Torres, Li Lioni is in a rustic setting with a large garden. All the meat dishes are cooked over an open fire in the fireplace. Try the macaroni with wild boar or mutton sauce, *culungiones*, and barbecued veal kebabs.

STINTINO

Silvestrino

Road map B2. Via Sassari 12.
📞 *079-52 30 07.* 🍴 🔓 🛗 🌿
V 🪑 🍽 *after 10pm in winter; weekly closing day variable, mid-Dec–mid-Jan.* 🌙 *AE, MC, V.* ⓁⒷ

In the center of Stintino, on the ground floor of a hotel, Silvestrino has a family atmosphere and more than 50 years of customer appreciation for its special lobster soup, grilled fish, and prize-winning *baci alla Silvestrino*: oven-baked croquettes with a cheese filling, topped with bechamel and tomatoes.

THE NORTH AND THE COSTA SMERALDA

ARZACHENA

Grazia Deledda

Road map D1. Road to Baia Sardinia.
📞 *0789-989 90.* 🔓 🪑 🍽
🍽 *Nov–Apr.* 🌙 *AE, DC, MC, V.*
ⓁⓁⒷ

Overlooking the beautiful bay of Cannigione, this restaurant is furnished with rare examples of Sardinian handicrafts. The cooking is sophisticated and includes soup of ovoli and porcini mushrooms, and *moscardini* (octopus) with Vermentino. High prices but the seafood is always superfresh.

Tiana

Road map D1. Località Tiana, road to Palau. 📞 *0789-821 95.* 🔓 🛗
🪑 🍽 *Mon.* 🌙 *AE, DC, MC, V.* ⓁⒷ

Varied seafood appetizers, spaghetti with lobster, mixed grilled and fried fish, baked dentex with shellfish, but above all specilties of the Gallura region. Tiana is only 2 km (1 mile) from the Costa Smeralda crowds.

CASTELSARDO

Fofò

Road map C2. Lungomare Anglona 1.
📞 *079-47 01 43.* 🍴 🔓 🛗
V 🪑 🍽 *Wed.* 🌙 *AE, DC, MC, V.*
ⓁⒷ

Lobsters from the nearby fish farm are prepared according to various recipes, such as Aragonese lobster soup. An alternative is risotto *alla corsara* with shellfish. If you order beforehand you can also have suckling pig or lamb.

LOIRI–PORTO SAN PAOLO

Cala Junco

Road map D2. Viale Pietro Nenni 8/10. 📞 *0789-402 60.* 🍴 🔓 🛗
V 🪑 🍽 🍽 *Tue in winter, 15 days in Jan.* 🌙 *AE, DC, MC, V.* ⓁⒷ

Cala Junca is by the sea, only 20 minutes from Olbia, and offers fish as well as many other traditional dishes. Among the first courses are soups such as *zuppa gallurese* and *minestra della nonna* with chard, and homemade pasta such as tagliatelle with mushrooms and mushroom sauce. Other choices include *mazzamurro* (a kind of flan made with bread soaked in milk, pecorino cheese and tomatoes), *fregula* with mussels, *pane frattau*, and lobster.

OLBIA

Bacchus 2

Road map D2. Via G D'Annunzio (Centro Martini). **(** 0789-216 12. ⛔ 🚻 **V** 🚻 🍴 ● *Sun in winter.* ○ *lunch only in summer, Feb–Nov.* 💳 *AE, DC, MC, V.* ⓁⓁ

Bacchus has antipasti with original combinations of vegetables and fish, *culungiones* stuffed with cheese and mint, rolled bundles of fillet of beef with smoked ham, stuffed squid, and a selection of special desserts.

Gallura

Road map D2. Corso Umberto 145. **(** 0789-246 48. 🚻 ⛔ **V** 🚻 🍴 ● *after 10pm, Mon, Oct 15-30, Dec 20–Jan 6.* 💳 *AE, DC, MC, V.* ⓁⓁⓁⓁ

Creativity is the key word here, beginning with the pasta (with sage, carrot, or saffron) and the delectable sauces (zucchini flowers and mussels). Main courses include meat and fish, and the desserts are delicious.

PALAU

Il Porticciolo

Road map D1. Piazza del Comune. **(** 0789-70 85 98. ⛔ 🚻 🚻 ● *Mon.* Ⓛ

This is a small, family-run trattoria, with a menu that changes daily, and choices dependent on the local market. Simple, good cooking, with both fish and meat offered. The *astice alla catalana* (Catalan-style lobster) is recommended. Among desserts, try the excellent tiramisù to finish.

Zio Nicola

Road map D1. Porticciolo Turistico. **(** 0789-70 85 20. ⛔ 🚻 🚻 ● *Wed in winter.* 💳 *DC, MC, V.* ⓁⓁ

Located in the port, this restaurant is run with great professionalism. The menu includes a range of meat and fish, grilled or panfried, prepared simply and with great care. There are plenty of tables outside in a large, tree-shaded garden. Rapid, good service.

La Gritta

Road map D1. I Faraglioni di Porto Faro. **(** 0789-70 80 45. 🚻 🚻 🚻 ● *Oct 15–Mar 15.* 💳 *AE, DC, MC, V.* ⓁⓁⓁ

One of Sardinia's top restaurants, with a large covered terrace overlooking the bay of Porto Rafael. Among many delicacies are stuffed squid with saffron sauce, linguine with delicate fish sauce and fish with potatoes and olives. Excellent wine list, and a special mention for the grappas.

PORTO CERVO

Gianni Pedrinelli

Road map D1. Località Piccolo Pevero. **(** 0789-924 36. 🍴 🚻 ⛔ 🚻 **V** 🚻 ● *lunchtime except Sat and Sun, Nov.* 💳 *AE, DC, MC, V.* ⓁⓁ

Fregula with mussels, fresh tomatoes, and clams, pasta with lobster, homemade gnocchi, fish in salt, and grilled suckling pig are the specials at Pedrinelli.

PORTO ROTONDO

Il Baretto

Road map D1. Piazzetta Rudalza. **(** 0789-340 18. 🍴 🚻 ⛔ 🚻 🚻 🍴 ● *Oct–Easter.* 💳 *AE, DC, MC, V.* ⓁⓁⓁ

This is a summer restaurant so most tables are outside, but there is also an air-conditioned room. Specials are first courses such as fresh fish or ricotta ravioli and seafood risotto, followed by fish cooked in foil and suckling pig.

SASSARI

L'Assassino

Road map B2. Vicolo Ospizio Cappuccini 1B. **(** 079-23 50 41. 🍴 🚻 ⛔ **V** 🚻 ● *Sun.* 💳 *AE, DC, MC, V.* Ⓛ

A typical Sassarese restaurant offering all kinds of meat dishes (including lamb, pork, and horse) and, in the winter, lamb's feet with herbs or various sauces.

Gianni e Amedeo

Road map B2. Via Alghero 69. **(** 079-27 45 98. ⛔ 🚻 🚻 ● *Sun, Aug.* 💳 *AE, DC, MC, V.* ⓁⓁⓁ

Furnished in rustic style, but the cooking is high quality in the best

tradition of fish and seafood cooking. Classic dishes like gnocchetti or Sardinian ravioli with pecorino, mint, and potato. To round off a delicious meal, try the *seadas* with a glass or two of Mirto (myrtle) liqueur.

SAN TEODORO

La Columbella

Road map D2. Piazzetta di Puntaldia. **(** 0784-86 41 76. 🚻 ⛔ 🚻 **V** 🚻 ● *Sun eve, Mon in winter.* 💳 *AE, DC, MC, V.* ⓁⓁⓁⓁ

This restaurant has a terrace overlooking the sea and offers elegant cuisine and atmosphere, featuring 50 dishes, mostly fish, from roast skate with raisins to seafood pesto sauce for the homemade pasta.

SANTA TERESA DI GALLURA

Canne al Vento

Road map C1. Via Nazionale 23. **(** 0789-75 42 19. 🚻 ⛔ 🚻 🚻 ● *lunch, after 10pm, Mon, Sep 30–Apr 1.* 💳 *MC, V.* ⓁⓁ

A family-run restaurant serving characteristic Sardinian dishes such as *zuppa cuata* soup with bread, cheeses, and mutton stock, lemon-flavored ravioli and mutton with herbs.

Riva

Road map C1. Via del Porto 29. **(** 0789-75 43 92. 🚻 🚻 ● *Wed in winter.* 💳 *AE, DC, MC, V.* ⓁⓁⓁ

Only 200 m (650 ft) from the port, Riva is a fish restaurant, but in the summer it also has suckling pig, *pane frattau* and *malloreddus*. The specialties are seafood risotto, razor-clam and mussel soup, fish ravioli, spaghetti with crab, and gilthead bream with Vermentino or Torbato wine.

TEMPIO PAUSANIA

Il Pizzicotto

Road map C2. Via Gramsci, 37. **(** 079-67 04 77. 🍴 🚻 ⛔ **V** 🚻 🍴 ● *Fri.* Ⓛ

Simple rustic cuisine: *zuppa gallurese* made with durum wheat bread, cheeses, and meat stock, homemade gnocchi, *seadas*, and a range of different kinds of pizza and flat bread.

For key to symbols *see p179*

SHOPS AND MARKETS

SARDINIA PRODUCES A GREAT variety of handicrafts that are hard to find in other regions of Italy. Among these are hand-woven rugs, linen napkins, *pibbiones* (embroidered fabrics), and baskets. Traditional materials and techniques are used for all these products, and while some are still made in the traditional style, others have been adapted to more modern tastes. Crafted goods are often made to a very

Local olives

high standard of design and workmanship, and include coral and filigree pins and brooches, pottery and crockery, and items made from cork and wrought iron.

In the larger towns and tourist resorts, traditional souvenirs are sold, such as ashtrays in the shape of nuraghi, costumed dolls, and seashell pictures. Specialties such as pecorino cheese, salted mullet roe, candies, and wine are also worth trying.

OPENING HOURS

SHOPS IN SARDINIA generally open in the morning at 9am and close at 1pm for lunch. Afternoon hours are 4–8pm (4:30–8:30pm in the summer). In the cities most shops close for two or three weeks in August while, on the coast, they tend to open on a seasonal basis, from June to September.

A potter at the wheel

HOW TO PAY

THE MAJORITY of the larger shops and department stores accept credit cards, but it is advisable to check in advance. The smaller shops and artisan's workshops will generally prefer payment in cash. You must get a receipt *(ricevuta fiscale)* when you pay; it is required by law and you may be asked to produce it as you leave the shop. It will also be needed should you want to return purchased articles later on.

DEPARTMENT STORES

THE MAIN DEPARTMENT store in Cagliari is **La Rinascente** in Via Roma. Other large stores are **Upim** and **Standa**, which you will also find in other Sardinian towns and cities. Recently, large shopping centers have grown up on the outskirts of towns, with a wide selection of goods available, from shoeshops and clothing stores to supermarkets and fast food restaurants.

HANDICRAFTS

LOCAL HANDICRAFTS are on sale all over Sardinia. In the villages, women display their wares, such as baskets, rugs, or ceramics, outside their homes.

Shops that belong to the *Istituto Sardo Organizzazione Lavoro Artigianale* (**ISOLA**), Sardinian Institute of Handicrafts, offer quality products from the local craftsmen's cooperatives, including rugs, tablecloths, leather, jewelry, baskets, pottery, carved wood,

Local handicrafts for sale in a certified ISOLA shop

and wrought-iron objects. All ISOLA products carry a seal of quality guaranteeing their origin and authenticity.

You can find good bargains at the *Fiera del Tappeto* (Carpet Fair), held at Mogoro in late July–August. Handicrafts can also be purchased at vacation farms. Other useful addresses can be found in the Esit publication *Sardegna – Un Mare di Tradizioni.*

A fish stand in Cagliari's covered market, San Benedetto

REGIONAL SPECIALTIES

Gastronomic specialties in Sardinia are sold in the food section of supermarkets as well as delicatessens and specialty shops or directly from the producers.

The **Mercato Coperto di San Benedetto**, an indoor market in Cagliari, offers an excellent choice of regional delicacies. *Bottarga* (mullet roe) can be bought at **Vaghi**, on Via Bayle, which also sells sea urchin pâté. Salted *bottarga* can be bought directly from the manufacturer at **Fratelli**

San Francesco's feast day celebrated at Lula with barbecued *porceddu*

A dish of typical
Sardinian honey

Manca in Cabras. Smoked fish is on sale at **Sarda Affumicati** in Buggerru.

Cakes and candies are also Sardinian specialties; a fine selection is offered in several shops, including **Sorelle Piccioni** in Quartu Sant'Elena, **Colomba Codias** in Olbia, and **Acciari** at Porto Torres.

A visit to a winery *(cantina)* to taste the wines before buying can prove both interesting and a bargain. It is sometimes possible to taste wines in a wine shop *(enoteca)*.

Other useful addresses of shops and workshops are listed in the publication by Esit, *Sardegna – Un Mare di Delizie*.

DIRECTORY

HANDICRAFTS

Alghero
ISOLA
Via Catalogna 54–6.
☎ 079-95 21 44.

Cagliari
ISOLA
Via Bacaredda 176–8.
☎ 070-49 27 56.

Nuoro
ISOLA
Via Monsignor Bua 10.
☎ 0784-315 07.

Olbia
Sardartis srl
SS125, km 313.
☎ 0789-669 33.

Cerasarda
Road for Palau, km 2,800.
☎ 0789-500 32.

Oristano
ISOLA
Via Tirso
& Via Lombardia.
☎ 0783-21 18 77.

Porto Cervo
ISOLA
Sottopiazza.
☎ 0789-944 28.

Sassari
ISOLA
Viale Mancini.
☎ 079-23 01 01.

REGIONAL SPECIALTIES

Alghero
Campu Fioridu
Via Sassari 4.
☎ 079-98 21 52.

Sella & Mosca
I Piani.
☎ 079-99 77 00.

Buggerru
Sarda Affumicati
Portixeddu.
☎ 0781-549 14.

Cabras
Fratelli Manca
Via Cima 5.
☎ 0783-29 08 48.

Cagliari
Mercato San Benedetto
Via San Benedetto.

Vaghi
Via Bayle 25.
☎ 070-65 17 60.

Olbia
Colomba Codias
Via Australia 12.
☎ 0789-682 26.

Ozieri
Pasticceria Pietro Pinna
Via Pastorino 35.
☎ 079-78 74 51.

Porto Torres
Acciaro
Corso Vittorio Emanuele 38.
☎ 079-51 46 05.

Quartu Sant'Elena
Sorelle Piccioni
Via Marconi 312.
☎ 070-81 01 12.

Sassari
Fratelli Rau
Via Gorizia 7.
☎ 079-29 22 64.

Tonara
Salvatore Pruneddu
Via Porru 7.
☎ 0784-638 05.

WINE

Cabras
Azienda Attilio Contini
Via Genova 48.
☎ 0783-29 08 06.

Cagliari
Enoteca Cagliaritana
Scalette Santa Chiara.
☎ 070-65 56 11.

Jerzu
Società Cooperativa
Vitivinicola di Jerzu
Via Umberto I 1.
☎ 0782-700 28.

Oristano
Cantina Sociale della Vernaccia
Stabilimento Rimedio.
☎ 0783-331 55.

Quartu Sant'Elena
Cantina Sociale
Via Marconi 489.
☎ 070-82 60 33.

Olbia
Enoteca e Ristorante Il Portico
Via Assisi.
☎ 0789-256 70.

Sant'Antioco
Cantina Sociale
Via Rinascita 46.
☎ 0781-830 55.

Sassari
Cantina Fratelli Dettori
Via Manunta 2.
☎ 079-39 55 01.

Serdiana
Cantina Argiolas
Via Roma 56.
☎ 070-74 06 06.

What to Buy in Sardinia

SARDINIA OFFERS A GREAT VARIETY of traditional island products and local handicrafts, ranging from hand-woven rugs, bedspreads, and pillowcases to baskets woven in asphodel, reed, or raffia. Some of the finest baskets are made in Flussio and Castelsardo. Other household articles, such as kitchenware and tableware, are made of cork or ceramics, materials that are also used to make large plates, statues, and bas-reliefs. Filigree and coral jewelry production is widespread and is worn by the women for festivals and weddings; the best jewelry is made in Alghero and Bosa.

Filigree pendant

Gold buttons

Pin and earrings

Brooch

Coral pin

JEWELRY

Traditional Sardinian jewelry, such as earrings, brooches, and buttons, often worn with local dress, is made of filigree and coral. Goldsmiths also make bracelets and necklaces in modern designs, including elegant coral spirals.

Circular amphora

Flower vase

At Calangianus, in the Gallura region of the Costa Smeralda, cork is used to make such household articles as boxes, umbrella stands, bowls, and ice buckets.

Cork ice bucket

Vases and jugs made to a modern design

POTTERY

Sardinian pottery is hand-thrown and glazed with natural colors. The most common articles are vases, plates, and jugs, and the designs are simple and fluid. Some potters have modified traditional designs to suit modern tastes.

Basket-weaving is an ancient craft that is still widely practiced. Baskets are made of straw, raffia, dwarf palm, asphodel, corn sheaves, or wicker in delicate, natural colors.

Rug made in Nule

Tapestry from Mogoro

A *pibbiones* rug

RUGS AND TAPESTRIES

Among the typical hand-woven articles are woolen rugs, linen bedspreads and napkins, and tapestries. The rugs are made from colored wool with lively geometric or floral designs. The *pibbiones* rugs consist of an embroidered raised pattern knitted with small needles on neutral colored fabric.

Wood carving *is an ancient Sardinian tradition. The most common articles produced are chests, kitchen tools, chopping boards, and ceremonial masks.*

Carved mask

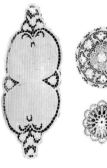

Lacework from Dorgali

Lace making *is a rare craft that requires great skill. At Oliena you can find delicate shawls made of black silk embroidered with bright colors. At Bosa you can still see women making filet lace.*

GASTRONOMIC DELICACIES

Typical Sardinian products include cakes and cheeses, which vary from region to region. Other specialties include jam, wine, and liqueurs, such as myrtle and lemon, salted mullet roe, and vegetables in oil.

Typical Sardinian cakes

Salted mullet roe

Myrtle liqueur

Typical Sardinian delicacies

SURVIVAL
GUIDE

PRACTICAL INFORMATION

BEACHES AND CLEAN BLUE sea are the principal attractions for visitors to Sardinia, and the coastline, especially in the northeast, gets very crowded from early July to late August. Visiting the island out of season can have its advantages, apart from avoiding the bustling crowds. The weather can be very hot in midsummer, and visits to the towns and countryside, rich in history, ancient culture, old traditions, and spellbinding scenery, are all the more easily appreciated in spring, early summer, and autumn.

Tourist information sign

Tourism is a relatively new phenomenon in Sardinia, and the familiar problems of funding and staffing for monuments and museums occur here as on the mainland. Do not be surprised to see signs such as *chiuso per restauro* (closed for restoration). Provision of information for travelers is far from perfect but is improving; there are now more tourist offices, opening at regular hours, able to provide maps and guides to help you plan your time. Attempts to speak Italian, however halting, are always appreciated.

Cooling off in midsummer

WHEN TO VISIT

IN JULY AND AUGUST practically the whole of Italy goes on vacation and everywhere is overcrowded, in particular the ferries to and from Olbia and Cagliari, and the seaside hotels and resorts. Prices are much higher, so you need to plan your visit ahead to make sure of accommodations. The most crowded areas are the Costa Smeralda, the beaches near the Golfo di Cagliari, and the area around Stintino.

The best months to visit the beautiful interior are May, June, and September. Spring is particularly delightful, when flowers are in bloom.

In winter the cold can be quite intense, especially at higher altitudes.

TOURIST INFORMATION

THERE ARE SEVERAL DIFFERENT categories of tourist office, depending on the size and status of each town. Each provincial capital has an **Ente Provinciale per il Turismo** (EPT), a provincial tourist office where information and literature are available. Some of the more famous sites have an **Azienda Autonoma di Soggiorno e Turismo** (AAST), or local tourist office. In small

towns and villages the Pro Loco, or local Town Hall, takes over the tourist information role. Information on tours and trips is issued at the EPT or the **Ente Sardo Industrie Turistiche** (ESIT), the Sardinian tourist board.

The local newspapers, *La Nuova Sardegna* and *L'Unione Sarda*, are also valuable sources of information, with complete day-by-day listings.

For those with access to the Internet, there is a useful website at www.sardinia.net where you can find all kinds of information on farm vacations as well as details of exhibitions and events.

IMMIGRATION AND CUSTOMS

EUROPEAN UNION (EU) residents and visitors from the United States, Canada, New Zealand, Australia, Japan, etc, need no visa for up to three months but must have one for a longer stay. Non-European Union citizens must carry a valid passport with them, while for EU citizens an ID will suffice. Non-EU citizens can bring in either 400 cigarettes or 100 cigars or 500 grams of tobacco, 1 liter of spirits, 2 liters of wine, and 50 grams of perfume. Valuable goods like cameras or watches may be imported only for personal use. Non-EU citizens can claim back sales tax (IVA) on purchases over L650,000.

Snowy scene in the interior, not unusual in midwinter

SHOPS, BANKS, AND POST OFFICES

THIS GUIDE provides the opening hours for the island's museums and archaeological sites. Shops are open from 8 or 9am to 1pm and from 3:30 or 4pm (in winter) or 5pm (in summer) to 7–8pm from Monday to Saturday, with one early closing day during the week. Banks are open from Monday to Friday from 8:30am–1:30pm and 3:30–4:30pm. Post offices are open from 9am–1pm and from 6–7pm. Italian mail is notoriously slow. The Italian national telephone company,

An elegant shop offering Sardinian crafts

Telecom Italia, runs both coin-operated and card (*scheda telefonica*) public telephones in all towns.

MUSEUMS AND MONUMENTS

NORMALLY museums and archaeological zones are open every morning except Monday, but many sites are also open in the afternoon and, in summer, opening hours are extended.

Museum entrance fees vary from L2,000–8,000 and, in line with EU rules, there are discounts or free entry for children, young people under 18, and senior citizens.

Churches in the interior are usually closed in the middle of the day and may be open only for mass. If a church is closed, the parish priest (*parroco*) or sexton may open it for you as a special favor for a short visit. A small contribution to church funds will always be welcome in return for assistance.

FESTIVALS

SARDINIA'S FESTIVALS HAVE a very long history and are colorful and unusual affairs. The busiest times of year for

Traditional rituals, still part of the community year in Sardinia

seeing traditional festivals are at Carnival and Easter. Tourist offices provide information on feast days and festivals, and dates are also given in the information for each town in this guide.

DISABLED TRAVELERS

UNFORTUNATELY, special facilities for the disabled are rare, even in the larger towns, and touring can be quite a frustrating experience for wheelchair users.

For more information on advice and assistance for the disabled, contact the ESIT offices in Cagliari.

Personal Security and Health

O N THE WHOLE, SARDINIA is a safe place for visitors and only a few precautions are needed for a pleasant stay. There is some petty crime, so be careful of money and belongings in the busy passenger terminals of the ports and in cities. Don't leave valuables in your car if the parking place is unsupervised. On the whole, rural areas are generally safer than cities. During the summer, forest fires are a very serious problem, so be sure to follow the instructions of the local police or firemen should an emergency arise. If you get sick, the nearest pharmacy *(farmacia)* is a good first stop.

CREDIT CARDS AND LOST PROPERTY

I T IS NEVER A GOOD IDEA to carry a lot of cash with you. The major credit cards (VISA, MasterCard, American Express, and Diners Club) are accepted by the majority of shops, restaurants, and hotels on the island. It is reasonably easy to find automatic cash machines *(bancomat)* in all the large cities, but interest will be charged on currency exchange withdrawals, so you may prefer to carry travelers' checks as well.

Generally speaking, it is safe to park where you like, as car theft is not common, especially in small towns. However, if anything is stolen, go immediately to the local police or carabinieri to report the theft; you will need the report for the insurance claim.

FIRE HAZARDS

U NFORTUNATELY, forest fires are a real problem in Sardinia, especially in the summer. Except for rare cases

Fire, a constant danger

of accidental fire that may be caused by a tossed cigarette, most fires on the island are started deliberately. In some instances forest and brush are destroyed to make way for more grazing land but, more often than not, the motive is to clear space for new buildings. In an attempt to stop the practice, a law has been passed prohibiting con-struction in areas destroyed by fire, but even this has not stopped arsonists. In the dry heat of summer, fire spreads rapidly in the undergrowth of the maquis, and the main

enemy of the firemen is the wind, which is capable of carrying the fire a long way in a very short time. Fire fighting is carried out by the local fire departments and the state forest rangers, volunteers, and specially equipped fire-fighting planes positioned in key areas of the island.

MEDICAL TREATMENT

I F YOU NEED medical assistance during your stay, Sardinia has a network of hospitals and emergency rooms *(pronto soccorso)* as well as pharmacies which can dispense advice as well as medicines. Visitors from the US should check with their insurance carriers before leaving home to make sure they are covered.

In all the tourist resorts there is a *Guardia Medica* (emergency treatment center) equipped to give medical attention to summer visitors. These offices are often closed in the winter so you will have to go to one of the main hospitals for emergencies.

Pharmacies in Sardinia are open from Monday to Friday, 9am–1pm and 4–7pm and Saturday morning. Lists of the night and holiday opening rotations for the local area are posted on the door.

FIRE PREVENTION RULES

1. Always be sure to extinguish cigarettes before discarding them.
2. Never light a fire except in areas where this is explicitly permitted.
3. If you see a fire, you must report it to the local firemen.
4. Do not stop or park your car to watch a fire; you may block the roads and interfere with fire-fighting operations.
5. Pay attention to the wind direction: it is highly dangerous to be down-wind of a fire, as it may spread quite rapidly and catch you unaware.

Policemen on horseback at the Poetto beach near Cagliari

COUNTRYSIDE CODES

DURING YOUR STAY you are likely to spend a good deal of time exploring outdoors, so be prepared for any problems that may occur.

In the summer, whether you are on the beach or in the interior, be wary of too much sun because it may cause serious burns and sunstroke. If it is windy, you may not be aware you are burning.

If a storm breaks and you need to take shelter, do not head for isolated trees or rocky peaks, which may attract lightning.

Although you cannot simply camp wherever you like, you can make private arrangements with landowners to pitch your tent away from official camping sites. Make sure you take away all your garbage, and do not light fires.

Bear in mind that grazing in the open countryside is still quite common in Sardinia: pigs, sheep, cows, and horses may well decide to see whether campers have anything good to eat in their tents. In hilly areas sheepdogs

Camping on the beach is forbidden in Sardinia, but private arrangements can be made on farmland with landowners

should be avoided, since they are trained to chase away any potential intruders.

While walking or trekking in the countryside you may come across gates or fences barring your way. It is always a good idea, if possible, to ask whether you can go through. Having done so, remember to close the gate so that animals are unable to escape. If you plan a lengthy hike, make sure you carry enough water with you, as villages may be few and far between. Despite the wildness, there are no poisonous snakes.

EMERGENCY TELEPHONE NUMBERS

General Emergencies
[113.

Police (Carabinieri Pronto Intervento)
[112.

Fire (Vigili del Fuoco)
[115.

Road Emergencies (Soccorso Stradale)
[116.

Medical Emergencies
[118.

Operator Information
[12.

Nautical Information
[196.

Mountain Emergencies (Soccorso Alpino)
[070-72 81 63 or 28 62 00 or 0784-3 10 70.

USING BANKS

BANK OPENING HOURS are usually 8:30am–1:30pm and 3–4:30pm from Monday to Friday. All banks close on weekends and public holidays. Credit cards, once regarded with suspicion in Sardinia, are now accepted without question by hotels, restaurants, and shops, especially those in the tourist areas. All the major credit cards are accepted, with the most popular cards being VISA and MasterCard (Access). There are automatic cash machines *(bancomat)* in the larger towns.

CURRENCY EXCHANGE

Foreign visitors will find automatic currency exchange machines at the airports. However, it is always a good idea to have some Italian currency before your departure for any immediate expenses. Because of lower commission rates, it costs less to exchange money in banks. Italy's currency is the *lira* (plural *lire*); banknotes come in denominations of L1,000, L2,000, L5,000, L10,000, L50,000, and L100,000. Large notes are not always acceptable for small purchases. If you use travelers' checks, buy them in a bank or from a well-known firm. It is not usually worthwhile changing small amounts because the rate of commission is fixed. The opening hours of foreign exchange offices are similar to many stores and may be useful when the banks are closed.

Current Italian banknotes

Water Sports

DESPITE THE IMPRESSIVE BEAUTY of its interior, Sardinia's fame is more strongly associated with the sea. The development of the tourist industry means that the island now offers a good range of facilities for water sports, in particular sailing, windsurfing, and scuba diving. There are diving centers and sailing schools in almost all the coastal resorts, and many of the resort villages are well equipped for water sports. Canoeing is a different matter, since the lack of navigable rivers limits your choice in the interior, and sea canoeing is practiced only in a few places along the coast.

Sailing along the coast

SAILING

WITH ITS MARVELOUS sea and coastline, Sardinia is regarded as a paradise for boating of all kinds, whether your preferred style is a billion-dollar luxury yacht on the Costa Smeralda or a simple dinghy rented from one of the more affordable centers. The conditions vary considerably and even experienced sailors find the Sardinian coast a challenge because of the strong and variable winds. A good source of useful information for a sailing vacation is volume 1A of *Portolano del Mediterraneo* (Mediterranean Pilot's Book), published by the Istituto Idrografico della Marina Militare. Another useful publication is the pamphlet *I Porti Turistici della Sardegna* (Sardinian Yacht Harbors), available from all tourist information offices. You need permission from the harbormaster to moor in most of Sardinia's harbors.

SCUBA DIVING

THE COASTLINE offers plenty of opportunities for experienced divers. Among the most famous spots for diving are the coasts of Asinara and Gallura, Capo Caccia, Carloforte, the Golfo di Orosei, and the area around the island of Tavolara. Many diving centers will organize diving trips. You can also buy or rent diving equipment and get advice on diving sites.

Diving in the crystal-clear waters of Sardinia

WINDSURFING

WINDSURFING EQUIPMENT is available for rent at almost all the tourist beaches. Some of the sailing centers also offer boards for rent and can organize lessons.

Windsurfing in the open sea

WINDSURFING BEACHES

The following beaches are the best on the island for windsurfing:

Bosa Marina
Poetto – Cagliari
Calagrande – Isola di Sant'Antioco
Saline – Isola di Sant'Antioco
Monti d'a Rena – La Maddalena
Porto Massimo – La Maddalena
Porto Taverna – Porto San Paolo
Lotzorai
Marinella – Olbia
Porto Istana – Olbia
Torre Grande – Oristano
Porto Pollo – Palau
Capo Testa – Santa Teresa di Gallura
La Cinta – San Teodoro
Putzu Idu – San Vero Milis
Platamona - Sorso
La Pelosa – Stintino

The Centro Velico Caprera sailing school

The safety rules for sailing also apply to this sport: the winds can be very strong and fickle (especially the mistral), so do not go too far out.

CANOEING

ALTHOUGH there are very few navigable rivers for canoeing in the interior – and the variable weather makes practicing the sport even more difficult – you can canoe in the lakes or along certain stretches of the coast.

OTHER SPORTS

THERE ARE NUMEROUS COVES along the Sardinian coasts where you can explore the rocks and the water and observe the varied marine life. Snorkeling is perhaps best left to the experienced: strong winds, and currents can easily create difficult and dangerous conditions.

Subaqua fishing with a harpoon and Aqua-Lungs are not permitted but freshwater fishing is possible in the lakes and reservoirs. You will need a permit to fish in the rivers.

In some resort villages water-based tours are offered to guests, and some even provide dinghys in which to explore the coastline.

Canoeing in the fabulous Cala Sisine cove

DIRECTORY

SAILING AND WINDSURFING CENTERS

Yacht Club Cagliari
Marina Piccola.
☎ 070-37 03 50.

Windsurfing Club Cagliari
Marina Piccola.
☎ 070-37 26 94.

Carloforte Yacht Club
☎ 0781-85 50 08.

Gruppo Vela LNI Carloforte
☎ 0781-85 56 18.

Windsurfing Vela Club Portoscuso
Portoscuso, Cagliari.
☎ 0781-50 95 38.

Centro Velico Caprera – La Maddalena
Porto Palma.
☎ 0789-73 85 29.

Club Nautico La Maddalena
Via G Cesare 20.
☎ 0789-73 83 32.

Gruppo Vela LNI Alghero
At the quay.
☎ 079-98 40 93.

Circolo Nautico Arbatax
☎ 0782-66 75 66.

Circolo Nautico Olbia
Via Genova 69.
☎ 0789-261 87.

Yacht Club Porto Rotondo
☎ 0789-340 10.

Yacht Club Alghero
☎ 079-95 20 74.

Yacht Club Costa Smeralda – Porto Cervo
Porto Cervo.
☎ 0789-913 32.

Circolo Nautico Oristano
Torregrande.
☎ 0783-21 01 72.

DIVING CENTERS

Acqua Pro Scuba Center
La Maddalena.
☎ 0789-73 53 85.

Area Mare Diving
Cannigione.
☎ 0789-884 28.

Nautilus
Palau.
☎ 0330-21 09 75.

Oyster Sub Diving Center
Palau.
☎ 0789-70 20 70.

Orso Diving Club – Porto Cervo
☎ 0789-990 01.

Time to Dive – Portisco
☎ 0789-335 12.

Centro Sub Isuledda Compagnia dell'Avventura
Cannigione, Arzachena.
☎ 0789-862 53.

Centro Sub Tavolara
Porto San Paolo.
☎ 0789-403 60.

Aqua Diving Center Puntaldia
Puntaldia,
San Teodoro.
☎ 0784-86 43 90.

Tanka Village Diving Center – Villasimius
☎ 070-79 51.

Air Sub Service – Villasimius
☎ 070-50 68 63.

Carloforte Tonnare Diving Center
Carloforte.
☎ 0781-85 48 40.

Centro Sub Caribù
c/o Villaggio Capo Caccia.
☎ 079-94 66 66.

L'Argonauta Diving Center
Cala Gonone.
☎ 0784-930 46.

CANOEING

Canoa Club Cagliari
☎ 070-65 13 18.

Associazione Italiana Kayak da Mare – Cagliari
☎ 070-66 04 89.

Scuola Canoa Cagliari
☎ 070-37 24 87.

Canoa Club Acque Selvagge – Cagliari
☎ 070-72 58 25.

Canoa Club Oristano
☎ 0783-21 03 35.

Outdoor Sports

NEGLECTED FOR YEARS because attention was focused on tourist development along the coast, the interior landscape of Sardinia offers plenty of opportunity to practice outdoor sports. The countryside can be explored on foot or on horseback – riding centers have made great advances in recent years and are in high demand. Facilities for hiking and rock climbing are good, and increasing numbers of mountain climbing routes are in the process of being marked out.

The Su Rei riding center in Sulcis

HORSEBACK RIDING

SARDINIA IS IDEALLY suited for trekking and riding. Horses have long been an integral part of the island's culture, as the animal has been part of local life since Phoenician times: many of the religious feast days and festivities include breakneck rides and horse races.

The many isolated minor roads, mule tracks, and paths, far away from traffic and noise, particularly in the interior, are ideal for pleasant rides, and many are not too difficult for beginners.

There are nearly 100 Sardinian equestrian clubs and centers, large and small, offering facilities for this sport. Most are equipped to organize lessons and rides for beginners as well as extended treks for experienced riders.

Most of the stables and clubs are located near Cagliari, Nuoro, and Oristano, but there has been an increase in the number of vacation farms *(see p170)* offering horseback riding and excursions for their guests, whatever their ability.

Supramonte, Giara di Gesturi, and the Valle della Luna are three of the most interesting and popular destinations for those who love long treks in the Sardinian countryside.

ROCK CLIMBING

IN THE 1960S THE Italian mountaineer Alessandro Gogna published *Mezzogiorno di Pietra* (Midday Stone), which opened up the possibilities for rock climbing in Sardinia. Since those days enthusiasm for the sport has grown considerably, and the island's most challenging

Cliffs at the seaside with facilities for rock climbing

rocks and cliffs are tackled by climbers from all over Italy and Europe. Among the most popular climbing areas are Supramonte (Surtana, l'Aguglia), the cliffs at Iglesiente (Domusnovas), where hand- and footholds have recently been placed, and the Isili area in Nuoro province.

Essential reading for rock climbers who decide to come here is *Pietra di Luna* (Moon Stone) by Maurizio Oviglia, the most up-to-date guide to rock climbing in Sardinia.

Additional information can be obtained at the **Sezione di Cagliari del Club Alpino Italiano**. Climbing lessons and special programs are organized by **Pietra di Luna** (070-28 87 46 or 29 18 28), by **Barbagia Insolita**, by the **Associazione La Montagna,** and by **Marcello Cominetti** (0471-83 65 94).

WALKING AND TREKKING

WILD MOUNTAINS, hills dotted with prehistoric ruins, forests, and maquis vegetation make up most of the terrain in the interior of Sardinia. The countryside is rugged but unspoiled and ideal for walking, hiking, and more strenuous treks. However, facilities are few and far between, clearly marked trails are rare, and there are very few shelters or stopping places. Yet every year more and more hikers come here rather than go to the "walkers' highway," as they refer to the Alps of northern Italy.

The most popular areas are Supramonte, the Gennargentu massif, and the Sulcis area (an unusual blend of hiking and industrial archaeology). Some stretches of the steep coastline are more suited to those with climbing experience.

In the Supramonte area experienced mountaineers can tackle the wild and precipitous Su Gorroppu gorges. The trek takes a few days, and special rock climbers' equipment is needed to make it down the vertical walls of the falls. This particular excursion is, therefore, not suitable for beginners.

THE SELVAGGIO BLU ROUTE

Its very name – Wild Blue – is the best possible description of this difficult route along the Golfo di Orosei, starting from Santa Maria Navarrese and ending at Cala Luna. The Selvaggio Blu was conceived a few years ago by Mario Verin and Peppino Cicalò. The course requires excellent physical condition and

preparation (since part of it consists of stretches of rock climbing, some of the descents are achieved by rapelling, and you have to carry along your own supply of water in your backpack), but the rewards are some of the most spectacular views of the Sardinian coast. The town of Baunei publishes a guide to Selvaggio Blu; for information, or if you would like to buy the book, call 0782-61 08 23.

A stretch of the Selvaggio Blu trail

Whether walking or climbing, or a combination of both, make sure you have the best map possible at hand (a good map is published by IGM). You should also carefully calculate the time the tour will take and how much food and water will be needed, as it is possible to walk for many miles without stumbling across a village.

SPELEOLOGY

THE MOUNTAINS OF SARDINIA are riddled with dozens of fascinating caves to be explored, some of which have tourist facilities. The temperature inside is likely to be relatively high, more or less the yearly average of the surrounding area. Bear in mind that some of the difficult caves, such as the Golgo abyss (at Su Sterru), the Grotta Verde at Capo Caccia, or the Su Palu cave near Orosei, are open only to experienced speleologists.

GOLF COURSES

SARDINIA has some famous golf courses, including the one at the **Pevero Golf Club** in Porto Cervo, designed by the architect Robert Trent Jones. This 18-hole golf course is internationally known for its tournaments.

OTHER SPORTS

THE ISLAND'S sports activities are not confined to the mountains and caves in its interior. More traditional sports such as tennis, soccer, swimming, and five-a-side soccer can be pursued on the many sports facilities and courts throughout the island.

The golf course at Pevero

DIRECTORY	WALKING TOURS	Keya	SPELEOLOGY

HORSEBACK RIDING

ANTE (Associazione Nazionale Turismo Equestre)
c/o Centro Vacanze Ala Birdi, Strada a Mare 24, Arborea.
☎ 0783-80 02 68.

FISE (Federazione Italiana Sport Equestri)
Via Cagliari 242, Oristano.
☎ 0783-30 29 32.

III (Istituto Incremento Ippico della Sardegna)
Piazza Borgia 4, Ozieri.
☎ 079-78 78 52
☎ 079-78 60 02.

WALKING TOURS

Club Alpino Italiano
Cagliari.
☎ 070-66 78 77.

Compagnia dell'Avventura
Cannigione.
☎ 0789-862 53.

Tramontana
Olbia.
☎ 0789-266 60.

Artrek Sardegna
Cagliari.
☎ 070-66 66 80.

L'Asfodelo
Cagliari.
☎ 070-65 76 91.

Segnavia
Cagliari.
☎ 070-91 651 38.

Keya
Quartu Sant'Elena.
☎ 070-82 71 93.

Scoprisardegna
Porto Torres.
☎ 079-51 22 09.

Cooperativa Ghivine
Dorgali.
☎ 0784-934 24.

Barbagia Insolita
Oliena.
☎ 0784-28 81 67.

Cooperativa Monte Maccione
Oliena.
☎ 0784-28 83 63.

Associazione La Montagna
Roma.
☎ 06 32-168 04.

SPELEOLOGY

Federazione Speleologica Sarda
Via De Magistris, Cagliari.
☎ 070-27 23 31.

Società Speleologica Italiana
Via Zamboni 61, Bologna.
☎ 051-25 00 49.

GOLF COURSES

Villaggio Arbatax Golf Club
☎ 0782-66 70 65.

Is Molas Golf Club
Santa Margherita di Pula.
☎ 070-92 410 13.

Pevero Golf Club
Porto Cervo.
☎ 0789-962 10.

TRAVEL INFORMATION

SARDINIA IS SERVED by Europe's major airlines, including the Sardinian Meridiana and the Italian carrier, Alitalia. In addition, there are many charter flights operating in the summer, often with low cost fares or as part of a package deal. The number of flights varies according to the season, with many more direct and charter flights during the busy summer months. If no direct flights or suitable connections are available, Alitalia and Meridiana provide regular domestic flights from

A Meridiana airlines plane

Italy's mainland cities throughout the year.

The island is also served by an excellent network of car and passenger ferries from ports on the Italian mainland. Slower ferries offer a long crossing, with berths for overnight trips, whereas the faster and more expensive ferry lines can cut the traveling time in half. During the peak summer season of July and August it is not easy to find places on passenger and, in particular, car ferries, so make sure to reserve your place well in advance.

ARRIVING BY AIR

THE MAIN AIRPORTS in Sardinia are Cagliari's **Elmas** airport, Alghero's **Fertilia** airport, and the **Olbia-Costa Smeralda** airport. These are not far from their respective city centers and offer public transportation into town as well as taxi services. In the summer there is also a coach service from Olbia airport to the towns in the Costa Smeralda.

Scheduled airlines such as British Airways, Alitalia, the Sardinian airline Meridiana, and other European carriers operate flights to the island from major European cities. Most of these, however, will

have a stopover in a city on mainland Italy. Charter airlines are more likely to offer direct flights during the summer. In general there are more flights to the island in the summer.

Long-haul passengers will almost inevitably have to change in an Italian mainland or other European city. If you are traveling from the United States, TWA, United Airlines, and Delta offer direct flights to Rome where you can get a connection to one of the island's airports. Canadian Airlines flies from Canada and Qantas flies from Australia. Alitalia also has a regular service between these countries and Rome.

A Sardinia Ferries car ferry

TICKETS AND FARES

APEX/SUPER APEX fares offer the best deals on scheduled flights to Italy, but they must be purchased well in advance. Fares vary greatly during the year, but the most

Olbia's airport serving the east and the Costa Smeralda

A Tirrenia line car ferry

expensive periods are summer, Christmas, and Easter holidays.

For intercontinental flights the most economical option is probably to take a budget flight to London, Frankfurt, Milan, or Rome and get a charter flight from there to the island.

FERRY SERVICES

SARDINIA IS EASILY reached by ferry from Italy's mainland ports. The crossing can be rather long (up to 16 hours from Naples to Cagliari, 7 hours between Civitavecchia and Olbia), although the more expensive ferry lines offer a much faster service. For overnight crossings, passengers can book a cabin.

Ferry services leave from Civitavecchia, Naples, Genoa, Livorno, Palermo, Trapani, and Tunis in Tunisia. They dock at Sardinia's major tourist ports of Cagliari, Olbia, Golfo Aranci, Palau, and Porto Torres. **Sardinia Ferries**' fast service connects Civitavecchia and Livorno with Golfo Aranci in just over four hours. **Tirrenia** offers a similar service from La Spezia and Civitavecchia to Olbia. This is a four- to five-hour trip. There are also ferries from Bonifacio in Corsica, bound for Santa Teresa di Gallura and between Palau and Porto Vecchio in Corsica during the tourist season.

PACKAGE TOURS

MOST TRAVEL AGENCIES, both in Italy and abroad, offer vacations to Sardinia. Obviously, the sea and coast are the greatest attraction, but there are also many options for vacations in the interior. Many resort villages provide a wide range of entertainment and sports facilities for their guests, including diving and windsurfing, sailing lessons, and horseback riding.

A Moby Lines ferry

DIRECTORY

AIRLINES

Meridiana

Cagliari
For information
070-65 13 81.
For reservations
070-66 91 61.
Elmas Airport,
Cagliari
070-24 01 69.
Olbia
For information
0789-529 99.
For reservations
0789-529 10.
Costa Smeralda Airport,
Olbia
0789-526 34.

Rome
06-47 80 42 33.
For reservations
06-47 80 41.
Milan
02-58 41 71.
For reservations
02-58 41 73 44.

Alitalia

Cagliari
070-601 01.
Elmas airport, Cagliari
070-24 00 79.
Sassari
079-29 27 85.
Alghero, Fertilia airport
079-93 50 33.
Rome
For reservations
06-656 41.
06-656 43.

Alitalia domestic flights
1478-656 41.
1478-656 43.

FERRY COMPANIES

Tirrenia

Cagliari
For information
070-65 46 64.
For reservations
070-66 60 65.
Olbia
0789-246 91.
Porto Torres
079-51 46 00.

Moby Lines

Milan
02-86 52 31.

Olbia
0789-279 27.
Cagliari
070-65 53 59.
Rome
06-444 05 27.

Ferrovie dello Stato

Cagliari, car ferry
information
070-65 79 94.

Sardinia Ferries

Olbia
0789-252 00.
Milan
02-72 00 03 24.
Genoa
010-59 33 01.
Livorno
0586-89 89 79.

Getting Around Sardinia

M ANY OF SARDINIA'S ROADS are characterized by an
interminable number of curves and tight bends:
annoying if you're in a hurry, but pleasant if you're on
vacation and can take time to enjoy the scenery. With
the exception of a few major roads, such as the N131,
which connects the four corners of the island, the roads
wind their way over hills and across plains so that,
even though the traffic outside the towns is light, always
calculate plenty of time when planning a tour. The
empty roads, on the other hand, are perfect for cyclists.

Avis ⓒ *167-86 30 63.*
Europcar ⓒ *167-86 80 88.*
Hertz ⓒ *167-82 20 99.*
Maggiore ⓒ *1478-670 67.*

ROAD RULES

T HE SPEED LIMITS are the
same as in the rest of Italy:
50 km/h (30 mph) in town,
90 km/h (55 mph) on normal
roads, 130 km/h (80 mph)
on highways. Motorists are
required to wear seat belts;
motorcyclists and moped
riders and passengers must
wear helmets. Traffic is usually
heaviest in cities and towns.

BOAT RENTAL

I N MANY PORTS it is possible to
charter yachts, with outings
of one day to one week. The
prices may include a crew or
simply the use of the boat.
Renting a boat enables you to
see the island away from the
busy resorts. For information,
make inquiries with the
harbor authorities.

A flock of sheep blocking a country road

BICYCLES AND MOUNTAIN BIKES

T HE QUIET ROADS along
the coast or the stunning
countryside in the interior are
ideal for outings or long trips
by bicycle. If you prefer more
arduous exercise, the steeper
mountain roads are suitable
for mountain bikes. Tourist
offices will have suggestions
for local bicycle routes and
several associations exist with
information about off-road
tours by mountain bike.

TRAVELING BY CAR

G IVEN THE INEFFICIENT public
transit system, and the
spectacular natural scenery,
traveling by car is the best
way to become acquainted
with the island.
It is important, however, to
be aware of the problems that
may occur. Minor roads will
often be blocked by flocks of
sheep, adding to your travel
time. Road signs are not always
clear and may be missing just
when you need them most.
Should this occur, the best
thing to do is to ask someone
on the way, as Sardinians are
courteous and will happily
help. Another potential
problem is fuel, because there
are not many gas stations in
the interior. You may often
find yourself forced to take
difficult dirt roads – which
Sardinians poetically call
"roads with natural paving" –
particularly when looking for
an out-of-the-way church or
archaeological site.
One way to be prepared for
these potential hindrances is
to carry a good, up-to-date
road map. One of the best is
published by the Touring Club
Italiano, to a scale of 1:200.000.

RENTING A CAR

T HE MAJORITY of international
car-rental companies are
represented in Sardinia, with
offices in the main port towns
(Olbia, Cagliari, Porto Torres)
and in the airports of Cagliari
Elmas, Olbia-Costa Smeralda,
and Alghero Fertilia. Hertz
offers discounts for those
who fly with Meridiana.
A number of tour com-
panies offer fly-drive deals
that allow you to fly to the
most convenient airport and
pick up a rented car on arrival.

Car rental, a convenient and comfortable way to see the island

A bicycle tour among the olive groves near Sassari

TOURING SARDINIA BY MOUNTAIN BIKE

Team Mountain Bike Orosei
(0784-913 30.

Società Ciclistica Mountain Bike
Dèsulo.
(0784-61 92 52.

Pool Bike Serramanna
(070-91 384 34.

Mountain Bike Club Taxus Baccata
Gonnasfanadiga.
(070-979 98 64.

Mountain Bike Team Sardegna
Sinnai.
(070-76 70 20.

Team Spakkaruote
Presso Superdue
Carbonia.
(0781-640 84.

Club Mountain Bike Città di Sassari
(079-27 37 47.

TRAVELING BY TRAIN

SARDINIAN TRAINS are narrow-gauge, making them more a tourist attraction than a true means of travel. The slow progress and inconvenient train times mean that trips to explore the island must be combined with the more efficient bus service run by the Azienda Regionale Sarda Trasporti (ARST) company.

A train ride in true late-19th-century style, such as on the Cagliari–Sòrgono route

(see p109), is an enjoyable and relaxing way to see the island's stunning scenery that has fascinated travelers and photographers from all over the world for many centuries.

In spring, the **Ferrovie della Sardegna** (Sardinian Railroad) organizes train rides from Cagliari to Mandas and Seui on the Trenino Verde *(see pp92–3).* "Vintage" cars from 1913 are pulled by steam locomotives from the 1930s.

Ferrovie della Sardegna
Via Cugia 1, Cagliari. (070-30 14 10 or 070-30 62 21.

TRAVELING BY BUS

THE AZIENDA REGIONALE Sarda Trasporti (ARST) bus company network covers almost all the towns, cities, and resorts in Sardinia. In order to meet the needs of the ever-growing number of visitors to the island, ARST has issued a tourist pass *(biglietto turistico),* available only to nonresidents, that allows you to travel on all ARST buses. The pass is valid for 7, 14, 21, or 28 days beginning with the first day you use it and costs L61,500, L105,000, L147,000, and L189,000 respectively.

ARST INFORMATION OFFICES

Cagliari (070-409 81.
   or 070-409 83 24.
Gùspini (070-97 02 36.
Lanusei (0782-402 92.
Nuoro (0784-322 01.
   or 0784-322 04.
Olbia (0789-247 29.
   or 0789-211 97.
Oristano (0783-717 76.
Sanluri (070-930 70 26.
Sassari (079-26 01 24.
Siniscola (0784-87 85 91.
Villacidro (070-93 22 40.

The narrow-gauge train known as the Trenino Verde

General Index

Phrase Book

IN AN EMERGENCY

Help!	**Aiuto!**	eye-**yoo**-toh
Stop!	**Fermate!**	fair-**mah**-teh
Call a doctor.	**Chiama un medico**	kee-**ah**-mah oon **meh**-dee-koh
Call an ambulance.	**Chiama un' ambulanza**	kee-**ah**-mah oon am-boo-**lan**-tsa
Call the police.	**Chiama la polizia**	kee-**ah**-mah lah pol-ee-**tsee**-ah
Call the fire department.	**Chiama i pompieri**	kee-**ah**-mah ee pom-pee-**air**-ee
Where is the telephone?	**Dov'è il telefono?**	dov-**eh** eel teh-**leh**-foh-noh?
The nearest hospital?	**L'ospedale più vicino?**	loss-peh-**dah**-leh pee-oo vee-**chee**-noh?

COMMUNICATION ESSENTIALS

Yes/No	**Sì/No**	see/ noh
Please	**Per favore**	pair fah-**vor**-eh
Thank you	**Grazie**	**grah**-tsee-eh
Excuse me	**Mi scusi**	mee **skoo**-zee
Hello	**Buon giorno**	bwon **jor**-noh
Goodbye	**Arrivederci**	ah-ree-veh-**dair**-chee
Good evening	**Buona sera**	**bwon**-ah **sair**-ah
morning	**la mattina**	lah mah-**tee**-nah
afternoon	**il pomeriggio**	eel poh-meh-**ree**-joh
evening	**la sera**	lah **sair**-ah
yesterday	**ieri**	ee-**air**-ee
today	**oggi**	**oh**-jee
tomorrow	**domani**	doh-**mah**-nee
here	**qui**	kwee
there	**la**	lah
What?	**Quale?**	**kwah**-leh?
When?	**Quando?**	**kwan**-doh?
Why?	**Perchè?**	pair-**keh**?
Where?	**Dove?**	**doh**-veh?

USEFUL PHRASES

How are you?	**Come sta?**	**koh**-meh stah?
Very well, thank you.	**Molto bene, grazie.**	**moll**-toh **beh**-neh **grah**-tsee-eh
Pleased to meet you.	**Piacere di conoscerla.**	pee-ah-**chair**-eh dee coh-**noh**-shair-lah
See you later.	**A più tardi.**	ah pee-**oo** tar-dee
That's fine.	**Va bene.**	va **beh**-neh
Where is/are ...?	**Dov'è/Dove sono ...?**	dov-**eh**/dov-eh **soh** noh?
How long does it take to get to ...?	**Quanto tempo ci vuole per andare a ...?**	**kwan**-toh **tem**-poh chee voo-**oh**-leh pair an-**dar**-eh ah ...?
How do I get to ...?	**Come faccio per arrivare a ...?**	koh-meh **fah**-choh pair arr-ee-**var**-eh ah..?
Do you speak English?	**Parla inglese?**	**par**-lah een-**gleh**zeh?
I don't understand.	**Non capisco.**	non ka-**pee**-skoh
Could you speak more slowly, please?	**Può parlare più lentamente, per favore?**	pwoh par-**lah**-reh pee-**oo** len-ta-**men**-teh pair fah-**vor**-eh?
I'm sorry.	**Mi dispiace.**	mee dee-spee-**ah**-cheh

USEFUL WORDS

big	**grande**	**gran**-deh
small	**piccolo**	**pee**-koh-loh
hot	**caldo**	**kal**-doh
cold	**freddo**	**fred**-doh
good	**buono**	**bwoh**-noh
bad	**cattivo**	kat-**tee**-voh
enough	**basta**	**bas**-tah
well	**bene**	**beh**-neh
open	**aperto**	ah-**pair**-toh
closed	**chiuso**	kee-**oo**-zoh
left	**a sinistra**	ah see-**nee**-strah
right	**a destra**	ah **dess**-trah
straight on	**sempre dritto**	**sem**-preh **dree**-toh
near	**vicino**	vee-**chee**-noh
far	**lontano**	lon-**tah**-noh
up	**su**	soo
down	**giù**	joo
early	**presto**	**press**-toh
late	**tardi**	**tar**-dee
entrance	**entrata**	en-**trah**-tah
exit	**uscita**	oo-**shee**-ta
toilet	**il gabinetto**	eel gah-bee-**net**-toh
free, unoccupied	**libero**	**lee**-bair-oh
free, no charge	**gratuito**	grah-**too**-ee-toh

MAKING A TELEPHONE CALL

I'd like to place a long-distance call.	**Vorrei fare una interurbana.**	vor-**ray far**-eh oona in-tair-oor-**bah**-nah
I'd like to make a reverse-charge call.	**Vorrei fare una telefonata a carico del destinatario.**	vor-**ray far**-eh oona teh-leh-fon-**ah**-tah ah **kar**-ee-koh dell dess-tee-nah-**tar**-ree-oh
I'll try again later.	**Ritelefono più tardi.**	ree-teh-**leh**-foh-noh pee-oo **tar**-dee
Can I leave a message?	**Posso lasciare un messaggio?**	**poss**-oh lash-**ah**-reh oon mess-**sah**-joh?
Hold on.	**Un attimo, per favore**	oon **ah**-tee-moh, pair fah-**vor**-eh
Could you speak up a little please?	**Può parlare più forte, per favore?**	pwoh par-**lah**-reh pee-**oo for**-teh, pair fah-**vor**-eh?
local call	**telefonata locale**	te-leh-fon-**ah**-tah loh-cah-leh

SHOPPING

How much does this cost?	**Quant'è, per favore?**	kwan-**teh** pair fah-**vor**-eh?
I would like ...	**Vorrei ...**	vor-**ray**
Do you have ...?	**Avete ...?**	ah-**veh**-teh.. ?
I'm just looking.	**Sto soltanto guardando.**	stoh sol-**tan**-toh gwar-**dan**-doh
Do you take credit cards?	**Accettate carte di credito?**	ah-chet-**tah**-teh kar-teh dee **creh**-dee-toh?
What time do you open/close?	**A che ora apre/ chiude?**	ah keh **or**-ah **ah**-preh/kee-**oo**-deh?
this one	**questo**	**kweh**-stoh
that one	**quello**	**kwell**-oh
expensive	**caro**	**kar**-oh
cheap	**a buon prezzo**	ah bwon **pret**-soh
size, clothes	**la taglia**	lah **tah**-lee-ah
size, shoes	**il numero**	eel **noo**-mair-oh
white	**bianco**	bee-**ang**-koh
black	**nero**	**neh**-roh
red	**rosso**	**ross**-oh
yellow	**giallo**	**jal**-loh
green	**verde**	**vair**-deh
blue	**blu**	bloo

TYPES OF SHOP

antique dealer	**l'antiquario**	lan-tee-**kwah**-ree-oh
bakery	**il forno /il panificio**	eel **forn**-oh /eel pan-ee-**fee**-choh
bank	**la banca**	lah **bang**-kah
bookstore	**la libreria**	lah lee-breh-**ree**-ah
butcher	**la macelleria**	lah mah-chell-eh-**ree**-ah
cake shop	**la pasticceria**	lah pas-tee-chair-**ee**-ah
delicatessen	**la salumeria**	lah sah-loo-meh-**ree**-ah
department store	**il grande magazzino**	eel **gran**-deh mag-gad-**zee**-noh
drugstore	**la farmacia**	lah far-mah-**chee**-ah
fishmonger	**il pescivendolo**	eel pesh-ee-**ven**-doh-loh
florist	**il fioraio**	eel fee-or-**eye**-oh
greengrocer	**il fruttivendolo**	eel froo-tee-**ven**-doh-loh
grocery	**alimentari**	ah-lee-men-**tah**-ree
hairdresser	**il parrucchiere**	eel par-oo-kee-**air**-eh
ice cream parlor	**la gelateria**	lah jel-lah-tair-**ree**-ah
market	**il mercato**	eel mair-**kah**-toh
newsstand	**l'edicola**	leh-**dee**-koh-lah
post office	**l'ufficio postale**	loo-**fee**-choh pos-**tah**-leh
shoe shop	**il negozio di scarpe**	eel neh-**goh**-tsioh dee **skar**-peh
supermarket	**il supermercato**	eel su-pair-mair-**kah**-toh
tobacconist	**il tabaccaio**	eel tah-bak-**eye**-oh
travel agency	**l'agenzia di viaggi**	lah-jen-**tsee**-ah dee vee-**ad**-jee

SIGHTSEEING

art gallery	**la pinacoteca**	lah peena-koh-**teh**-kah
bus stop	**la fermata dell'autobus**	lah fair-**mah**-tah dell **ow**-toh-booss
church	**la chiesa**	lah kee-**eh**-zah
	la basilica	lah bah-**seel**-i-kah
closed for holidays	**chiuso per le ferie**	kee-**oo**-zoh pair leh **fair**-ee-eh
garden	**il giardino**	eel jar-**dee**-no
library	**la biblioteca**	lah beeb-lee-oh-**teh**-kah
museum	**il museo**	eel moo-**zeh**-oh
train station	**la stazione**	lah stah-tsee-**oh**-neh
tourist information	**l'ufficio di turismo**	loo-**fee**-choh dee too-**ree**-smoh

NUMBERS

1	uno	oo-noh
2	due	doo-eh
3	tre	treh
4	quattro	kwat-roh
5	cinque	ching-kweh
6	sei	say-ee
7	sette	set-teh
8	otto	ot-toh
9	nove	noh-veh
10	dieci	dee-eh-chee
11	undici	oon-dee-chee
12	dodici	doh-dee-chee
13	tredici	tray-dee-chee
14	quattordici	kwat-tor-dee-chee
15	quindici	kwin-dee-chee
16	sedici	say-dee-chee
17	diciassette	dee-chah-set-teh
18	diciotto	dee-chot-toh
19	diciannove	dee-chah-noh-veh
20	venti	ven-tee
30	trenta	tren-tah
40	quaranta	kwah-ran-tah
50	cinquanta	ching-kwan-tah
60	sessanta	sess-an-tah
70	settanta	set-tan-tah
80	ottanta	ot-tan-tah
90	novanta	noh-van-tah
100	cento	chen-toh
1,000	mille	mee-leh
2,000	duemila	doo-eh mee-lah
5,000	cinquemila	ching-kweh mee-lah
1,000,000	un milione	oon meel-yoh-neh

TIME, DAYS, MONTHS, SEASONS

one minute	un minuto	oon mee-noo-toh
one hour	un'ora	oon or-ah
half an hour	mezz'ora	medz-or-ah
a day	un giorno	oon jor-noh
a week	una settimana	oona set-tee-mah-nah
Monday	lunedì	loo-neh-dee
Tuesday	martedì	mar-teh-dee
Wednesday	mercoledì	mair-koh-leh-dee
Thursday	giovedì	joh-veh-dee
Friday	venerdì	ven-air-dee
Saturday	sabato	sah-bah-toh
Sunday	domenica	doh-meh-nee-kah
January	gennaio	jen-nah-yo
February	febbraio	feb-bra-yo
March	marzo	mar-tzo
April	aprile	a-pree-leh
May	maggio	mah-jo
June	giugno	joo-nyo
July	luglio	loo-lyo
August	agosto	ag-os-toh
September	settembre	set-tem-bre
October	ottobre	ot-toh-bre
November	novembre	no-vem-bre
December	dicembre	dee-chem-bre
Spring	primavera	pree-mah-veh-ra
Summer	estate	es-tah-te
Autumn	autunno	ow-toon-noh
Winter	inverno	een-vair-no
Christmas	Natale	nah-tah-le
Christmas Eve	la Vigilia	vee-jee-lya
	di Natale	dee nah-tah-le
Good Friday	Venerdì Santo	ven-air-dee san-toh
Easter	Pasqua	pas-kwa
New Year	Capodanno	kah-poh-dah-noh
New Year's Eve	San Silvestro	san seel-ves-tro
Pentecost	Pentecoste	pente-kos-te

TRAVELING

adult	l'adulto	ad-ool-toh
airport	l'aeroporto	a-air-oh-por-toh
baggage clam	il ritiro bagagli	ree-tee-roh bah-gal-yee
baggage room	il deposito bagagli	deh-poh-zee-toh bah-gal-yee
boarding card	la carta d'imbarco	kar-tah deem-bar-koh
boat	la barca	bar-kah
booking office	la biglietteria	beel-yet-teh-ree-ah
bus	l'autobus	ow-toh-booss
bus stop	la fermata	fer-mah-tah
	dell'autobus	del-ow-toh-booss
check-in desk	l'accettazione	achet-ah-tzyoh-neh
luggage	i bagagli	bah-gal-yee
child (male)	il bambino	bam-bee-noh
child (female)	la bambina	bam-bee-nah

coach (bus)	la corriera	kor-ee-air-ah
connection	la coincidenza	ko-een-chee-den-tza
customs	la dogana	doh-gah-nah
delay	ritardo	ree-tar-doh
domestic	nazionale	natz-yoh-nah-leh
fare	la tariffa	tah-reef-fah
ferry	il traghetto	trah-get-toh
first class	prima classe	pree-mah klas-seh
flight	il volo	voh-loh
gate	l'uscita	oo-shee-tah
lost property	l'ufficio oggetti smarriti	oof-fee-cho ojet-tee zmar-ree-tee
luggage cart	il carrello	kar-rel-loh
nonsmoking	non fumatori	noh-n foo-mah-toh-ree
passport	il passaporto	pas-sah-por-toh
platform	il binario	bee-nah-ree-o
railroad	la ferrovia	fer-roh-vee-a
reservation	la prenotazione	pre-noh-tatz-yoh-neh
return ticket	andata e ritorno	an-dah-tah ay ree-tor-no
seat	il posto	poss-toh
second class	seconda classe	sek-on-da klas-seh
single ticket	solo andata	soh-loh an-dah-tah
sleeper	la cuccetta	koo-chet-tah
smoking	fumatori	foo-mah-toh-ree
station	la stazione	statz-yoh-neh
subway	la metropolitana	met-roh-poh-lee-tah-nah
supplement	il supplemento	soop-leh-men-toh
taxi	il taxi	tak-si
ticket	il biglietto	beel-yet-to
timetable	l'orario	oh-rah-ry-oh
train	il treno	treh-noh

DRIVING

Fill up	il pieno	eel pyeh-noh
Do you do repairs?	Effettua riparazioni?	ef-fet-tua ree-paratz-yoh-nee?
I'd like to rent a car	Vorrei noleggiare una macchina	vor-ray noh-ledg-ah-re oona mah-keena
automatic	con il cambio automatico	kon eel kam-bee-oh ow-toh-mah-tee-koh
trunk	il portabagagli	porta-bah-gal-yee
car	l'automobile, la macchina	ow-toh-moh-bee-leh, mah-kee-nah
car ferry	il traghetto	trah-geh-to
diesel oil	gasolio	gaz-oh-lyo
garage (repairs)	il meccanico	mek-ah-neeko
gas	la benzina	ben-dzeena
gas station	la stazione di servizio	statz-yoh-neh dee sair-veetz-yo
four-star gas	benzina super	ben-dzee-na soo-per
highway	l'autostrada	ow-toh-strah-da
license	la patente	pah-ten-teh
motorbike	la motocicletta	moh-toh-chee-kleh-ta
ring road	raccordo anulare	rak-or-do an-oo-lah-re
road	la strada	strah-da
traffic lights	il semaforo	sem-ah-foh-roh
unleaded gas	benzina senza piombo	ben-dzeena sen-dza peeom-boh

SIGNS YOU MAY SEE ON THE ROAD

accendere i fari	ach-en-deh-reh ee fah-ree	headlights on
caduta massi	kah-doo-tah mah-see	falling rocks
divieto di accesso	dee-vyeh-toh dee ach-eh-so	no entry
divieto di sosta	dee-vyeh-toh dee sos-tah	no stopping
dogana	dog-ah-nah	customs
escluso residenti	es-kloo-so reh-zi-den-ti	residents only
ghiaccio	gyah-cho	ice
lavori in corso	lah-voh-ree een kor-so	roadworks
nebbia	neb-bya	fog
parcheggio a pagamento	par-kej-yo a pah-gah-men-toh	paying parking lot
parcheggio custodito	par-kej-yo koo-sto-dee-toh	parking lot with attendant
pedaggio	peh-daj-oh	toll
pericolo	peh-ree-koh-loh	danger
rallentare	rah-lehn-tah-reh	reduce speed
senso unico	sen-tzo oo-nee-ko	one way
uscita camion	oo-shee-tah kah-myon	truck entrance
zona pedonale	dzoh-na peh-doh-nah-leh	pedestrian area

STAYING IN A HOTEL

Do you have any vacant rooms?	**Avete camere libere?**	ah-**veh**-teh **kah**-mair-eh **lee**-bair-eh?
double room	**una camera doppia**	oona **kah**-mair-ah **doh**-pee-ah
with double bed	**con letto matrimoniale**	kon **let**-toh mah-tree-moh-nee-**ah**-leh
twin room	**una camera con due letti**	oona **kah**-mair-ah kon **doo**-eh **let**-tee
single room	**una camera singola**	oona **kah**-mair-ah **sing**-goh-lah
room with a bath, shower	**una camera con bagno, con doccia**	oona **kah**-mair-ah kon **ban**-yoh, kon **dot**-chah
I have a reservation.	**Ho fatto una prenotazione.**	oh **fat**-toh oona preh-noh-tah-tsee-**oh**-neh
balcony	**balcone**	bal-**coh**-neh
breakfast	**prima colazione**	**pree**-ma coh-lah-**tzyoh**-neh
key	**la chiave**	lah kee-**ah**-veh
porter	**il facchino**	eel fah-**kee**-noh
room service	**servizio in camera**	ser-**vitz**-yoh een **cah**-meh-rah

EATING OUT

Have you got a table for ...?	**Avete una tavola per ... ?**	ah-**veh**-teh oona **tah**-voh-lah pair ...?
I'd like to reserve a table.	**Vorrei riservare una tavola.**	vor-**ray** ree-sair-**vah**-reh oona **tah**-voh-lah
the bill, please.	**il conto, per favore.**	**kon**-toh pair fah-**vor**-eh
I am a vegetarian.	**Sono vegetariano/a.**	**soh**-noh **veh**-jeh-tar-ee-**ah**-noh/nah
beer	**la birra**	**bee**-rah
bread	**il pane**	**pah**-neh
bottle	**la bottiglia**	bot-**teel**-yah
breakfast	**la prima colazione**	**pree**-mah koh-lah-tsee- **oh**-neh
butter	**il burro**	**boor**-roh
carafe	**la caraffa**	kah-rah-**fah**
child's portion	**una porzione per bambini**	portz-**yoh**-neh pair bam-**bee**-nee
coffee	**il caffè**	kaf-**feh**
cover charge	**il coperto**	koh-**pair**-toh
cup	**la tazza**	**tat**-zah
dessert	**il dessert**	des-**ser**
dinner	**cena**	**cheh**-nah
dish of the day	**piatto del giorno**	pee-**ah**-toh dell **jor**-no
first course	**il primo**	**pree**-moh
fixed price menu	**il menù a prezzo fisso**	meh-**noo** ah **pret**-soh **fee**-soh
fork	**la forchetta**	for-**ket**-tah
glass	**il bicchiere**	bee-kee-**air**-eh
half-liter	**da mezzo litro**	da **met**-zoh **lee**-troh
knife	**il coltello**	kol-**tel**-loh
liter	**un litro**	**lee**-troh
lunch	**pranzo**	**pran**-tsoh
main course	**il secondo**	seh-**kon**-doh
medium *(meat)*	**al punto**	al **poon**- toh
menu	**il menù**	meh-**noo**
milk	**il latte**	**lat**-teh
napkin	**il tovagliolo**	toh-val-**yoh**-loh
pepper	**il pepe**	**peh**-peh
plate	**il piatto**	p-**yat**-toh
rare *(meat)*	**al sangue**	al **sang**-gweh
receipt *(in bars)*	**lo scontrino**	skon-**tree**-noh
(in restaurants)	**la ricevuta**	ree-cheh-**voo**-tah
restaurant	**il ristorante**	rees-toh-**ran**-teh
salad	**l'insalata**	een-sah-**lah**-tah
salt	**il sale**	**sah**-leh
sandwich	**il panino**	pan-**ee**-noh
snack	**lo spuntino**	spoon-**tee**-noh
soup	**la minestra**	mee-**nes**-trah
spoon	**il cucchiaio**	koo-kee- **eye**-oh
starter	**l'antipasto**	an-tee-**pas**-toh
sugar	**lo zucchero**	**dzoo**-keh-roh
tea	**il tè**	**teh**
teaspoon	**il cucchiaino**	kook-yah-**ee**-noh
tip	**la mancia**	**man**-cha
vegetables	**il contorno**	eel kon-**tor**-noh
waitress	**cameriera**	kah-mair-ee-**air**-ah
waiter	**cameriere**	kah-mair-ee-**air**-eh
water	**l'acqua**	**ak**-wah
fizzy/still	**gassata/naturale**	gah-**zah**-tah/ nah-too-**rah**-leh
well done *(meat)*	**ben cotto**	ben **kot**-toh
wine	**il vino**	**vee**-noh
wine list	**la lista dei vini**	**lee**-stah day **vee**-nee

MENU DECODER

abbacchio	ab-**ak**-yoh	spring lamb
acciughe	ach-**oo**-geh	anchovies
aceto	ach-**eh**-toh	vinegar
acqua minerale	**ah**-kwah mee-nair-	mineral water
gassata/naturale	**ah**-leh gah-**zah**-tah/ nah-too-**rah**-leh	fizzy/still
aglio	**al**-ee-oh	garlic
agnello	ah-**niell**-oh	lamb
al forno	al **for**-noh	baked
alla griglia	ah-lah **greel**-yah	grilled
albicocche	al-bee-**kok**-eh	apricots
ananas	**an**-an-ass	pineapple
anatra	**an**-at-rah	duck
anguria	an-**goo**-rya	watermelon
antipasti	ahn-ti-**pas**-ti	starters
aperitivo	apeh-ree-**tee**-voh	aperitif
aragosta	ara-**goss**-tah	lobster
arancia	ah-**ran**-cha	orange
aringa	ah-**reen**-gah	herring
arrosto	ar-**ross**-toh	roast
asparagi	as-**pah**-rah-ji	asparagus
baccalà	bak-al-**la**	dried cod
basilico	bas-**ee**-lee-ko	basil
besciamella	besh-ah-**mel**-ah	white sauce
birra	**beer**-rah	beer
bistecca	bees-**tek**-ka	steak
bottarga	bot-**ahr**-gah	salted mullet roe
branzino	bran-**zee**-no	sea bass
brasato	bra-**sah**-toh	braised beef
bresaola	breh-**sah**-oh-lah	slices of cold, wind-dried beef with oil and lemon
brioche	bri-**osh**	type of croissant
brodo	**broh**-doh	clear broth
budino	boo-**dee**-noh	pudding
burro	**boor**-oh	butter
caffè	kah-**feh**	espresso coffee
caffè corretto	kah-**feh** koh-**reh**-toh	espresso coffee with a dash of liqueur
caffè lungo	kah-**feh** loon-goh	weak espresso coffee
caffè macchiato	kah-**feh** mak-**yah**-toh	espresso coffee with a dash of milk
caffè ristretto	kah-**feh** ree-**streh**-toh	strong espresso coffee
caffelatte	kah-**feh**-lah-teh	half coffee, half milk
calamari	kah-lah-**mah**-ree	squid
calzone	kal-**zoh**-neh	folded pizza filled with tomato and mozzarella
camomilla	kah-moh-**mee**-lah	camomile tea
cannella	kan-**el**-lah	cinnamon
cannelloni	kan-eh-**loh**-nee	stuffed pasta tubes
cappuccino	kap-oo-**chee**-noh	coffee with foaming milk
carciofi	kar-**choh**-fee	artichokes
carne	**kar**-neh	meat
carote	kar-**roh**-teh	carrots
castagne	kas-**tan**-yeh	chestnuts
cavolfiore	kavol-**fyoh**-reh	cauliflower
cavolo	**kah**-voh-loh	cabbage
cefalo	**che**-fah-loh	gray mullet
cernia	**cher**-nya	grouper *(fish)*
ciambella	cham-**bella**	ring-shaped cake
cicoria	chih-**kor**-ya	chicory
ciliege	chil-**yej**-eh	cherries
cioccolata	choc-oh-**lah**-tah	chocolate
cipolle	chip-**oh**-leh	onions
coniglio	kon-**ee**-lyo	rabbit
contorni	kon-**tor**-nee	vegetables
coperto	kop-**er**-toh	cover charge
coppa	**koh**-pah	cured pork, sliced finely and eaten cold
cordula	**kor**-doo-lah	Sardinian spit-roasted braided lamb entrails
cotoletta	kot-oh-**let**-ta	pork or lamb chop
cozze	**kot**-zeh	mussels
crema	**kreh**-mah	custard dessert
crespella	**kres**-pel-lah	savory pancake
crostata di frutta	kros-**tah**-tah dee **froo**-tah	fruit tart
datteri	**dat**-eh-ree	dates
digestivo	dee-jes-**tee**-voh	digestive liqueur
dolci	**dol**-chi	desserts, cakes
espresso	es-**pres**-soh	strong black coffee
fagiano	fah-**jah**-noh	pheasant
fagioli	fah-**joh**-lee	beans
fagiolini	fah-joh-**lee**-nee	long, green beans
fegato	**feh**-gah-toh	liver
fettuccine	feh-too-**chee**-neh	ribbon-shaped pasta
fichi	**fee**-kee	figs

filetto	fee-**leh**-toh	fillet (of beef)
finocchio	fee-**noh**-kyo	fennel
formaggio	for-**maj**-yo	cheese
fragole	**frah**-goh-leh	strawberries
frappé	frap-**eh**	whisked fruit or milk drink with ice
fregula	**freh**-goo-lah	small, granular pasta
frittata	free-**tah**-tah	type of omelette
fritto	**free**-toh	deep fried
fritto misto	**free**-toh **mees**-toh	seafood in batter
frittura di pesce	free-toh dee **pesh**-eh	variety of fried fish
frutta	**froo**-tah	fruit
frutta secca	**froo**-tah sek-kah	dried fruit
frutti di mare	**froo**-tee dee **mah**-reh	seafood
funghi	**foon**-g-ee	mushrooms
gamberetti	gam-beh-**reh**-tee	shrimp
gamberi	**gam**-beh-ree	prawns
gamberoni	gam-beh-**roh**-nee	jumbo shrimp
gelato	gel-**ah**-toh	ice cream
gnocchi	**nyok**-ee	small flour and potato dumplings
gorgonzola	gor-gon-**zoh**-lah	strong, soft blue cheese
granchio	**gran**-kyo	crab
granita	gra-**nee**-tah	drink with crushed ice
grissini	**gree**-**see**-nee	thin, crisp breadsticks
insalata	een-sah-**lah**-tah	salad
involtini	een-vol-**tee**-nee	meat rolls stuffed with ham and herbs
lamponi	lam-**poh**-nee	raspberries
latte	**lah**-teh	milk
lattuga	lah-**too**-gah	lettuce
leggero	leh-**jeh**-roh	light
legumi	leh-**goo**-mee	legumes
lenticchie	len-**teek**-yeh	lentils
lesso	**less**-oh	boiled
lepre	**leh**-preh	hare
limone	lee-**moh**-neh	lemon
lingua	**leen**-gwa	tongue
macedonia di frutta	mach-eh-**doh**-nya dee **froo**-tah	fruit salad
maiale	mah-**yah**-leh	pork
mandarino	man-dah-**ree**-noh	mandarin
mandorla	**man**-dor-lah	almond
manzo	**man**-dzo	beef
mascarpone	mah-skar-**poh**-neh	soft, sweet cheese
mela	**meh**-lah	apple
melanzane	meh-lan-**zah**-neh	eggplant
melone	meh-**loh**-neh	melon
menta	**men**-tah	mint
merluzzo	mer-**loo**-tzoh	cod
minestrone	mee-nes-**troh**-neh	thick vegetable soup
mirtilli	meer-**tee**-lee	blueberries
more	**mor**-eh	blackberries
nasello	nah-**seh**-loh	hake
nocciole	noch-**oh**-leh	hazelnuts
noce moscata	**noh**-che mos-**kah**-tah	nutmeg
noci	**noh**-chi	walnuts
olio	**oh**-lyo	oil
orata	oh-**rah**-tah	gilthead bream
origano	oh-**ree**-gah-noh	oregano
ossobuco	os-oh-**boo**-ko	stewed shin of veal
ostriche	**os**-tree-keh	oysters
pane	**pah**-neh	bread
carasau	cah-rah-**sahw**	crisp, circular bread
panino	pah-**nee**-noh	filled roll
panna	**pah**-nah	cream
parmigiana di melanzane	par-mee-**jah**-nah dee meh-lan-zah-neh	eggplant, tomato, mozarella and parmesan bake
parmigiano	par-mee-**jah**-noh	parmesan cheese
pasticcio	pas-**tich**-oh	pasta and meat bake
patate	pah-**tah**-teh	potatoes
pecorino	peh-coh-**ree**-noh	strong, hard ewe's milk cheese
penne	peh-**neh**	pasta quills
pepe	peh-**peh**	pepper (spice)
peperoncino	peh-peh-**ron**-chee-noh	cayenne pepper
peperoni	peh-peh-**roh**-nee	peppers
pera	peh-**rah**	pear
pesca	pes-kah	peach
pesce	pesh-**ch**	fish
piselli	pee-**seh**-lee	peas
polenta	poh-**len**-tah	boiled cornmeal with meat or vegetables
pollo	**poh**-loh	chicken
polpette	pol-**peh**-teh	meatballs
polpettone	pol-**peh**-toh-neh	meatloaf

pomodori	poh-moh-**doh**-ree	tomatoes
pompelmo	pom-**pel**-moh	grapefruit
porceddu	por-**ched**-doo	roast suckling pig
porri	**poh**-ree	leeks
prezzemolo	pretz-**eh**-moh-loh	parsley
primi piatti	**pree**-mee **pyah**-tee	first courses
prosciutto cotto/crudo	pro-**shoo**-toh **kot**-toh/**kroo**-doh	ham cooked/cured
prugne	**proo**-nyeh	plums
radicchio	rah-**deek**-yo	radicchio
ragù	rah-**goo**	mince and tomato sauce
ravanelli	rah-vah-**neh**-lee	radishes
ravioli	rah-vee-**oh**-lee	square-shaped egg pasta filled with meat
razza	**rah**-tzah	skate
ricotta	ree-**kot**-tah	white, soft cheese
ripieno	**ree**-pyeh-noh	stuffed
riso	**ree**-soh	rice
risotto	ree-**soh**-toh	rice cooked in stock
rognone	ron-**yoh**-neh	kidney
rosato	roh-**sah**-toh	rosé wine
rosolato	roh-soh-**lah**-toh	fried
rosmarino	ros-mah-**ree**-noh	rosemary
salame	sah-**lah**-meh	salami
sale	**sah**-leh	salt
salsa	**sal**-sah	sauce
salsiccia	sal-**see**-cha	sausage
salvia	**sal**-vya	sage
scaloppine	skah-loh-**pee**-neh	veal scallops
seadas	say-**ah**-dahs	sweet cheese and lemon fritters
secco	**seh**-koh	dry
secondi piatti	seh-**kon**-dee **pyat**-ee	main courses
sedano	**seh**-dah-noh	celery
selvaggina	sel-vah-**jee**-nah	game
semifreddo	**seh**-mee-**freh**-doh	ice cream and sponge dessert
senape	**seh**-nah-peh	mustard
seppie	**sep**-pee-eh	cuttlefish
servizio compreso	ser-**vitz**-yo com-**preh**-soh	tip included
servizio escluso	ser-**vitz**-yo es-**cloo**-so	tip not included
sogliola	**sol**-yoh-lah	sole
sorbetto	sor-**bet**-oh	sorbet
speck	sp-**ek**	cured, smoked ham
spezzatino	spetz-ah-**tee**-noh	stew
spiedini	spyeh-**dee**-nee	meat or fish on a spit
spinaci	spee-**nah**-chee	spinach
spremuta	spreh-**moo**-tah	freshly squeezed juice
spumante	spoo-**man**-teh	sparkling wine
stufato	stoo-**fah**-toh	casserole
tacchino	tak-**ee**-noh	turkey
tagliatelle	tah-lyah-**teh**-leh	flat strips of egg pasta
tartine	tar-**tee**-neh	small sandwiches
tartufo	tar-**too**-foh	ice cream covered in cocoa
tè	**teh**	tea
tiramisù	tee-rah-mee-**soo**	dessert of coffee-soaked sponge, Marsala and mascarpone
tisana	tee-**zah**-nah	herbal tea
tonno	toh-**noh**	tuna
torta	**tor**-tah	tart, cake
torta salata	**tor**-tah sah-**lah**-tah	meat pie
tortellini	tor-teh-**lee**-nee	stuffed pasta shapes
triglie	**tree**-lya	red mullet
trippa	**tree**-**pah**	tripe
trota	**troh**-tah	trout
uova	oo-**wo**-va	eggs
uova sode	oo-**wo**-va **soh**-deh	hard-boiled eggs
uva	**oo**-va	grapes
verdura	ver-**doo**-rah	vegetables
vino	**vee**-noh	wine
vino bianco	**vee**-noh **byan**-ko	white wine
vino da dessert	**vee**-noh dah deh-**ser**	dessert wine
vino da pasto	**vee**-noh dah **pas**-toh	table wine
vino da tavola	**vee**-noh dah **tah**-voh-lah	table wine
vino rosso	**vee**-noh **ros**-soh	red wine
vitello	vee-**tel**-loh	veal
vongole	**von**-goh-leh	clams
zafferano	zah-fair-**ah**-noh	saffron
zucca	**dzoo**-kah	pumpkin
zucchero	**dzoo**-kair-oh	sugar
zucchine	dzoo-**kee**-neh	zucchini
zuppa	**dzoo**-pah	soup
zuppa inglese	dzoo-**pah** een-**gleh**-seh	trifle

Acknowledgments

DORLING KINDERSLEY would like to thank the following organizations and people whose contributions have made the preparation of this book possible:

SPECIAL ASSISTANCE
Agriturismo di Lucia Sotgiu, Agriturismo Sa Perda Marcada, Hertz, Claire Littlejohn, Hotel Mediterraneo, Greca Mattan, Meridiana, Anna Chiara Montefusco, Filomena Rosato, Anna Sacripanti, Terranostra Sardegna.

DESIGN AND EDITORIAL ASSISTANCE
Samantha Borland, Antonugo Cerletti, Michelle Clark for proofreading, Lee Redmond, Tiziana Tuveri.

PICTURE CREDITS
Key: t=top; tl=top left; tlc=top left center; tc= top center; trc=top right center; tr=top right; cla=center left above; ca=center above; cra=center right above; cl=center left; tc=center cr=center right; clb=center left below; crb=center right below; cb=center below; bl=bottom left; br=bottom right; b=bottom; bc=bottom center; bcl=bottom center left; bcr=bottom center right.

All the photographs were taken by the photographic agency OVERSEAS S.r.l., except for the following:

FABRIZIO ARDITO, Rome: 22tr, 22br, 23cr, 32cr, 33bl, 33br, 37t, 59b, 82b, 83b, 85b, 85c, 96b, 99c, 99cr, 102b, 103cl, 104t, 104bl, 105t, 106tl, 106cr, 106b, 108c, 111tl, 111cr, 116tr, 116cl, 119cl, 120t, 121t, 124l, 124c, 124b, 125t, 150t, 151tr, 151cr, 151br, 151cl, 152tl, 153tl, 155cr, 156tl, 156tr, 156c, 156b, 157tl, 157tr, 157c, 157b, 158tr, 158c, 158b, 159tl, 159tr, 159b, 164cr, 165t, 165c, 170b.

RACCOLTA DELLE STAMPE ACHILLE BERTARELLI, Milan: 30b, 36, 37c, 38c, 38b.

FABIO BRAIBANTI, Milan: 139, 147tr, 179c, 188cl, 191bl, 191tr, 191crb.

FABIO DE ANGELIS, Milan: 32tr, 32cra, 143bl, 190c, 191cr.

CRISTINA GAMBARO, Milan: 23b, 70cl, 70c, 91c, 108t, 109cl, 140b.

ILISSO EDIZIONI, Nuoro: 159cra, 159crb.

IMAGE BANK, Milan: 127, 130t, 138.

ALFIO ELIO QUATTROCCHI, Cagliari: 20tr, 39t, 42cl, 53t, 62b, 70tr, 106tr, 109cr, 145t, 149t, 165b, 190bl, 191br.

FRANCINE RECULEZ, Milan: 180, 181, 191bc.

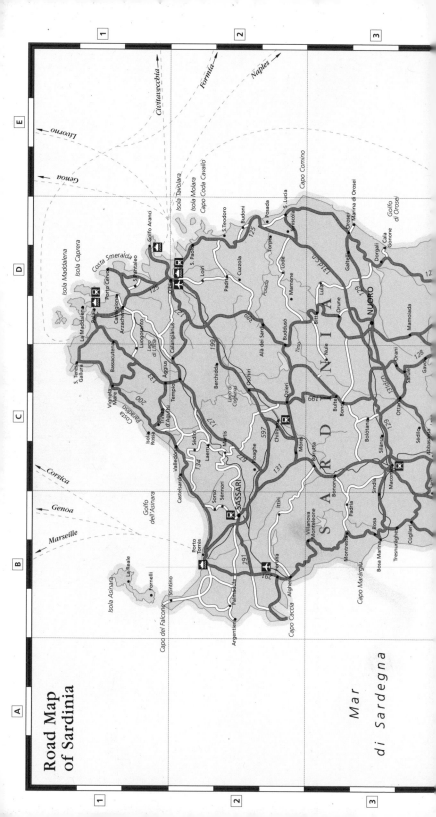

Road Map of Sardinia